Georgia Coach, GPS Edition
Standards-Based Instruction
Physical Science

Coach™
America's Best for Student Success®

Triumph Learning®

Georgia Coach, GPS Edition, Standards-Based Instruction, Physical Science
107GA
ISBN-10: 1-59823-669-5
ISBN-13: 978-1-59823-669-9

Cover Image: The Georgia peach. ©Jerry Errico/FoodPix/JupiterImages

Triumph Learning® 136 Madison Avenue, 7th Floor, New York, NY 10016
Kevin McAliley, President and Chief Executive Officer

©2008 Triumph Learning, LLC
A Haights Cross Communications, Inc. company

Printed in the United States of America.

10 9 8 7

Table of Contents

Letter to the Student

Dear Student,

Welcome to the **Georgia GPS Edition Coach, Standards-Based Instruction, Physical Science**. This book will help you as you prepare to strengthen your physical science skills this year. *Coach* also provides practice with the kinds of questions you will have to answer on tests, including the state test.

The *Coach* book is divided into chapters and lessons. Before you begin the first chapter, you may want to take the Pretest at the beginning of the book. The Pretest will show you your strengths and weaknesses in the skills and strategies you need to know this year. This way, you will be aware of what you need to concentrate on to be successful. At the end of the *Coach* book is a Posttest that will allow you and your teacher to evaluate how much you have learned. We have tried to match the style of the state test in the Pretest and Posttest for better test practice.

The lessons in this book will help you review and practice your skills and get you ready to take tests. Some of the practice will be in the style of the state test. You will be answering multiple-choice questions. Questions like these may appear on your state test. Practicing with these types of questions will give you a good idea of what you need to review to triumph.

Here are some tips that will help you as you work through this book. Remembering these tips will also help you do well on the state test

- Listen closely to your teacher's directions
- Read each choice carefully before choosing the BEST answer
- Time yourself so that you have the time at the end of a test to check your answers.

We hope you will enjoy using *Coach* and that you will have a fun and rewarding year!

Letter to the Family

Dear Parents and Families,

The *Coach* series of workbooks is designed to prepare your child to master grade-appropriate skills in physical science and to take the Georgia End-of-Course Test in Physical Science, which is the test administered each year in the state of Georgia. In your state, the grade-appropriate skills are called Performance Standards. These are the skills the state has chosen as the building blocks of your child's education in physical science, and these are the skills that will be tested on the Georgia EOCT in Physical Science. Your child's success will be measured by how well he or she masters these skills.

You are an important factor in your child's ability to learn and succeed. Get involved! We invite you to be our partner in making learning a priority in your child's life. To help ensure success, we suggest that you review the lessons in this book with your child. While teachers will guide your child through the book in class, your support at home is also vital to your child's comprehension.

Please encourage your child to read and study this book at home, and take the time to go over the sample questions and homework together. The more students practice, the better they do on the actual exam and on all the tests they will take in school. Try talking about what your child has learned in school. Perhaps you can show your children real-life applications of what they have learned. For example, you could discuss why science skills are important in life and how scientific concepts apply to everyday situations.

You will also want to foster good study habits. Students should set aside quiet time every day to do their homework and study for tests. Students need to learn to pace themselves to avoid cramming, or last minute preparing, for the challenges they will face in school.

We ask you to work with us this year to help your child triumph. Together, we can make a difference!

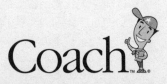

Georgia Performance Standards Correlation Chart

Performance Standard	Lesson
SCSh1. Students will evaluate the importance of curiosity, honesty, openness, and skepticism in science. a. Exhibit the above traits in their own scientific activities. b. Recognize that different explanations often can be given for the same evidence. c. Explain that further understanding of scientific problems relies on the design and execution of new experiments which may reinforce or weaken opposing explanations.	1
SCSh2. Students will use standard safety practices for all classroom laboratory and field investigations. a. Follow correct procedures for use of scientific apparatus. b. Demonstrate appropriate techniques in all laboratory situations. c. Follow correct protocol for identifying and reporting safety problems and violations.	2
SCSh3. Students will identify and investigate problems scientifically a. Suggest reasonable hypotheses for identified problems. b. Develop procedures for solving scientific problems c. Collect, organize and record appropriate data d. Graphically compare and analyze data points and/or summary statistics. e. Develop reasonable conclusions based on data collected. f. Evaluate whether conclusions are reasonable by reviewing the process and checking against other available information	3, 4
SCSh4. Students will use tools and instruments for observing, measuring, and manipulating scientific equipment and materials. a. Develop and use systematic procedures for recording and organizing information. b. Use technology to produce tables and graphs. c. Use technology to develop, test, and revise experimental or mathematical models.	3
SCSh5. Students will demonstrate the computation and estimation skills necessary for analyzing data and developing reasonable scientific explanations. a. Trace the source on any large disparity between estimated and calculated answers to problems. b. Consider possible effects of measurement errors on calculations. c. Recognize the relationship between accuracy and precision. d. Express appropriate numbers of significant figures for calculated data, using scientific notation where appropriate. e. Solve scientific problems by substituting quantitative values, using dimensional analysis, and/or simple algebraic formulas as appropriate.	5
SCSh6. Students will communicate scientific investigations and information clearly. a. Write clear, coherent laboratory reports related to scientific investigations. c. Use data as evidence to support scientific arguments and claims in written or oral presentations. d. Participate in group discussions of scientific investigation and current scientific issues.	6
SCSh7. Students will analyze how scientific knowledge is developed a. The universe is a vast single system in which the basic principles are the same everywhere. b. Universal principles are discovered through observation and experimental verification. c. From time to time, major shifts occur in the scientific view of how the world works. More often, however, the changes that take place in the body of scientific knowledge are small modifications of prior knowledge. Major shifts in scientific views typically occur after the observation of a new phenomenon or an insightful interpretation of existing data by an individual or research group. d. Hypotheses often cause scientists to develop new experiments that produce additional data. e. Testing, revising, and occasionally rejecting new and old theories never ends.	7

SCSh8. Students will understand important features of the process of scientific inquiry. a. Scientific investigators control the conditions of their experiments in order to produce valuable data. b. Scientific researchers are expected to critically assess the quality of data including possible sources of bias in their investigations' hypotheses, observations, data analyses, and interpretations. c. Scientists use practices such as peer review and publication to reinforce the integrity of scientific activity and reporting. d. The merit of a new theory is judged by how well scientific data are explained by the new theory. e. The ultimate goal of science is to develop an understanding of the natural universe which is free of biases. f. Science disciplines and traditions differ from one another in what is studied, techniques used, and outcomes sought	8, 9, 10
SCSh9. Students will enhance reading in all curriculum areas by: a. Reading in All Curriculum Areas • Read a minimum of 25 grade-level appropriate books per year from a variety of subject disciplines and participate in discussions related to curricular learning in all areas. • Read both informational and fictional texts in a variety of genres and modes of discourse. • Read technical texts related to various subject areas. b. Discussing books • Discuss messages and themes from books in all subject areas. • Respond to a variety of texts in multiple modes of discourse. • Relate messages and themes from one subject area to messages and themes in another area. • Evaluate the merit of texts in every subject discipline. • Examine author's purpose in writing. • Recognize the features of disciplinary texts. c. Building vocabulary knowledge • Demonstrate an understanding of contextual vocabulary in various subjects. • Use content vocabulary in writing and speaking. • Explore understanding of new words found in subject area texts. d. Establishing context • Explore life experiences related to subject area content. • Discuss in both writing and speaking how certain words are subject area related • Determine strategies for finding content and contextual meaning for unknown words.	11
SPS1. Students will investigate our current understanding of the atom. a. Examine the structure of the atom in terms of • proton, electron, and neutron locations. • atomic mass and atomic number. • atoms with different numbers of neutrons (isotopes). • explain the relationship of the proton number to the element's identity. b. Compare and contrast ionic and covalent bonds in terms of electron movement.	12, 13
SPS2. Students will explore the nature of matter, its classifications, and its system for naming types of matter. a. Calculate density when given a means to determine a substance's mass and volume b. Predict formulas for stable binary ionic compounds based on balance of charges. c. Use IUPAC nomenclature for transition between chemical names and chemical formulas of • binary ionic compounds (containing representative elements). • binary covalent compounds (i.e. carbon dioxide, carbon tetrachloride). d. Demonstrate the Law of Conservation of Matter in a chemical reaction. e. Apply the Law of Conservation of Matter by balancing the following types of chemical equations: • Synthesis • Decomposition • Single Replacement • Double Replacement	14, 15, 16

SPS3. Students will distinguish the characteristics and components of radioactivity. a. Differentiate among alpha and beta particles and gamma radiation. b. Differentiate between fission and fusion. c. Explain the process half-life as related to radioactive decay. d. Describe nuclear energy, its practical application as an alternative energy source, and its potential problems.	17

SPS4. Students will investigate the arrangement of the Periodic Table
a. Determine the trends of the following:
    • Number of valence electrons
    • Types of ions formed by representative elements
    • Location of metals, nonmetals, and metalloids
    • Phases at room temperature
b. Use the Periodic Table to predict the above properties for representative elements.
	18

SPS5. Students will compare and contrast the phases of matter as they relate to atomic and molecular motion. a. Compare and contrast the atomic/molecular motion of solids, liquids, gases and plasmas. b. Relate temperature, pressure, and volume of gases to the behavior of gases.	19, 20

SPS6. Students will investigate the properties of solutions.
a. Describe solutions in terms of
    • solute/solvent
    • conductivity
    • concentration
b. Observe factors affecting the rate a solute dissolves in a specific solvent.
c. Demonstrate that solubility is related to temperature by constructing a solubility curve.
d. Compare and contrast the components and properties of acids and bases.
e. Determine whether common household substances are acidic, basic, or neutral.
	21

SPS7. Students will relate transformations and flow of energy within a system.
a. Identify energy transformations within a system (e.g. lighting of a match
b. Apply Newton's three laws to everyday situations by explaining the following:
    • Inertia
    • Relationship between force, mass and acceleration
    • Equal and opposite forces
c. Determine the heat capacity of a substance   using mass, specific heat, and temperature.
d. Explain the flow of energy in phase changes through the use of a phase diagram.
	27, 28, 29

SPS8. Students will determine relationships among force, mass, and motion.
a. Calculate velocity and acceleration
b. Apply Newton's three laws to everyday situations by explaining the following:
   • Inertia
   • Relationship between force, mass and acceleration
   • Equal and opposite forces
c. Relate falling objects to gravitational force
d. Explain the difference in mass and weight.
e. Calculate amounts of work and mechanical advantage using simple machines.
	22, 23, 24, 25, 26

SPS9. Students will investigate the properties of waves. a. Recognize that all waves transfer energy. b. Relate frequency and wavelength to the energy of different types of electromagnetic wave and mechanical waves. c. Compare and contrast the characteristics of electromagnetic and mechanical (sound) waves. d. Compare and contrast the characteristics of electromagnetic and mechanical (sound) waves e. Relate the speed of sound to different mediums. f. Explain the Doppler Effect in terms of everyday interactions.	30, 31, 32, 33

SPS10. Students will investigate the properties of electricity and magnetism.
a. Investigate static electricity in terms of
   • friction
   • induction
   • conduction
b. Explain the flow of electrons in terms of
   • the relationship among voltage, resistance and current.
   • simple series and parallel circuits
b. Explain the flow of electrons in terms of
   • alternating and direct current.
c. Investigate applications of magnetism and/or its relationship to the movement of electrical charge as it relates to
   • electromagnets
   • simple motors
   • permanent magnets
	34, 35, 36, 37

Georgia GPS Edition Coach, Standards-Based Instruction, Physical Science

PRETEST

Name: _____

Directions:

Today you will be taking a test modeled on the Physical Science End-of-Course Test. Read each question carefully and then choose the *best* answer.

Be sure that the question number on the answer sheet matches the number on the test. Then mark your answer by filling in the circle on your answer sheet. If you do not know the answer to a question, skip it and go on. You may return to it later if time permits.

If you need to change an answer on your answer sheet, be sure to erase your first mark completely. Do not make any stray marks on the answer sheet.

If you finish the section of the test early, you may review your answers in that section only. You may not go on to the next section or return to a previous section.

SECTION 1

1. The diagram below shows the reactants and products of a chemical reaction. What property of reactions does this diagram illustrate?

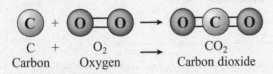

C + O₂ → CO₂
Carbon + Oxygen → Carbon dioxide

A. Energy is always produced in a synthesis reaction.

B. Atoms are always conserved during chemical reactions.

C. The number of bonds always increases in a chemical reaction.

D. Only gases can react to produce gases in a chemical reaction.

2. Which of the following phase changes is exothermic?

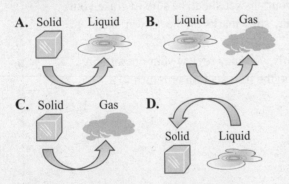

A. Solid → Liquid

B. Liquid → Gas

C. Solid → Gas

D. Solid → Liquid

3. Enrique is planning an experiment in which he will study how the angle of a ramp affects an object's acceleration. To do this, he will measure the final speed that a toy car travels at five different angles. What type of equipment will he use?

A. stopwatch

B. graduated cylinder

C. spring scale

D. triple beam balance

4. According to the graph below, what is the approximate half-life of thorium-234?

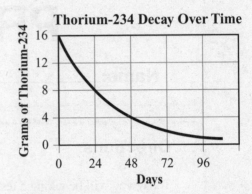

Thorium-234 Decay Over Time

A. 8 days

B. 16 days

C. 24 days

D. 96 days

5. Which of the following subatomic particles contributes significantly to the mass of an atom but does not contribute to its electrical charge?

A. proton

B. quarks

C. electron

D. neutron

6. Which statement below does not correctly match the type of element with its location on the periodic table?

A. Noble gases are located in the far right-hand column.

B. Metals are located on the left side of the periodic table.

C. Nonmetals are located on the right side of the periodic table.

D. Metalloids are located in the bottom two rows of the periodic table.

Go On

7. The diagrams below show the arrangement of water molecules in liquid water and solid water. Which of the following statements BEST explains the difference between the particles in these two phases of water?

H₂O liquid   H₂O solid

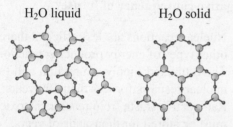

A. For a liquid to form a liquid, energy is needed to overcome the forces that hold particles in their fixed positions in the solid state.

B. For a solid to form a liquid, energy is needed to overcome the forces that hold particles in their fixed positions in the liquid state.

C. In their fixed positions in the solid state, water molecules form a more open structure that is less dense than that of liquid water.

D. In their fixed positions in the liquid state, water molecules form a more open structure that is less dense than that of solid water.

8. The table below shows the results of an experiment Jack conducted to determine how temperature affects a ball's bounciness. In the experiment, he measured how high a ball bounced when it was 0°C and 30°C He changed nothing else about the ball in between trials. Jack knows that ball bouncing height is influenced by pressure. A ball with a greater internal pressure tends to bounce higher than a ball with lower pressure. How might Jack explain his results?

Temperature of Ball (°C)	Height of Bounce (cm)			
	Trial 1	Trial 2	Trial 3	Average
0	32	38	34	34.7
30	67	65	68	66.7

A. According to Charles's Law, the lower temperature will result in a higher pressure, which means a lower height of bounce.

B. According to Boyle's Law, the lower temperature will result in a lower pressure, which means a greater height of bounce.

C. According to Gay-Lussac's Law, the lower temperature will result in a lower pressure, which means a lower height of bounce.

D. According to Charles's Law, the lower temperature will result in a greater volume, which means a lower height of bounce.

9. Which group in the periodic table forms ions that have a valence of 2-?

A. 1
B. 2
C. 16
D. 17

Go On

PHYSICAL SCIENCE

10. How much heat is needed to raise a 5 gram sample of liquid water from 25°C to 35°C?

Specific Heat of Common Substances

Substance	Specific Heat (J/g • °C)
Water (liquid)	4.18
Ethanol	2.44
Water (solid)	2.06
Aluminum	0.897
Lead	0.129

A. 50 J
B. 209 J
C. 522.5 J
D. 731.5 J

11. Ohm's law states the relationship between voltage (V), current (I), and resistance (R). It can be stated mathematically as V = IR. If the current remains constant but the voltage through the circuit increases, what will happen to the resistance?

A. The resistance will increase.
B. The resistance will decrease.
C. The resistance will remain the same.
D. The resistance will drop to zero

12. Chlorine is a halogen found in group 17 and period 3. How many valence electrons does chlorine have?

A. 6
B. 7
C. 11
D. 17

13. Modern technology allows humans to use energy from nuclear reactions to produce electricity. Nuclear power plants now produce nearly 20 percent of the energy used by humans. Which of the following aspects of nuclear power technology represents a true negative consequence of its use?

A. Nuclear reactions are less efficient than other types of energy producing reactions.
B. The estimated supply of uranium will fuel nuclear reactors for less than 100 years.
C. Radioactive waste from reactors is toxic and must be stored for thousands of years.
D. Steam from nuclear reactors contains low-level radiation that may accumulate in the environment.

14. Examine the diagram below.

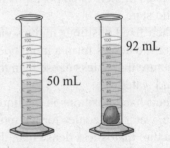

50 mL   92 mL

If the mass of the solid object is 63 g, what is the density of the solid object in g/mL?

A. 0.4
B. 0.7
C. 1.3
D. 1.5

Go On

15. Samantha is making a solution of lemonade by dissolving a package of powdered lemonade mix in a glass of water, as shown below.

What is the solvent in this solution?

A. acid
B. drink powder
C. lemon
D. water

16. **Study the diagram below.**

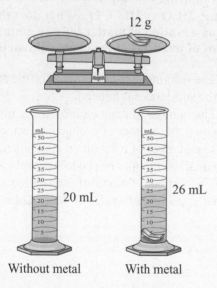

Without metal   With metal

Which of the following could be an observation made in this investigation?

A. Most metals sink in water.
B. Water has a density of 2 g/mL.
C. The metal has a density of 2 g/mL.
D. Most metals have a density greater than 2 g/mL.

17. Glucose is produced by plants through a series of chemical reactions collectively known as photosynthesis. The formula for glucose is $C_6H_{12}O_6$. Which is correct about glucose?

A. Glucose is a mixture, not a compound.
B. The correct formula for glucose is CH_2O.
C. The ratio of carbon to oxygen atoms is 1:1.
D. Each glucose molecule is composed of 6 atoms.

18. Helen uses a force of 200 N to push a cart a distance of 20 meters. How much work did she do on the cart?

A. 0.1 J
B. 10 J
C. 180 J
D. 4000 J

19. Which of the following statements correctly compares the pressure of the gas in each can and the reason for that pressure difference?

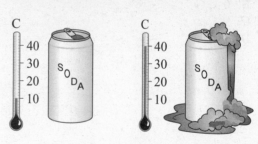

A. According to Boyle's Law, the colder can will have a higher pressure.
B. According to Boyle's Law, the warmer can will have a higher pressure.
C. According to Charles's Law, the colder can will have a higher pressure.
D. According to Gay-Lussac's Law, the warmer can will have a higher pressure.

Go On

PHYSICAL SCIENCE

PRETEST

20. **What type of arrangement and motion do particles in a gas have?**

   A. Particles are closely packed together and vibrating.
   B. Particles are not in contact with one another and are moving very slowly.
   C. Particles are moving very quickly and their only contact is when they collide.
   D. Particles are in contact with each other but they are able to slip past one another.

21. **What is the name for the ionic compound Mg_3P_2?**

   A. magnesium phosphide
   B. trimagnesium diphosphide
   C. magnesium diphosphide
   D. magnesium(III) phosphide(II)

22. **What is the mechanical advantage of a wedge that requires an input force of 3 N to do 9 N of work?**

   A. 3
   B. 6
   C. 9
   D. 18

23. **When iron atoms come into contact with oxygen gas, they can form rust, a mixture that includes particles of iron (II) oxide. The reaction is illustrated in the diagram below.**

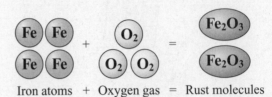

Iron atoms + Oxygen gas = Rust molecules

Keeping in mind conservation of mass, which equation BEST illustrates this reaction?

   A. $Fe + O_2 \rightarrow Fe + O_3$
   B. $Fe + O_2 \rightarrow FeO_3$
   C. $4Fe + 3O \rightarrow 2FeO$
   D. $4Fe + 3O_2 \rightarrow 2Fe_2O_3$

24. **When electricity is passed through water, the following decomposition reaction can occur: $2H_2O \rightarrow 2H_2 + O_2$. What does the law of conservation of matter tell you about the ratios of particles in the chemical reaction?**

   A. The reacting substances must be the same as the substances produced.
   B. The number of reactant molecules must equal the number of product molecules.
   C. The number of reactant compounds must equal the number of product compounds.
   D. The number of atoms of each element must be equal on both sides of the reaction arrow.

Go On

25. An unusual metal substance was found at a crime scene and evaluated in the lab. The metal was found to have a density of somewhere between 9 and 11. These results were compared with known data in the bar graph shown below.

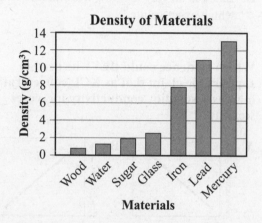

Density of Materials

Which conclusion can be made?

A. The substance could be lead.
B. The substance could be water.
C. The substance could be mercury.
D. The substance could not be a metal.

26. Salt dissolves in water forming a solution with sodium (Na+) and chloride (Cl-) ions. What could be done to speed up the rate at which salt dissolves?

A. heat the water
B. remove the ions
C. do not stir the solution
D. put in a larger piece of salt

27. Students tested 6 different common household products and found that the pH paper for 3 liquids turned blue and the pH paper for 3 liquids turned red. Red is an indication that a substance is an acid, and blue is an indication that the substance is a base. If lemon juice was one of the liquids that caused the pH paper to turn red, using the chart below, which other substance would have the same effect?

The pH scale

Acidic

0	hydrochloric acid
1	stomach acid
2	lemon juice
3	cola
4	vinegar
5	coffee
6	rainwater
7	pure water
8	seawater
9	baking soda
10	bleach
11	household ammonia
12	bicarbonate
13	oven cleaner
14	drain cleaner

Neutral — 7 pure water

Alkaline

A. Ammonia would turn the pH paper red.
B. Vinegar would turn the pH paper red.
C. Baking soda would turn the pH paper red.
D. Bleach would turn the pH paper red.

Go On

PHYSICAL SCIENCE

28. During a phase change from a liquid to a solid, what happens to the temperature of the liquid and to the amount of energy during the process?

  A. The temperature decreases as the energy increases.
  B. The temperature decreases as the energy decreases.
  C. The temperature remains constant as the energy increases.
  D. The temperature remains constant as the energy decreases.

29. Santos is given this graph of the relationship between temperature and pressure.

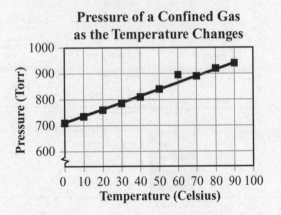

Pressure of a Confined Gas as the Temperature Changes

Which conclusion can be made about the graph?

  A. Temperature and pressure show an inverse relationship.
  B. Temperature was the dependent variable in this investigation.
  C. As the temperature increases, pressure remains generally the same.
  D. For each increase in temperature, there is a proportional increase in pressure

30. In general, what happens to the solubility of a solid solute as temperature decreases?

  A. The solubility decreases.
  B. The solubility increases.
  C. The solubility remains the same.
  D. There is no way to know without knowing which exact solute.

31. Which evidence could BEST be used to support the claim that as KCL concentration increases steadily, conductivity increases steadily?

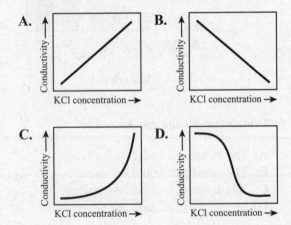

32. Which of the following BEST describes a base?

  A. It has a pH less than 7.
  B. It turns litmus paper red.
  C. It does not mix well with water.
  D. It releases OH- ions when forming a solution.

Go On

33. Hannah wants to find the density of a liquid. She knows that calculating density requires knowing the mass and volume of a substance. Which pieces of equipment will she need?

A. spring scale and beaker
B. stopwatch and meter stick
C. thermometer and pan balance
D. graduated cylinder and triple beam balance

34. The illustration below shows the conditions before and after a chemical reaction has taken place. What law is demonstrated by this experiment?

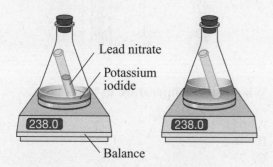

A. law of conservation of charge
B. law of conservation of energy
C. law of conservation of mass
D. law of conservation of momentum

35. What law relates the temperature and volume of a gas at a fixed pressure?

A. Boyle's law
B. Charles's law
C. Gay-Lussac's law
D. Newton's First law

36. A new runway is being constructed at the Hartsfield-Jackson Atlanta International Airport. If the smaller planes travel at an average velocity of 50m/s, and it takes 5 seconds for the planes to get to the end of the runway, what is the minimum length that the runway should be?

A. The runway should be at least 100 meters long.
B. The runway should be at least 150 meters long.
C. The runway should be at least 200 meters long.
D. The runway should be at least 250 meters long.

37. How much heat is needed to raise a 100 gram sample of lead from 5°C to 15°C?

Specific Heat of Common Substances

Substance	Specific Heat (J/g • °C)
Water (liquid)	4.18
Ethanol	2.44
Water (solid)	2.06
Aluminum	0.897
Lead	0.129

A. 12.9 J
B. 64.5 J
C. 129 J
D. 193.5 J

Go On

PHYSICAL SCIENCE

38. Which one of Newton's three laws of motion is being illustrated in the drawing below?

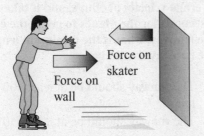

Force on skater

Force on wall

A. Newton's law of universal gravitation
B. Newton's first law of motion, the law of inertia
C. Newton's second law of motion, F = ma
D. Newton's third law of motion, action = reaction

39. Which is a correct explanation of how the wall acquired an electrical charge?

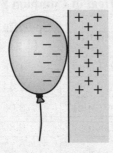

A. The wall became charged when it was constructed.
B. The wall became charged when its protons were knocked off.
C. The wall became charged when it was rubbed with a cloth.
D. The wall became charged when the balloon touched it.

40. In an experiment to determine the relationship between pressure and temperature of a gas, a chemist measured the temperature of a sample of hydrogen using the thermometer shown below.

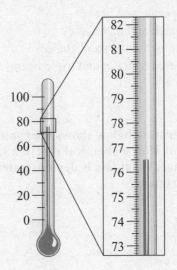

What is the temperature in °C?

A. 67.0
B. 76.5
C. 77.5
D. 80.0

41. A chemist is carrying out a reaction that releases a lot of energy. The bottle of one of the reactants has the following symbol

What does this symbol mean?

A. Contents are sharp.
B. This chemical is poisonous.
C. This chemical is flammable.
D. Know the location of the eye wash station.

Go On

PHYSICAL SCIENCE

42. The diagram below shows the water cycle. Which part of the diagram represents the change of state from a liquid to a gas?

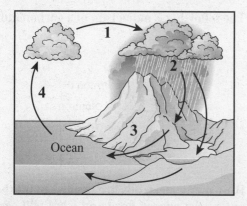

A. 1
B. 2
C. 3
D. 4

43. Jupiter is the largest planet in our solar system. An asteroid passing by Earth at a determined distance might not be pulled into our atmosphere, but if the same asteroid were passing by Jupiter at the same distance, it might be pulled into Jupiter's atmosphere. What is the BEST explanation for this?

A. Jupiter's mass is greater than the mass of Earth, and therefore, the gravitational pull of Jupiter is greater.
B. Jupiter's mass is greater than the mass of Earth, and therefore, the gravitational pull is less than that of Earth.
C. Earth's distance from the sun is less than the distance of Jupiter to the sun and therefore, Jupiter has less gravity.
D. Earth's distance from the sun is less than the distance of Jupiter to the sun and therefore, Jupiter has more gravity.

44. A car has a uniformly accelerated motion. If the car started from rest, traveled for 4 seconds and reached a final velocity of 20 meters/second, what was the car's acceleration?

A. 1 meter/sec^2
B. 2 meter/sec^2
C. 5 meter/sec^2
D. 10 meter/sec^2

45. If bulb 1 in the circuit shown stops working, what will happen to the light from bulb 2?

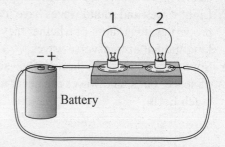

A. Bulb 2 will not glow.
B. Bulb 2 will glow brighter.
C. Bulb 2 will glow, but it will be dimmer.
D. Bulb 2 will glow for a while and then stop.

PHYSICAL SCIENCE

SECTION 2

46. Although light is visible from stars, we cannot hear the sound created from the explosions on those stars. Light is a transverse wave and sound waves are longitudinal waves. Which statement is correct about light and sound waves?

   A. Light waves are transverse waves and they cannot move through the vacuum of space.
   B. Sound waves are longitudinal waves and they cannot move through the vacuum of space.
   C. Light waves and sound waves have identical properties, regardless of whether they are longitudinal or transverse waves.
   D. Sound and light travel through the vacuum of space, but sound waves are never able to reach Earth.

47. What happens to the number of energy levels as you travel from top to bottom in a group on the periodic table?

   A. The number of energy levels increases.
   B. The number of energy levels decreases.
   C. The number of energy levels stays the same.
   D. The number of energy levels is random as you go down a group.

48. Which term identifies the type of interference shown in the diagram below?

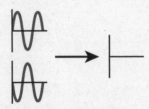

Waves are out of phase

   A. standing
   B. destructive
   C. constructive
   D. transverse

49. The following is a diagram of a carbon atom.

Carbon Atom

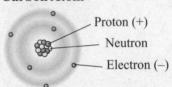

Proton (+)
Neutron
Electron (−)

How many electrons are needed to fill the outermost energy level and what will occur when it is full?

   A. One electron would fill the outermost energy level leading to the formation of an isotope.
   B. Two electrons would fill the outermost energy level, making this atom radioactive.
   C. Four electrons would fill the outermost energy level, leading to chemical stability.
   D. Six electrons would fill the outermost energy level, making carbon unreactive.

50. Which of the following is a stable molecule formed when atoms share electrons?

   A. F_2 C. HCl
   B. NaCl   D. $CaCl_2$

51. Ions are charged particles formed when an atom gains or loses electrons. Which of the following is NOT a characteristic of ionic compounds like sodium chloride (table salt)?

   A. Ionic compounds are good conductors of electricity when dissolved.
   B. Ionic compounds are formed when ions of opposite charges attract.
   C. Ionic compounds form structures called crystal lattices.
   D. Ionic compounds make good insulators.

Go On

52. Eddy and Gamby traveled during the holidays to visit their family members in Atlanta. The distance and driving time are shown in the graph that follows.

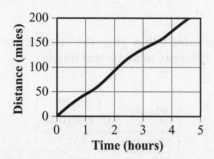

Which conclusion can be made from the graph?

A. They stopped often along the way.
B. They traveled at a fairly constant velocity.
C. There were different drivers at different times during the journey.
D. They were driving slowly at first, but their velocity increased every hour.

53. Imagine an object sitting on a frictionless surface. If a 16 N force is applied to the object and its acceleration is 2 m/sec/sec, what is the mass of the object?
Force = mass × acceleration

A. 4 kg   C. 16 kg

B. 8 kg   D. 32 kg

54. Which two properties determine the force of gravity between two objects?

A. their masses and their velocities
B. their inertia and their accelerations
C. their weights and their accelerations
D. their masses and the distance between them

55. Which of the following is accurate when comparing alternating current (AC) and direct current (DC)?

A. The flow of electrons goes back and forth in different directions in direct current.
B. With direct current, the flow of electrons through the wire is in one direction only.
C. The flow of electrons is the same in alternating and direct current but they are used differently.
D. With alternating current, the flow of electrons through the wire is in one direction only.

56. Fusion and fission are different types of nuclear reactions. Although the mechanisms of the reactions are very different, both reactions release a great deal of energy. What is another similarity between the two nuclear reaction types?

A. Both reactions occur at similar temperatures and pressures.
B. Both reactions involve the combining of atomic nuclei.
C. Both reactions create the same amount of energy.
D. Both reactions result in a loss of mass.

Go On

PHYSICAL SCIENCE

PRETEST

57. Sara took her first skydiving lessons. Her acceleration after 4 seconds is listed in the table below.

Acceleration Due to Gravity

Time	Velocity
1 second	9.8 meters/second
2 seconds	19.6 meters/second
3 seconds	29.4 meters/second
4 seconds	39.2 meters/second

Which conclusion can be made about her velocity?

A. It is constant for all 4 seconds.

B. It decreases over time.

C. It increases every second.

D. It is not related to acceleration

58. What type of nuclear reaction results in a single nucleus undergoing a decrease in atomic number, no change in mass number, and the release of high energy light?

A. alpha decay   C. gamma radiation

B. beta decay   D. nuclear fusion

59. What important distinction between mass and weight is illustrated in the diagram below?

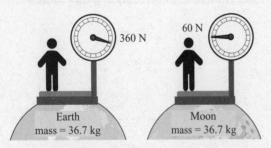

A. Your mass is always 1/6 lighter than your weight on the moon.

B. Your mass is greater on the moon, while your weight is less on the moon.

C. Mass is the same everywhere in the universe but weight depends on the force of gravity.

D. Mass and weight are the same everywhere in the universe, but they are measured in different units.

60. Which subatomic particles are involved in chemical reactions?

A. electronss   C. nuclei

B. neutrons   D. protons

61. The table below gives the relative gravities of different solar system objects.

Planet	Gravity (× Earth's)
Mercury	0.38
Venus	0.91
Earth	1.00
Mars	0.38
Jupiter	2.53
Saturn	1.14
Uranus	0.9
Neptune	1.14
Pluto	0.08

How does your mass compare on Jupiter and on Saturn?

A. Your mass is the same.

B. Your mass is 1.14 times greater on Jupiter.

C. Your mass is 2.22 times greater on Jupiter.

D. Your mass is 2.53 times greater on Saturn.

Go On

62. Sonar uses sound waves to map the ocean floor. A sonar device sends sound waves toward the ocean bottom. The waves bounce off the ocean floor and return to the boat. A computer measures the amount of time it takes the returning waves to come back and calculates how deep the ocean floor is from the sonar device. What wave interaction does a sonar device rely on?

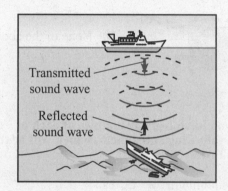

Transmitted sound wave

Reflected sound wave

A. constructive interference

B. diffraction

C. reflection

D. refraction

63. The picture below shows an effect of light waves. What is happening to make the pencil appear broken?

A. destructive interference

B. diffraction

C. reflection

D. refraction

64. What is the mechanical advantage of a wheel and axle that requires an input force of 2.5 N to do 5 N of work?

A. 0.5   C. 5

B. 2   D. 12.5

65. Where would a girl on a playground have the GREATEST amount of gravitational potential energy?

A. standing on the ground

B. sitting on the bottom of the slide

C. halfway up the ladder

D. at the top of the slide

66. Photosynthesis is one of the most important chemical reactions on Earth. The general formula for photosynthesis is shown below.

$$6CO_2 + 6H_2O + Energy \rightarrow C_6H_{12}O_6 + 6O_2$$

Which of the following BEST describes this reaction?

A. It transforms light energy into chemical energy.

B. It transforms chemical energy into light energy.

C. It transforms mechanical energy into kinetic energy.

D. It transforms potential energy into mechanical energy.

67. Which of the following is a good conductor of thermal energy?

A. animal fur   C. copper tea kettle

B. cloth potholder   D. foam insulation

Go On

PHYSICAL SCIENCE

68. A lava lamp contains two liquids that do not mix. When the lava lamp is turned on, its base will heat the liquids at the bottom of the glass container. What process causes the liquids to move up and down within the glass container?

   A. Radiation of light causes the entire glass container to have the same temperature.
   B. Conduction from the lamp base causes the liquids to gain thermal energy and boil rapidly.
   C. Conduction from the lamp base causes the entire glass container to have the same temperature.
   D. Convection currents cause the liquids to rise when they are heated and sink when they are cooled.

69. Which of the following statements is true of the laboratory setup shown in the diagram below?

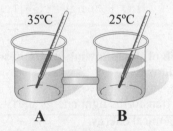

   A. Heat will flow through conduction from beaker A to beaker B.
   B. Heat will flow through conduction from beaker B to beaker A.
   C. Radiation will cause both beakers to become the same temperature.
   D. Both beakers will remain the same temperature until cooled by the surrounding air.

70. Which of the following images shows an object being heated through radiation?

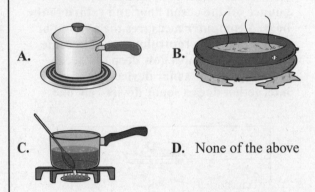

   D. None of the above

71. If you have 1-gram samples of each of the following substances, which will heat the fastest?

   A. aluminum   C. lead
   B. ethanol   D. liquid water

72. Which energy transformation represents light energy changing to chemical energy?

Energy Transformations

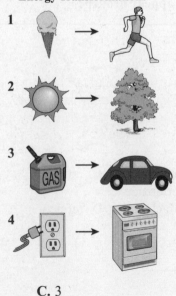

   A. 1   C. 3
   B. 2   D. 4

Go On

PHYSICAL SCIENCE

73. Which type of mechanical wave is shown in the drawing below?

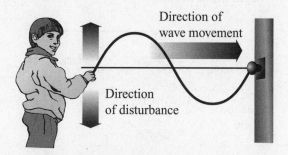

Direction of wave movement

Direction of disturbance

A. a compression wave
B. a longitudinal wave
C. a surface wave
D. a transverse wave

74. As light waves pass through water and then through air, the speed of the light wave changes. Which of the following refers to the bending of light waves as they pass through different materials?

A. interference   C. refraction

B. reflection   D. diffraction

75. Which of the following statements BEST describes the interaction of a longitudinal sound wave and matter?

A. Sound waves can transfer energy only through open space or a vacuum.
B. Sound waves can travel through a vacuum and are slowed down by matter.
C. Sound waves transfer energy by carrying matter parallel in the direction of the wave.
D. Sound waves transfer energy through matter, but the matter does not travel with them.

76. What does the name iron(II) oxide tell you about the iron ions in the compound?

A. Each iron ion in the compound has a +2 charge.
B. There is only one type of stable positive iron ion.
C. There are two of iron ions for every O_2- ion in the compound.
D. The formula for the compound has a subscript after the symbol for iron.

77. If the heavy arrow in the diagram below represents the incident light wave, at what angle will the reflecting light wave bounce off the smooth surface?

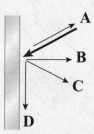

A. angle A   angle C
B. angle B   D. angle D

78. A sound wave travels 200 meters in 5 seconds in a certain medium. Use the formula $s = d/t$ to determine its speed.

A. s = 5 meters per second
B. s = 10 meters per second
C. s = 40 meters per second
D. s = 200 meters per second

Go On

PHYSICAL SCIENCE

79. What happens when you remove one of the light bulbs in a parallel circuit?

A. Only that light bulb will go dark.
B. All of the light bulbs will go dark.
C. The current in the circuit will increase.
D. The resistance in the circuit will increase.

80. The diagram below shows how a speaker is constructed. When an electric current runs through the wire (in either direction), the voice coil rapidly moves away from then back toward the permanent magnet. This vibration creates sound.

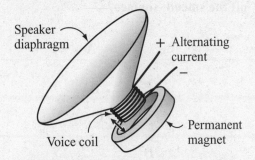

Which statement is correct about the construction of a speaker?

A. It demonstrates an effect of the Doppler effect and the flow of ions.
B. It demonstrates the production of sound waves and generators.
C. It demonstrates an effect of alternating current and magnetism.
D. It demonstrates an effect of direct current and light waves

81. A construction worker accidentally drops a piece of wood from the top of a building he is repairing. Under ideal conditions, what would be the velocity of the piece of wood after three seconds?

A. 3.0 m/sec   C. 29 m/sec

B. 9.8 m/sec   D. 940 m/sec

82. Which principle of physical science is MOST closely associated with the illustration below?

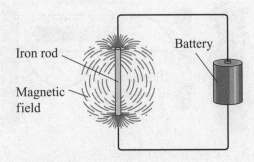

A. Einstein's theory of relativity
B. Newton's second law of motion
C Newton's law of universal gravitation
D. the relationship of magnetism and electricity

83. Which illustration below shows balls that have like charges?

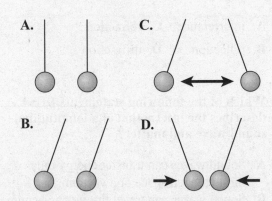

Go On

84. Carbon-12 is very stable. However, carbon-14 is an unstable element. The graph below provides evidence that carbon-14 is an unstable element.

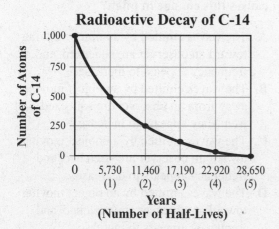

Radioactive Decay of C-14

Years
(Number of Half-Lives)

Which is the best explanation of the results illustrated on the graph?

A. The amount of carbon-12 increases over time.
B. The amount of carbon-12 decreases over time.
C. The amount of carbon-14 increases over time.
D. The amount of carbon-14 decreases over time.

85. Tamika filled a shallow baking pan with water. She floated a stick in the water, and rolled the stick lightly back and forth to create transverse waves on the surface of the water. She observed that the faster she rolled the stick back and forth, the shorter the wavelength of the waves she created. Tamika's investigation shows that there is a relationship between

A. a wave's energy and wavelength.
B. a wave's wavelength and amplitude.
C. a wave's medium and the distance the wave travels.
D. a wave's type and the medium through which it travels.

86. Examine the diagram below.

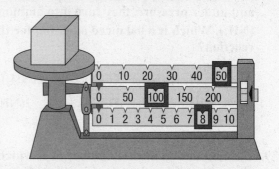

If the length of one side of this cube is 3 cm, what is the density of the cube?

A. 5.9 g/cm^3 C. 52.7 g/cm^3
B. 17.6 g/cm^3 D. 158g/cm^3

87. The atomic number of the element fluorine is 9. The isotope Fluorine-18 has a mass of 18 and fluorine-19 has a mass of 19. What is the reason for their mass differences?

A. Fluorine-18 has a different number of protons than fluorine-19
B. Fluorine-18 has a different number of neutrons than fluorine-19
C. Fluorine-18 has a different number of electrons than fluorine-19
D. Fluorine-18 has a different number of protons and electrons than fluorine-19

Go On

PHYSICAL SCIENCE

88. When nitrogen gas (N_2) and hydrogen gas (H_2) are combined at a high temperature and under pressure, they turn into ammonia (NH_3). Which is a balanced equation for this reaction?

    A. $N_2 + 2H_2 \rightarrow 2(NH_3)$ C. $N + 3H_2 \rightarrow 2(NH_3)$

    B. $N_2 + 3H_2 \rightarrow 2(NH_3)$ D. $2N_2 + 3H_2 \rightarrow 2(NH_3)$

89. Lithium has an atomic number of 3, which means that it has 3 protons in its nucleus and 3 orbiting electrons. If it loses its outermost electron to another element, what will be the electrical charge?

    A. Lithium will have a +1 charge.
    B. Lithium will have a −1 charge.
    C. Lithium will have a +2 charge.
    D. Lithium will have a −2 charge.

90. When an ambulance passes by, the siren's pitch changes. The sound becomes higher-pitched as it approaches, and then the pitch lowers as it gets further away. This change in pitch is known as the Doppler effect. What causes this change in pitch?

    A. The waves emitted by an object moving toward an observer are squeezed, and frequency appears to increase.
    B. The waves emitted by an object moving away from an observer are squeezed, and frequency appears to increase.
    C. The waves emitted by an object moving toward an observer are stretched, and frequency appears to decrease.
    D. The waves emitted by an object moving toward an observer are stretched, and frequency appears to increase.

CHAPTER 1

Habits of Mind

Evidence and Explanations

SCSh1.a-c

Getting the Idea

Key Words

scientific method
hypothesis
experiment
observation
conclusion
inference
prediction
mechanism

Having a scientific habit of mind means being curious, honest, open, skeptical, and logical when investigating nature. Scientists investigate nature by using a scientific method. A **scientific method** is a series of steps that a scientist follows in order to find an answer to a question. As part of a scientific method, scientists both describe what they have seen in an investigation and try to give an explanation for their observations. They also question the explanations that other scientists have given for an event. They require that explanations be backed up by evidence.

Not all scientific investigations follow the same series of steps. However, the chart below describes steps that are frequently followed

The Steps of a Scientific Method

Steps in a Scientific Method

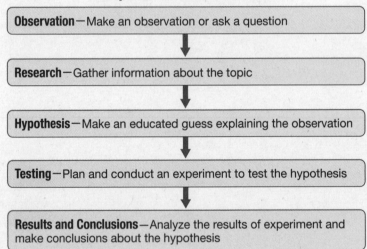

Observation—Make an observation or ask a question

Research—Gather information about the topic

Hypothesis—Make an educated guess explaining the observation

Testing—Plan and conduct an experiment to test the hypothesis

Results and Conclusions—Analyze the results of experiment and make conclusions about the hypothesis

The process most often starts with an observation that stimulates the curiosity of the scientist. This prompts the scientist to ask a question. The question must be capable of being answered using scientific processes. The question might begin with the words "how come…?" The scientist then might do some library or Internet research to find out whether other scientists have asked a similar question and what they did to try to find an answer. The following charts give examples of good and poor scientific questions.

Asking Questions

Good Scientific Questions	Poor Scientific Questions
• What is the average height of a shih tzu? • Which has a lower freezing point—alcohol or fresh water? • Does salt water slow growth in tomato plants?	• Do shih tzus make better pets than poodles? • Is blue a nicer color than beige? • Do roses smell better than petunias?

Common Phrases in Scientific Questions
What is…? What causes…? How does…?
When…? How long…?
Why…? What happens if…?
How are two things alike and/or different?
Which works better…? What is the best way to…?

Next, the scientist might formulate a **hypothesis**. A hypothesis is a suggested explanation for an observation. To test a hypothesis, that is, to find out whether it makes sense as an explanation for an observation, a scientist can perform an experiment.

An **experiment** is a test that uses controlled conditions to find support, or lack of support, for a hypothesis. After scientists have gathered evidence in an experiment, they give a description of what they have found and come up with an explanation for their findings.

The results of the experiment can be a list of **observations**, a summary of the quantitative data gathered during the experiment or descriptive notes about what took place. The results can be displayed in tables, graphs, lists, or descriptive sentences. They are simply a description of what took place during the investigation.

A **conclusion** applies what was observed during the experiment to answer the original question and evaluates any preliminary explanation the scientist had before conducting the experiment. In a conclusion, you can make an inference about the results. An **inference** is an idea that follows logically from observations. In a conclusion, you can also make a prediction of what might happen if certain variables are changed. A **prediction** is a guess about the future based on facts or data. Also, in a conclusion, you can comment on the significance of the results, or how important they are in a particular area of science. Finally, you can suggest an explanation or mechanism for how the results came about. A **mechanism** is a description of the process that explains how something happens.

Consider how a scientist may make observations about the pictures below of a curb at the end of someone's driveway.

The picture on the left shows how the curb appeared on Monday, Tuesday, and Wednesday mornings. The one of the right shows how the curb appeared on Thursday and Friday mornings. From the pictures, a scientist would observe that the trash was gone in the later part of the week. The scientist might infer that the city's waste removal service took away the trash at some time early on Thursday morning. That inference is supported by the evidence (the pictures and the times they were taken). However, the scientist cannot be certain that this explanation is true. The trash might have been removed on Wednesday evening. To test the explanation, the scientist would have to make further observations or set up an experiment to determine the exact time that the trash is removed.

Very often, different explanations can be offered for the same observation. When this happens, to further understand the scientific problem, scientists must design and carry out new experiments that may strengthen or weaken an explanation. A weak explanation may be replaced by a stronger explanation that has more evidence to support it. The results of a later experiment may overturn that stronger explanation by providing new evidence that supports an even stronger explanation.

DISCUSSION QUESTION

A scientist wants to know what mixture of antifreeze and water is best for use in a car in a cold region. She finds that a very dilute mixture will freeze at 0°C and a concentrated mixture will freeze at -40°C. How might she determine the best mixture in a region that has temperatures no lower than -10°C?

LESSON REVIEW

1. Which of the following could be an observation in an investigation?

    A. Oil is not a good solvent for salt.

    B. The oil did not dissolve the salt sample.

    C. With enough mixing, the oil will probably dissolve salt.

    D. Oil deep beneath the surface of the earth could leach salt from rocks.

2. Study the diagram of the investigation below.

Which of the following sentences could be a reasonable conclusion drawn from this investigation?

A. A diet soft drink is less dense than a regular soft drink.

B. Both cans of soft drink were at the same temperature as the water.

C. The can of diet soft drink floated, while the can of regular soft drink sank.

D. Which will float in water, a can of diet soft drink or a can of regular soft drink?

3. How is an observation different from a conclusion?

A. An observation answers questions, while a conclusion generates more questions.

B. Observations can be numerical or descriptive, while conclusions can be only numerical.

C. An observation is a description, while a conclusion applies what is observed to answer a question.

D. A conclusion involves an inference, a prediction, or a mechanism, while an observation is an explanation of events.

4. Which of the following traits does not represent a scientific way of thinking?

A. being curious

B. being honest

C. being skeptical

D. being trusting

5. What do scientists do when there are two opposing explanations for how the world works?

A. They see which explanation is more popular with the public.

B. They randomly choose one of explanations to be the official explanation.

C. They agree that both explanations get equal representation in publications.

D. They do more experiments to gather evidence in support of the best explanation.

2 Safety and Use of Laboratory Equipment

 SCSh2.a-c

Getting the Idea

Key Words

personal protective equipment

triple beam balance

graduated cylinder

The nature of scientific research sometimes requires scientists to use potentially hazardous equipment or to be exposed to dangerous chemicals, live viruses, and other toxic substances. However, the use of such potentially dangerous equipment and materials can be essential to good research. So scientists must use equipment properly and carefully follow standard safety guidelines and procedures. These procedures protect scientists from injury and illness. They also help scientists make precise and accurate measurements.

Recognizing and Avoiding Potential Hazards

Laboratory safety is not a subject to be taken lightly. All laboratory workers need to take responsibility for their own safety and for the safety of their coworkers. The best way to ensure laboratory safety is for everyone in the laboratory to use **personal protective equipment** (PPE). The following table lists the most important pieces of PPE, which everyone should wear whenever they set foot in the laboratory

Personal Protective Equipment
Eye protection—safety glasses with side shields or goggles. Most school labs require the use of eye protection.
Clothing—lab coats or aprons when indicated. Never wear lab coats or aprons outside of the lab. Always wear closed-toe shoes in the lab.
Gloves—protective gloves for handling chemicals. Always wear gloves when working with potentially infectious living organisms.

PPE use depends upon the kind of chemicals, biological agents, and procedures being used within the laboratory. However, the regulations for their use are set by the federal government and apply to schools as well as commercial laboratories. In addition to PPE requirements, labs usually have safeguards in place just in case an accident should occur. Such safeguards include emergency eyewash stations and showers so that scientists can flush their eyes or their skin should they come into contact with a harmful substance. Near the eyewash and shower stations, labs usually have emergency clean-up kits for spills that occur within the lab.

Additionally, labs usually have fume hoods, which use a vacuum to remove harmful chemical fumes so that scientists do not inhale them. Obviously, labs must have fire extinguishers and fire blankets just in case a fire should occur.

Personal protective equipment provides a measure of safety for everyone and helps to keep the potential for accidents to a minimum. The following is a standard list of laboratory rules and regulations that protect people working in and around laboratories.

Lab Safety Rules

1. Know the location of the first aid kit, eyewash, shower, and fire equipment.

2. Wear eye protection whenever glassware or solutions are heated or when fumes may be present. Avoid wearing contact lenses. Use goggles and other PPE as indicated by the instructor.

3. Assume all chemicals are dangerous. Read the labels on chemical bottles, and make sure you understand safety precautions. Clean spills from skin and surfaces immediately. Dispose of chemicals properly.

4. Many chemicals are flammable. Do not use them near open flames. Avoid inhaling chemical fumes.

5. No eating, drinking, or smoking in the lab. Never let any lab equipment touch your mouth.

6. Avoid wearing excessively loose clothing and jewelry. Long hair should be tied back. Do not wear sandals or opened-toe shoes.

7. Come to the lab prepared for the experiments you will be doing. Uncertainty can be dangerous! If you are not sure about a procedure, ask your instructor before proceeding.

8. Absolutely no horseplay. IMMEDIATELY report any and all incidents including spills, broken glass, or personal injuries, however minor, to your instructor.

Safely Manipulate Materials and Equipment

Part of remaining safe in the laboratory is knowing how to manipulate materials and equipment properly. Symbols are often included in laboratory procedures to warn you about safety precautions that must be taken when using certain equipment. They might also identify emergency stations and other locations around the lab.

This symbol indicates the presence of poisonous chemicals.

This symbol indicates the presence of flammable chemicals.

This symbol indicates the presence of sharp objects.

This symbol indicates the location of the eyewash station.

This symbol indicates a shower or running water.

This symbol indicates the location of a fire alarm.

Compressed gases present danger in the lab because they are extremely flammable. Flammable gases, such as acetylene, butane, ethylene, hydrogen, methylamine, and vinyl chloride, can burn or explode under certain conditions. Extreme care must be taken when working with compressed gases, too, because high-pressure cylinders can become airborne missiles if their valves are damaged.

Corrosives are extremely dangerous as well. Many chemicals commonly used in the laboratory are corrosive or irritating to body tissue. They present a hazard to the eyes and skin by direct contact, to the respiratory tract by inhalation, or to the gastrointestinal system by ingestion. Bromine, sodium hydroxide, sulfuric acid, and concentrated hydrogen peroxide are examples of highly corrosive liquids that represent a significant hazard because skin or eye contact can readily occur from splashes and spills.

Basic Laboratory Equipment

Scientific research and experimental design must be both accurate and specific. In order to minimize the possibility of outside factors affecting experimental results, scientists must control the conditions of their experiments in order to produce reliable data. They do this by using certain tools to make sure their work is as safe and accurate as possible.

The well-equipped scientific laboratory contains many important pieces of equipment. An important part of many scientific experiments involves accurately weighing and measuring. As a result, the most common laboratory items include extremely sensitive scales and **triple beam balances**, which are used to measure weights and masses accurately. **Graduated cylinders** are used to measure the volume of liquids accurately

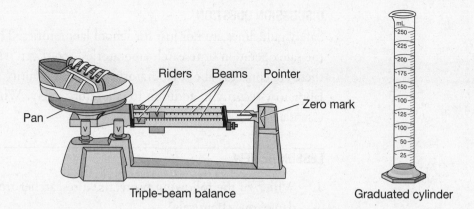

Triple-beam balance

Graduated cylinder

Because temperature is an important factor in physical processes, scientists need tools to monitor temperature and to increase or decrease it as necessary. Laboratories are equipped with sensitive thermometers for measuring temperature, water baths for keeping liquids warm, and gas burners for raising temperatures quickly.

The following tools are part of a well-stocked physical science laboratory. Can you imagine a use for each instrument?

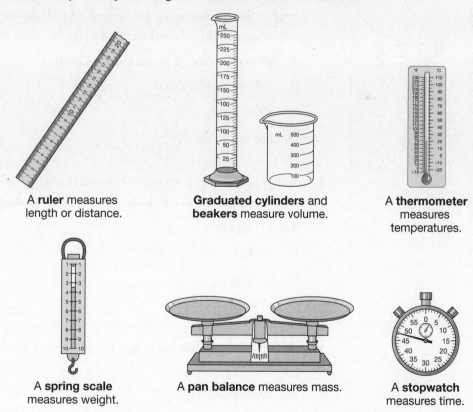

A **ruler** measures length or distance.

Graduated cylinders and **beakers** measure volume.

A **thermometer** measures temperatures.

A **spring scale** measures weight.

A **pan balance** measures mass.

A **stopwatch** measures time.

DISCUSSION QUESTION

Safety guidelines are not just for school laboratories. They are essential to the safe operation of research laboratories, too. Even with clear guidelines, there are concerns about laboratory safety and security. Discuss the need for laboratory security in addition to laboratory safety. Why is laboratory security essential?

LESSON REVIEW

1. Which of the following protect(s) a researcher from inhalation of dangerous chemicals?

   A. safety glasses or goggles

   B. a fire blanket

   C. a fume hood

   D. a spill kit

2. In the event that during a laboratory experiment someone's clothing catches fire or chemicals are spilled on that person, which of the following should be used immediately?

   A. a large beaker of liquid on the counter

   B. the eyewash fountain

   C. a fire extinguisher

   D. the safety shower

3. When measuring a volume of liquid that requires an exact measurement, what would be the best tool to use?

   A. balance

   B. beaker

   C. goggles

   D. graduated cylinder

4. Which of the following pieces of equipment keeps liquids warm in the laboratory?

   A. triple beam balance

   B. thermometer

   C. fume hood

   D. water bath

3 Processing Data

 SCSh3.c-f, SCSh4.a-c

Getting the Idea

Just as scientists use tools and instruments to conduct their investigations, they use mathematics to analyze, compare, and present the information they discover. **Mathematics** is the science of the properties and manipulation of numbers. It includes using graphs, calculations, forming conclusions from data, and determining the validity of data.

Mathematics is useful when presenting scientific data because it shows quantitative changes that occur during an investigation. A quantitative change, such as a change in mass or temperature, is expressed in numbers. For example, imagine an experiment in which scientists are testing whether super premium gasoline increases the efficiency of an automobile. The best way to show whether super premium gasoline increases driving efficiency is to show the fuel mileage of the control group beside that of the experimental group. Numbers, in this situation, are essential for showing the amount of mileage recorded in each group. They are important for accessing and understanding the results of a study quickly and easily.

Organizing and Presenting Data

Some investigations will produce a large amount of data. It will be difficult to analyze the data without organizing them in a useful way. In order to organize data, it is important to look for patterns. How are things alike or different? Is there a steady increase, decrease, or no change at all? What common features are there? Scientists use graphs and tables to organize their data because seeing patterns in data is easier when looking at a graphic representation.

Volume–Temperature Relationship

Temperature (°C)	Volume (L)
0	0.9
100	1.2
200	1.5
300	1.8
400	2.1
500	2.4

A **table** can display a large amount of numerical data in one place.

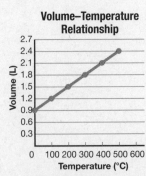

A **line graph** can let you see trends among those data.

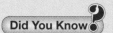

It is often important to judge the reasonableness of an answer. One way to do this is to estimate the answer. An estimate is a number close to the actual number but not exactly. By estimating what the answer will be, you can recognize whether or not you made a mistake when entering information into a calculator or computer.

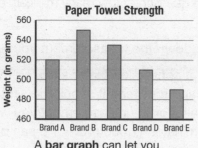

A **bar graph** can let you compare data points.

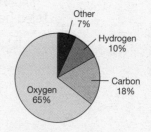

A **circle graph** allows you to compare parts, or percentages, of a whole.

Whenever creating a table or chart, follow these basic rules:

- Organize the data sequentially, or in numerical order.

- Include a title for the table or chart.

- Label the columns and include units for measurements.

Whenever creating a graph, follow these basic rules:

- Include a title or caption and other labels as needed.

- Choose an appropriate number scale, if necessary.

- For bar and line graphs, put the independent variable (the one controlled by the researcher) on the horizontal axis, or *x*-axis, and the dependent variable (the one that results) on the vertical axis, or *y*-axis.

Scientists also often use **models** to describe what they are researching. Examples include drawings, computer simulations, and mathematical descriptions. For instance, several different models of the atom have been formulated over the years. Each of these was based on the data available to the scientists of the time and has been modified as more data became available due to technological advances.

Calculations

Mathematics is the language of science. Many relationships in nature can be analyzed and described using formulas. A **formula** is a mathematical statement or equation. It is usually expressed in algebraic symbols. A formula can illustrate the relationship between different quantities. For example, consider the formula for weight: $W = mg$. To determine the weight of an object, the object's mass (m) is multiplied by the force of gravity (g) acting upon it.

Sometimes quantities are measured using different units. Suppose a cat that has a mass of 6 kg gains 32 g. What is its new mass? The answer cannot be found by adding 6 kg and 32 g. **Dimensional analysis** must be used to change one unit of measurement into another, in this case all of the units must be converted into grams or kilograms. Converting to grams is simple since 1 kg = 1000 g. Thus, 6 kg = 6000 g. So 6000 g + 32 g = 6032 g.

To answer the question, "How many milliliters are in 5 liters?" use the steps listed below.

1. Write down the measurement you want to convert. (5 L)

2. Write a conversion factor showing the relationship between liters and milliliters. It should be written as a fraction with the units for the measurement you want to convert in the denominator. (1,000 mL = 1 L can be written as 1,000 mL /1 L)

3. Multiply the measurement you want to convert by the fraction. The units in the measurement you want to convert should cancel the units in the fraction's denominator. (5 L × 1,000 mL/ 1 L = 5,000 mL)

Statistical Analysis

In order to determine the likelihood of a certain result occurring again, scientists use statistical analyses. Statistical analysis helps scientists make important decisions about whether or not an experiment should or can be replicated. Statistics is an area of applied mathematics. Statistical methods and procedures help scientists make their data clear, concise, and understandable for others who might read them. Scientists in all fields use statistics to help them organize, describe, and evaluate data.

The graph below is a scatter plot. If you look carefully at the scatter plot you will observe an outlier, a plotted point that falls outside the typical location of all of the other data points. Outliers can show that some results are not valid, or they can show important instances where data are different from what is expected. It is important to show all outliers in scientific results, even when they go against an expected trend.

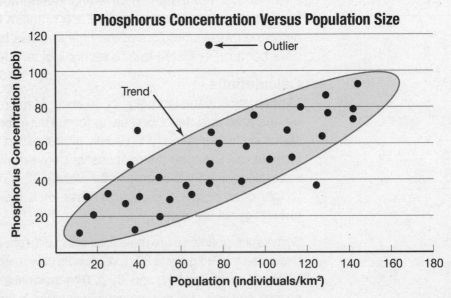

Phosphorus Concentration Versus Population Size

DISCUSSION QUESTION

200 students at a Georgia high school were asked to identify their favorite academic subject. The table below shows the results of the survey.

Subject	Number of students	Percentage
English	50	25%
Math	24	12%
History	62	31%
Science	38	19%
Foreign Language	26	13%

Discuss whether the data could be represented in a line graph, a bar graph, or a circle graph. What conclusions can you make?

LESSON REVIEW

1. Why are graphic organizers essential in scientific reporting?

   A. They shorten scientific reports considerably.

   B. They are accessible to people who cannot read.

   C. They make scientific reports more interesting to read.

   D. They show data trends and relationships clearly.

2. Which graphic organizer would best show the changes in the temperature of water as it is heated over a period of 20 minutes?

   A. a line graph   C. a bar graph

   B. a scatter plot   D. a circle graph

3. A book has a mass of 3.2 kilograms. If there are 1000 grams in 1 kilogram and 1000 milligrams in 1 gram, what is the mass of the book in milligrams?

   A. 0.0032   C. 3,200,000

   B. 3,200   D. 0.0000032

4. How do outliers affect a scientist's results?

   A. They should always be disregarded.

   B. They make the results more accurate.

   C. They sometimes cause the scientist to rethink a hypothesis.

   D. They allow the scientist to feel more confident in his or her results.

4 Generating and Verifying Hypotheses

 SCSh3.a-b

Getting the Idea

Key Words

science
scientific method
observation
scientific question
hypothesis
data
theory

As you discovered in Lesson 1, scientists follow strict procedures in their search for answers to nature's puzzles, riddles, and mysteries. Among these procedures is that of generating and verifying hypotheses, or possible explanations for observations.

Science, in the broadest sense of the word, refers to the study of anything related to the natural world. A **scientific method** refers to the process of inquiry and investigation that researchers use to gain knowledge and to understand the natural world around them better. Review the illustration at the beginning of Lesson 1 that outlines the steps in a scientific method.

Making Observations

When beginning an inquiry or an experiment, a scientist collects data (singular: datum), or information, by making careful observations. An **observation** is a record or note made by studying something using the senses. An observation might include how something looks, sounds, or feels. It can also be mathematical measurement such as temperature or distance. Observations can be performed in the laboratory under controlled conditions or in the "field" (any natural environment in which an event or object is observed).

No matter where and how the observations are made, they should be carefully recorded for later analysis. Observations should be described as they occur. Recording observations from memory increases the possibility of introducing errors. In order to be accurate, scientists should record everything they see when studying a topic. This includes the expected results as well as any surprises. Even if a scientist does not understand an observation, it should be recorded and interpreted later. Scientists should also mention any mistakes that were made in making the observations.

The observations that scientists make usually lead to **scientific questions**—questions that can be studied through further observation, testing, and analysis. People have always searched for explanations about the physical processes in the world around them. Scientific study is a systematic, repeatable, testable approach to finding those explanations. It relies on observation, experimentation, and experience.

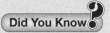
Did You Know

Development of a Hypothesis

An essential part of any scientific investigation is the formulation of a hypothesis. A **hypothesis** is a possible explanation or tentative answer to the question being investigated. In other words, a hypothesis is a best guess at the answer to the question.

The hypothesis is not reached without basis. A sound hypothesis is developed through logical reasoning, direct observations, and research using scientific literature. Reading is crucial to developing a credible hypothesis. Scientists must examine the available literature on the topic and gather as much information as is available. Sources may include scientific journals as well as the published research results of other scientists. The literature that becomes the basis for a hypothesis must be accurate, credible, and relevant.

Suppose, for example, a scientist wants to know whether thermal heat released through hot wastewater from an industrial plant affects the chemistry of a river. After researching similar experiments and information about how thermal pollution affects water temperature and dissolved oxygen content, the scientist might develop a hypothesis. The hypothesis might be that thermal pollution decreases dissolved oxygen content in rivers and thus causes an increase in acidity.

An essential element of any hypothesis is that it must be falsifiable. This means that it must be possible to test the hypothesis to prove it false. A hypothesis cannot be a statement that is impossible to test. For example, a hypothesis suggesting that sheep are happier on sunny days is impossible to test and is therefore not a valid scientific hypothesis.

Verifying or Refuting a Hypothesis

Once a testable hypothesis is established, a test must be designed After designing an experimental model, scientists collect data. Data are information collected through scientific research and inquiry. Once scientists have collected data, they compare their findings to their original hypothesis. A hypothesis can be accepted until in is proven otherwise.

If many observations yield the same explanation repeatedly, over time, the related hypothesis may become part of a theory. A **theory** is a hypothesis that has been tested several times and in several different ways. It is a broad explanation that ties together a range of observations and ideas about how processes are thought to occur. The flow chart below demonstrates the cyclical nature of research. Many cycles of proving or disproving hypotheses ultimately lead to the development of theories through experimental research.

Scientific Method

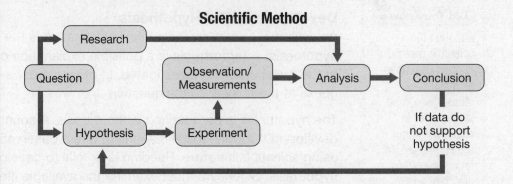

DISCUSSION QUESTION

A hypothesis is proposed by a single scientist, but a theory is more likely to be the product of more than one scientist. Why is this statement true?

LESSON REVIEW

1. How is field study different from laboratory study?

   A. Field study is not conducted by scientists.

   B. Field study involves observations of living things.

   C. Field study does not result in data that can be analyzed.

   D. Field study involves observing in the natural environment.

2. What is the BEST definition of a hypothesis?

   A. an educated prediction

   B. a random, detailed guess

   C. an experimental question

   D. a single, important observation

3. If scientific experiments repeatedly yield results that are consistent with the expectations of a hypothesis, what should the scientist do with the hypothesis?

   A. reject it

   B. accept it

   C. test it again

   D. modify or change it

4. Which of the following shows the correct order of steps in a scientific method?

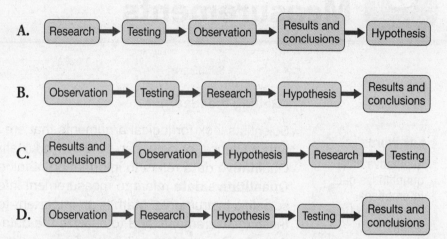

A. Research → Testing → Observation → Results and conclusions → Hypothesis

B. Observation → Testing → Research → Hypothesis → Results and conclusions

C. Results and conclusions → Observation → Hypothesis → Research → Testing

D. Observation → Research → Hypothesis → Testing → Results and conclusions

5 Making and Analyzing Measurements

SCSh5.a-e

Getting the Idea

Key Words

qualitative data
quantitative data
International
  System of Units
length
mass
volume
meniscus
accuracy
precision
significant figures
procedural errors
measurement
  errors

Scientists look for logical arguments that are supported by evidence. This evidence, or data, can be either qualitative or quantitative. **Qualitative data** refers to information obtained by using the senses. **Quantitative data** refers to measurement information obtained by using scientific instruments. Math is an important tool used to communicate these measurements and to analyze the data that have been collected. It is important that scientists are familiar with using the appropriate metric units that reflect precision and accuracy. The chart shows some differences between qualitative and quantitative data.

International System of Units

In order to ensure that scientists are able to communicate and share information easily, it is important that they all use a similar system of measurement. The **International System of Units** (SI) is the standard system of measurement used by scientists around the world. It is based on multiples of 10, with each unit being ten times larger than the next smaller unit (or ten times smaller than the next largest unit). There are a variety of prefixes that are used with some of the most common measurements used in SI.

Base Units

Length	Meter	m
Mass	Gram	g
Time	Second	s
Temperature	Degrees Celsius	°C
Amount of Substance	Mole	mol
Electric Current	Ampere	A
Fluid Volume	Liter	L

SI Prefixes

Common Prefixes	Meaning	Decimal
Milli-	One-thousandth	0.001
Centi-	One-hundredth	0.01
Kilo-	One thousand	1,000

There are a variety of scientific instruments that are used to measure objects and events. To measure **length**, or the distance between two points, a metric ruler or meter stick can be used. The largest lines on the metric ruler represent centimeters (cm) while the smaller, unnumbered lines represent millimeters (mm). In the diagram, the pencil would measure 17.8 cm or 17 cm and 8 mm.

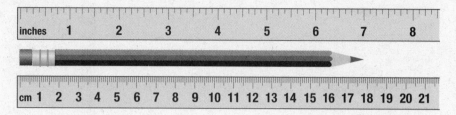

Mass, the amount of matter in an object, can be measured by using a triple beam balance. Triple beam balances are able to measure to the tenths of a gram (g). In the diagram, the block has a mass of 158.0 grams.

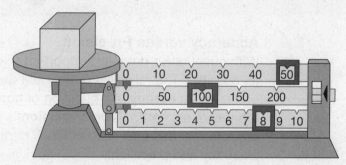

To measure the **volume** of a liquid, or the amount of space it takes up, a graduated cylinder can be used. In a graduated cylinder, the liquid in the cylinder appears to have a curved surface. This curved surface is called a **meniscus**. To get the most accurate measurement for a given volume, the liquid level is read at the lowest point on the meniscus. The graduated cylinder in the diagram shows a volume of 5.9 mL.

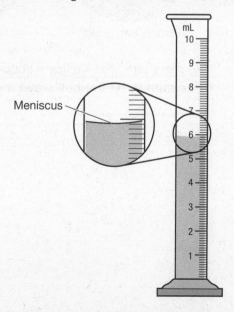

Meniscus

The temperature of a substance can be determined by using a thermometer. While we in the United States generally refer to everyday temperatures on the Fahrenheit scale, scientists use the Celsius scale. The thermometer shows a reading of 38°C

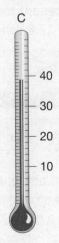

Accuracy versus Precision

With quantitative data, it is important that measurements be as reliable as possible. The reliability of the data depends on their accuracy and precision. **Accuracy** is a question of how close a measurement is to the real or accepted value. **Precision** is a matter of how close the measurements are to each other. A dartboard is often used to compare accuracy and precision.

Precise, not accurate   Accurate, not precise   Precise and accurate

Archery can also illustrate accuracy and precision. An archer must be accurate to hit the bull's-eye and precise to hit it more than once.

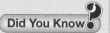
Did You Know

Observations can be quantitative (numerical) or qualitative (descriptive). Some qualitative observations, such as "The rock is very hard," can be made quantitative by developing a scale. The Mohs hardness scale assigns numbers to different degrees of hardness to make quantitative observations about the hardness of rock samples.

Significant Figures

The precision of a measurement depends on the instrument used. For example, if the smallest unit on a ruler is the millimeter then the most precise measurement will be in millimeters. Precision is represented by the number of significant figures recorded in the measurement. They include:

- digits other than zero

- final zeros after a decimal point (4.560 m)

- zeros between any other digits (4.056 m)

Zeros that are at the beginning of a number are not significant (0.0456 m). Calculations can be only as precise as the number with the least amount of significant figures. The answer must be rounded to reflect the least precise measurement.

Consider the following multiplication problem:

$3.14 \times 7.8 = 24.492$. The number 3.14 has three significant figures while 7.8 has two. Because 7.8 has the fewest figures, the answer should reflect only two figures. In this case, 24.492 should be rounded to 24.

When you add or subtract, the answer's place value should be determined by the number that is least precise, or has the least number of place values. Consider the following subtraction problem: $9.06 - 5.4 = 3.66$. The number 9.02 is written to the hundredth place while 5.6 is written to the tenth place. The answer should therefore be rounded to the tenth place, or 3.7.

Sources of Error

Sometimes procedural or measurement errors can cause a scientist's calculations to be incorrect. Procedural errors involve mistakes made in conducting the experiment, while measurement errors are mistakes made in using or reading measuring tools, For example if a thermometer in an ice bath mistakenly reads 5°C instead of 0°C all the measurements will be off by 5°C Using correct measurements is essential in other occupations. If an engineer makes an error in measurement when designing a bridge, it may affect certain calculations such as the amount of weight the bridge can hold.

DISCUSSION QUESTION

Imagine a scenario in which a scientist does not use adequate records and precise equipment in the laboratory. What might the consequences be? How might research and development be affected?

LESSON REVIEW

1. The diagram below shows a picture of a graduated cylinder filled with a liquid.

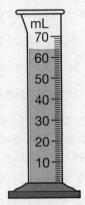

   What is the volume of the liquid?

   A. 60 mL

   B. 63 mL

   C. 64 mL

   D. 65 mL

2. The thermometer in a water bath reads 20.36°C. A researcher increases the temperature by 15.5°C. Which of the following final temperatures is the MOST precise?

   A. 35.8°C

   B. 35.86°C

   C. 35.9°C

   D. 36°C

3. Marco and his classmates practice archery during their physical education period. He hits the bull's-eye on his first try. Which term BEST describes his shot?

   A. accurate

   B. estimated

   C. precise

   D. quantitative

4. In a Friday night baseball game the pitcher throws a ball four times. Which of the following data (shown in miles/hour) would show the MOST precision?

   A. 89, 91, 90, 91

   B. 90, 92, 94, 95

   C. 95, 97, 93, 91

   D. 92, 98, 96, 90

6 Communicating Scientific Information

SCSh6.a-d

Getting the Idea

Key Words

peer review
fraud
lab report

In their work, scientists often develop new ideas, uncover new information, and explore new phenomena that may be of value to other scientists and to the public. Scientists also examine, analyze, and repeat work done by other scientists. For science to advance, the results of such studies must be truthfully reported to the scientific community and reviewed by other scientists. Communicating scientific information is therefore an important skill that anyone working in science must master.

Communicating Scientific Results

Communicating scientific results does more than just give scientists credit for their achievements. Whether it is through discussions with colleagues, presentations at conferences, published articles, news interviews, or teaching classes, sharing scientific information is an important part of a scientist's work. Scientists must communicate what they learn so that other scientists can build upon their work. As one scientific team learns about a subject, other scientific teams may apply those results to their own studies. Scientists also keep the public informed of scientific progress so that society can understand and benefit from their work. This is especially true, when the input of citizens can influence governmental policies that are based on scientific findings, such as those affecting climate change and stem cell research. Finally, scientists communicate their methods and results so that other scientists can evaluate their work.

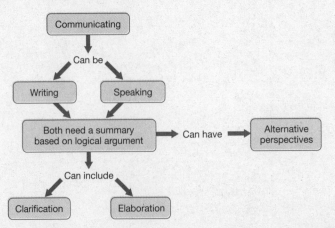

Before an article is published in a scientific journal, it undergoes **peer review**, a process in which the article is sent to knowledgeable scientists who review the procedures and conclusions of the investigation. After this peer review, acceptable articles are published, giving the entire scientific community access to the information. After a scientist's research is published, other scientists can review the investigation and benefit from the information learned by it. In some cases, flaws are discovered even in an investigation that proceeds this far. When this occurs, the flaws may be exposed and discussed to determine their impact on the research. In this way, the peer review process provides the best hope that only accurate information is added to scientific knowledge about a topic.

Through sharing experimental methods and results with peers, scientists do more than just undergo evaluation of their methods. The process also allows other scientific teams to replicate experimental results. When other scientists use the published methods to get the same results, they are verifying that the results are not mistaken or fraudulent. Fraud is the falsification of research findings through lying, omitting data, or hiding logical weaknesses. Including a description of methods in a scientific report is very important so that others can use the same methods for verification.

Finally, scientists present their data so that they can support their ideas. The strongest scientific arguments and ideas are those that are backed up by strong evidence. Evidence is what separates a scientific fact from an opinion. Solid evidence also separates weak explanations from strong explanations.

Preparing a Lab Report

As a student, you will practice scientific communication by preparing a lab report that describes what happened in an experiment. A **lab report** shows how an investigator followed the steps of a scientific method. Lab reports can take many forms, but the chart below shows the parts of a typical lab report.

Parts of a Lab Report

Section	Purpose
Purpose	States the goal of the investigation
Procedure	Describes the design of the experiment
Observations	Describes what happened during the experiment; includes raw data
Data	Organizes measurements into charts, graphs, and tables; analyzes the data
Conclusion	States and justifies the answer to the original question

A lab report should have a purpose, a procedure, observations, data, and a conclusion. The purpose describes the question that you are trying to answer and can give an educated guess as to what the answer might be. The procedure gives a step-by-step description of the methods used to carry out the experiment. In the procedure, you might also list the materials used and any special information about where the materials came from. Someone should be able to use your procedural description to repeat your investigation. The observations section includes all of the data you collected. These data can be summarized or reorganized in tables or graphs in the data section. Some lab report formats combine the observations and data sections into a single section called results. After displaying the results, your lab report should present a conclusion, in which you explain how your research has helped address the original question. How you choose to present your evidence is important. The chart below describes different ways of presenting scientific information.

Common Ways to Present Information

Chart/Table	Summarizes data in rows and columns
Diagram/Model	Uses pictures to explain or show detail
Bar Graph	Uses bars to show the magnitude of the data
Line Graph	Uses a line to relate two sets of data or show how data change over time
Circle Graph	Divides a circle into wedges to show how parts relate to the whole
Flow Chart	Series of boxes that show the order of steps or how different steps relate
Scatter Plot	Plots a series of points against two axes to show the relationship between two or more sets of numerical data

Depending on what kind of data you have collected, you might choose to present your results in different ways. For example, if you want to highlight how much of a mixture is made up of water, you might use a circle graph. But if you want to show that one sample has a much greater mass than all the other samples, you might use a bar graph. A line graph can show how data change over time. Tables can show a lot of data, but graphs are often a better visual way of showing trends.

Consider the data in the table and graph below. You can see the relationship between volume and temperature very clearly in the graph. Not only does volume go up when temperature goes up, but they increase together at a steady rate. You cannot see this relationship as well in the table.

Volume–Temperature Relationship

Temperature (°C)	Volume (L)
0	0.9
100	1.2
200	1.5
300	1.8
400	2.1
500	2.4

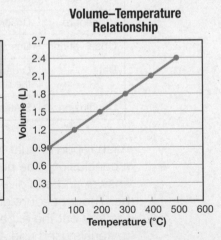

Volume–Temperature Relationship

DISCUSSION QUESTION

Two scientists follow the same procedure and get different results.
One scientist claims that the difference is due to fraud. The other scientist did
not use proper methods. How might the scientists resolve their disagreement?

LESSON REVIEW

1. What is a role that peer review plays in science?

   A. It allows scientists to get jobs in different cities.

   B. It helps make scientists famous.

   C. It allows other scientists to evaluate an investigation.

   D. It protects scientists from people who claim ownership of their ideas.

2. Why is it important to include the procedure or methods in a lab report?

   A. so that the conclusions drawn are valid

   B. so that others know how to repeat the investigation

   C. so that the experimental question is fully answered

   D. so that others can see trends in any numerical results

3. Which circle graph supports the conclusion that hamsters are the
   MOST popular pet in the apartment building?

   A. **Number of Pets in an Apartment Building**

   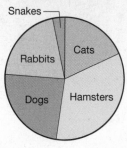

   C. **Number of Pets in an Apartment Building**

   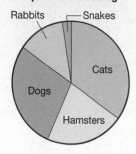

   B. **Number of Pets in an Apartment Building**

   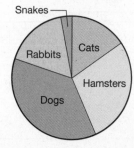

   D. **Number of Pets in an Apartment Building**

   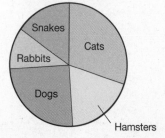

4. Which graph supports the claim that velocity increases and then decreases over time?

A.

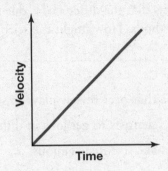

B.

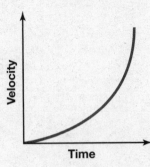

C.

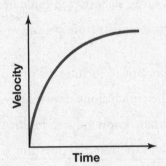

D.

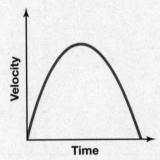

EOCT Review

1. **Which of the following could be an observation in an investigation?**

   A. Not all ceramics can conduct electricity.
   B. The new ceramic does not conduct electricity.
   C. By adding iron powder, ceramics can be made to conduct electricity.
   D. At high temperatures, the new ceramic will probably conduct electricity.

2. **The diagram below shows a log while it is burning and after it has become ash.**

   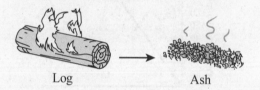

   Log   Ash

   Which of the following sentences could be a conclusion drawn from this observation?

   A. Ash is a product of a burning log.
   B. What happens to a log when it burns?
   C. The ash will have less mass than the burning log.
   D. The log produced yellow flames when it burned.

3. **A scientist wants to add a particular volume of sulfuric acid to a beaker. Which of the following would be the BEST measuring instrument to use?**

   A. balance
   B. testtube
   C. scale
   D. graduated cylinder

4. **Gerald wants to find out how temperature affects the volume of a liquid. Which pieces of equipment will he need?**

   A. graduated cylinder and beaker
   B. thermometer and meterstick
   C. thermometer and pan balance
   D. graduated cylinder and thermometer

5. **The symbol shown below appears in the discussion of a laboratory procedure.**

   What does this symbol mean?

   A. Sharp objects will be used.
   B. Poisonous chemicals will be used.
   C. Flammable chemicals will be used.
   D. Know the location of the eye wash station.

6. **Biao performs an experiment in which he compares the melting point of various elements found within a single group in the periodic table. What would be the BEST way to visually communicate his data?**

   A. line graph
   B. bar graph
   C. flow chart
   D. circle graph

7. Evelyn was investigating whether objects of different masses fall at different rates. She hypothesizes that the more massive object will fall faster than the less massive object. She climbs up a ladder and drops both objects from equal heights at the same time. They both hit the ground simultaneously. As a result of this research, what would be the BEST step for her to take next?

A. accept her hypothesis
B. revise her hypothesis
C. move on to another experiment
D. create a theory about how mass affects the rate at which different objects fall

8. Peter rode his bike 18.48 miles on Saturday. On Sunday he rode 4.2 miles less. Which of the following is the most precise difference for how many miles he rode Sunday?

A. 14.3
B. 14.28
C. 22.68
D. 22.7

9. Through what process do scientists make sure that each other's work is valid?

A. intuition
B. peer review
C. ethics
D. scholarships

10. Examine the graphs below. They show a relationship between receipt of a flu vaccine and the subsequent number of flu cases. Which graph supports the claim that the vaccine greatly reduced the number of flu cases until its tenth year of use?

A.

B.

C.

D.

Key: ———— People receiving vaccine
      .... Number of flu cases

CHAPTER 2

The Nature of Science

7 Developing Scientific Knowledge

 SCSh7.a-e

Getting the Idea

Understanding the world around us involves both the careful study of old scientific knowledge and rigorous questioning and testing in order to develop new knowledge. As scientists develop new ideas, they also check on and revise old ideas. Scientists constantly experiment to confirm what others have long accepted to be true, which is just as important as exploring new phenomena.

The Universe Is a System

Science is the systematic study of the world around us. To be systematic is to use a method, or a series of carefully designed steps. As discussed in an earlier lesson, the method that scientists use to study the world is a scientific method. Physical scientists use a **scientific method** to develop and discover rules about how the physical world works.

These rules, or universal principles, are true for every part of the universe. For example, the rules governing the way that objects are attracted to one another by the force of gravity are true everywhere on Earth. They are also true on other planets in our Solar System and on planets that revolve around distant stars. Scientists don't always look at every part of the universe at once, of course, but they keep in mind the broader rules when developing ideas about the details that they study. The rules of gravity, for example, are true for galaxies millions of times larger than Earth and for atoms millions of times smaller than a poppy seed.

Hypotheses Drive Experimentation

Part of the scientific method involves developing a hypothesis. Recall that a **hypothesis** is a possible explanation or tentative answer to the question being investigated. In other words, a hypothesis is a best guess at the answer to the question. A hypothesis must be testable, which means it must be possible for a scientist to design an experiment that verifies or disproves the hypothesis. In a well designed investigation, the results will either be consistent or inconsistent with the hypothesis.

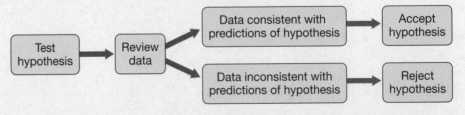

Test Tips . . .

Dress comfortably on the day of the exam. Be prepared for warm or cold conditions. You do not want to be distracted by physical discomfort on the day of the exam.

When scientists get data that do not support the hypothesis, they must reject or revise the hypothesis. But these data can still be valuable. They can help scientists develop a better hypothesis or design new experiments that better test hypotheses. In this way, hypotheses often cause scientists to develop new experiments that produce additional data.

Experimentation Never Ends

If many observations yield the same explanation repeatedly, over time, a hypothesis may become a theory. A **theory** is a hypothesis that has been tested many times, in different ways, with the same results. It is a broad explanation that ties together a range of observations and ideas about how processes are thought to occur.

But while theories are important explanations that result from many investigations, they can still be revised or even rejected. Scientists are constantly questioning old theories and testing new ideas. Sometimes they develop new ways to test an old theory. Results that confirm the theory strengthen its standing, and results that do not support the theory can lead to a revision of the theory or a rejection of it.

The flow chart below shows the never ending cycle of scientific research. Many cycles of testing hypotheses ultimately lead to the development of theories through experimental research. And any new data that call into question the validity of an old, established theory can also start the cycle all over again.

Scientific Method

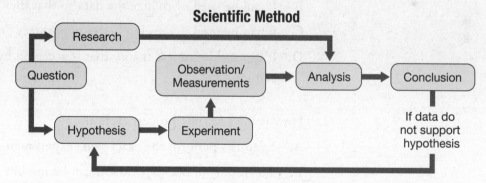

Scientific Understanding Is Always Changing

Scientists are always building on knowledge gained through the experiments of other scientists—their modern-day peers, as well as scientists who are no longer living. Sometimes, this knowledge remains uncontested for centuries. Sometimes, a scientific idea may be revised very soon after it is developed. Most changes to scientific knowledge are very small. For example, a single research team might publish a paper that outlines the details of a process specific to their town. Or a scientist might revise a very small part of a much larger theory.

But from time to time, there may occur major shifts in how scientists view how the world works. These major shifts are rare, but they can be very far reaching. Because universal principles are often interrelated, a shift in one idea can lead to a shift in many ideas. For example, quantum mechanics is a field of study that looks at how atoms and the particles that make up atoms behave. Before quantum mechanics was developed, scientists thought that atoms behaved exactly like larger objects, such as balls or planets. However, the new understanding of how they behave changed how scientists viewed the world With new evidence to support their ideas, scientists were able to revise or reject old ideas about how such tiny particles behave. These kinds of major shifts in scientific views result from new observations, new events, or even a new way of thinking that sheds light on old ideas.

DISCUSSION QUESTION

How do scientists go about exploring the physical world? What systematic procedure do they use?

LESSON REVIEW

1. How can a hypothesis that is inconsistent with experimental data be useful?

    A. It can identify scientists who are not good at their jobs.

    B. It can be used to change the data so that they match better.

    C. It can be used to develop better hypotheses or new experiments.

    D. It can still become a theory that is accepted by the scientific community.

2. How is the scientific process cyclical?

    A. Scientists perform the exact same experiments over and over.

    B. The results of one experiment can be used to develop new experiments.

    C. All scientific hypotheses become theories that are used to develop new hypotheses.

    D. Scientists learn from other scientists and then teach young people who may grow up to be scientists.

3. Which of the following terms is a possible explanation or tentative answer to a scientific question?

   A. hypothesis

   B. scientific method

   C. theory

   D. universal principle

4. Which of the following is true of scientific understanding?

   A. Scientists rarely work from knowledge that they did not discover themselves.

   B. Occasionally, there are major shifts in how scientists view how the world works.

   C. There is only one way to carry out the scientific method in order to develop a theory.

   D. Scientists never throw out a theory once it has been accepted by the scientific community.

8 Designing Investigations

SCSh8.a

Getting the Idea

Even very young children have questions about the natural world around them. They wonder why the sky is blue, why we fall "down" instead of fly off into space, or how puddles evaporate. All of these questions, along with thousands of others are valid and important scientific questions that generate opportunities for studying science. A scientific method is a process that all scientists, regardless of what they study, use to solve problems and develop scientific knowledge. It works best when the problem, question, or phenomena being studied can be isolated. A scientist uses a hypothesis to design a fair test to investigate a question. The experimental design describes the steps that will be taken to conduct the test. The Universe Is a System.

Key Words

experimental design
variable
independent variable
dependent variable
experimental group
control group
trials

Starting the Scientific Process

A scientific method is a process that guides the search for answers to a question. Although there is no single order in which the steps of the scientific method must be performed, there are some general parts that should be conducted in order to carry out an investigation. When beginning an inquiry or an experiment, scientists always begin with an observation, or something they have noticed. They follow that observation with a hypothesis. It is based on background knowledge and previous scientific research. A hypothesis is a scientific statement or idea that can be tested with research.

After the formation of a sound hypothesis, scientists develop an experimental design to test it. The **experimental design** is the plan for the research study. It must be carefully constructed so that other scientists can replicate it to test its validity and reliability.

Identify Variables

In the development of an experiment, scientists must identify conditions to be changed in the experiment and conditions to be controlled, or kept the same. A fair test examines only one factor, or variable, at a time. A **variable** is anything that might affect the outcome of the test, or it is a factor that changes during a test. There are two kinds of variables—the independent variable, or manipulated variable, and the dependent variable, or responding variable. The **independent variable** is the one that the scientist changes or manipulates. The **dependent variable** responds to changes in the independent variable. It measures the effects of the independent variable (if any). The table below shows the independent and dependent variables for different scienctific questions.

Examples of Independent and Dependent Variables

Question	Independent Variable	Dependent Variable
How does salt affect water's freezing point?	Amount of salt in the water	Freezing temperature
Which fertilizer grows the largest apples?	Type of fertilizer	Volume or mass of the apples
What size parachute slows a free fall fastest?	Area of the parachute	Speed of the free fall

Using a Control Group

How will a scientist know that the dependent variable changed as a result of the manipulated variable? For example, it might simply be coincidence that a particular amount of salt in the water affected its freezing temperature. To avoid such a possibility, every good experiment should have two groups to be studied—the **experimental group** and the **control group**. The two groups should be identical except for the fact that the experimental group undergoes a change in its independent variable. Every other factor must stay the same.

In the salt water example, the control and the experimental group would have identical conditions of water amount, starting temperature, location, etc., but the control group would have no salt and the experimental group would have varying amounts of salt.

Accepting or Rejecting a Hypothesis

A scientist usually repeats an experiment with the same conditions many times. These repetitions are called **trials**. After analyzing the data from the trials, the scientist will determine if the experimental results are consistent with the hypothesis. If there are discrepancies, scientists will modify the hypothesis and conduct additional controlled experiments to test the new hypothesis. This process continues until the predicted and observed results are the same, and then a sound conclusion is formed.

A great strength of the scientific method is that it is a verifiable process. Since scientists must use clear statements of the hypothesis being tested and provide detailed records, other scientists are able to verify the findings. This process of verification allows the scientific community to accept the findings as true. Until experimental results can be replicated and verified, the scientific community is reluctant to accept results as facts.

DISCUSSION QUESTION

An experiment is designed to test a new sneaker. The scientists have designed the sneaker to perform well on a variety of surfaces (trails, tracks, and gym equipment). Each time the sneaker is tested on a different surface, it is tested by the same athlete, tied to the same tightness, and worn for the same length of time. Why wouldn't the scientists use different athletes and for different lengths of time as well?

LESSON REVIEW

1. An experiment tests the effect of ramp height on toy car speed Ramp height in this case is the

   A. independent variable

   B. dependent variable

   C. control

   D. constant

2. In the experimental data below, which variable appears to cause the water to boil at a higher temperature?

Salt Concentration and Boiling Point

Solution	Boiling Point Trial 1	Boiling Point Trial 2	Boiling Point Trial 3
1 L water	100°C	100°C	100°C
1 L water + 1 tablespoon salt	102.1°C	101.9°C	101.6°C
1 L water + 2 tablespoons salt	103.5°C	103.4°C	103.4°C

   A. amount of water

   B. amount of salt

   C. container size

   D. time of day

3. Tom investigated whether sugar raises the boiling point of water. He put 2 liters of water at 20°C and 2 cups of sugar in a pot, heated the solution over a flame, and measured the temperature when the water reached a rolling boil. He repeated the experiment three times and recorded the same result each time. He concluded the sugar raises the boiling point of water by 5°C. Where did Tom err in his experimental design?

   A. He did not boil a pot of water without sugar.

   B. He did not conduct the trials at the same time.

   C. He waited until the water reached a rolling boil.

   D. He should have repeated the measurement several more times.

4. Alice studied the flow of water through different types of soil. She set up identical volumes of samples of different types of soil in each of five different beakers. One by one, she poured a measured volume of water into the samples and measured the time it took for the water to drain through the samples. In this investigation, what is the dependent variable?

   A. the number of samples she used

   B. the amount of water she poured

   C. the type of soil she selected

   D. the drainage time

9 Theories and Bias

 SCSh8.b-e

Getting the Idea

Because scientists rely on each other's work to build on scientific understanding, honesty in science is important. Honesty can involve a conscious effort to report scientific results truthfully. It can also involve an effort to eliminate unconscious desires to have an investigation come out in a certain way. Such an unconscious desire, or bias, to influence or interpret the results of an investigation, will be discussed later in this lesson.

Key Words
objective
bias

Honesty in Science

Ethical guidelines require scientists to conduct investigations responsibly and with integrity. One way scientists achieve this goal is by doing experiments that make use of procedures that other scientists agree are fair and honest. Experiments are planned to honestly test the validity of a hypothesis. Reasonable efforts are made to eliminate personal feelings or prejudices that may taint the investigation's results. Data are accurately recorded Data are also interpreted honestly—even when they contradict the expectations of the researcher.

Ethical behavior is equally important after an investigation is completed Consider the consequences, for example, of a scientist who conducts an investigation and obtains unexpected and unwanted results. An unethical scientist might fail to report the results or claim that the results are invalid However, unexpected results are often as important and informative as expected results. For example, the discovery of one of the most effective weapons against infections, the antibiotic penicillin, was an unexpected result of an investigation. In addition, future research builds and depends on the results of current research. Scientists therefore have an obligation to report their results honestly, even when the results are not what they had hoped to find.

Avoiding Bias

An underlying requirement of scientific inquiry is that it be **objective**—based on facts and free of bias. **Bias** is a personal prejudice or preconceived idea that may favor a particular point of view or outcome. Bias is the opposite of objectivity.

Scientists are human, so it can sometimes be difficult for a scientist to recognize or admit that an idea is inaccurate, wrong, or unsupported by evidence. One way scientists try to eliminate bias is by conducting

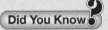
experiments that make use of procedures that other scientists agree are fair and honest. For example, hypothesis testing and controlled experimentation help scientists step back from their beliefs and test ideas objectively. Using mathematics to confirm and verify findings also helps to fight bias.

Many experiments need a control, or an unchanged sample, to avoid bias. Experiments often involve observing how changes in a certain variable affect an object or event. A control would not be subject to these changes. Without a control, the results may be tainted without the researcher realizing it. A control may not be needed for research that involves only simple measurements or observing patterns in nature.

Scientists try to develop an awareness of their biases and set them aside as they do their work. Some scientists work in collaboration with others to try to reduce bias in their research. Working as part of a team does not always totally eliminate the risk of bias. However, team members can reduce bias by challenging each other about untested assumptions.

When an investigation is complete, allowing researchers in other groups to review the results is important. Researchers who are part of a different team will often have different backgrounds and personal opinions about topics. Other teams may also have somewhat different experimental techniques. Allowing others to review an experiment's procedures and the interpretation of results will likely expose any unintentional biases in the experiment.

Unintentional bias may also be avoided by performing what is known as a double-blind experiment. This is often done when studying the effect of experimental medicines on human subjects. In a double-blind experiment the experimental medicine is given to some patients and a solution containing nothing but an ineffective substance, such as sugarwater, to other patients. Neither the scientists nor the patients know which group is receiving the medicine and which the sugarwater. In other words, both groups are "blind" as to who is getting the independent variable, the medicine. Such a procedure helps eliminate unintentional bias.

Judging the Merit of a New Theory

When scientists judge whether a theory has merit, they look at how well it explains results from unbiased experiments or observations. When experimental results or observations do not agree with a theory, scientists may question, reject, or revise the theory. They may also develop new experiments to further test the validity of the theory. The ultimate goal of science is to develop an understanding of the world that is based on experimental evidence, observation, or logic. The chart below shows some characteristics that scientists look for to give them confidence in their conclusions.

Confidence Characteristics

Confidence results from . . .
- past experiences
- repeatable patterns
- logical analysis
- well-collected data
- well-analyzed conclusions
- many repeated trials or experiments
- a sound experimental design
- sound and accurate mathematical analysis
- independent review by other scientists

DISCUSSION QUESTION

What are some ways that scientists try to overcome bias as they conduct investigations?

LESSON REVIEW

1. You conduct an experiment and find that your data do not support your hypothesis. What should you do?

    A. report the data and conclusion honestly

    B. change both the data and the hypothesis

    C. change the data to support the hypothesis

    D. change the hypothesis to one that is supported by the data

2. Which of the following is NOT a tool scientists use to overcome bias during investigations?

    A. conduct experiments that make use of procedures that other scientists agree are fair and honest

    B. discard data that do not support the hypothesis

    C. carry out controlled experiments

    D. use mathematical analyses

3. Which of the following is a description of bias?

    A. a personal prejudice that may favor a particular point of view

    B. a theory that is based on facts or evidence gathered in an experiment

    C. a method of analyzing data that uses mathematics instead of qualitative description

    D. a process in which knowledgeable scientists review the procedures and conclusions of an investigation

4. What is the BEST way to convince a scientist that a theory is valid?

    A. publish the theory in an article

    B. describe how many years it has been in existence

    C. list several prominent scientists who think the theory is valid

    D. show data collected from unbiased experiments that support the theory

Scientific Disciplines

 SCSh8.f

Getting the Idea

Physical science is the study of nonliving systems. Physical scientists study matter and how it interacts with energy. **Matter** has mass and takes up space. It is what all substances are made of. Rocks, plants, metals, liquids, and even you are made up of matter. **Energy** is the ability to do work. When objects move, when they give off heat, when they make sounds, when they produce light, matter is interacting with energy.

Branches of Physical Science

There are many types of physical science. They differ in what topics scientists study and how they go about studying those topics. Two main branches of physical science are chemistry and physics.

Chemistry is the science of what substances are made of and how they interact with energy and each other. Chemists study the particles that make up different materials. They study how different chemicals react, how energy plays a role in such reactions, and the conditions that cause substances to change into new substances. Some chemists, biochemists, study the chemistry of living systems. Other chemists, physical chemists, study the processes that cause atoms and molecules to behave the way they do. For example, a physical chemist might investigate the factors that affect the solubility of one substance, such as sugar, in another substance, such as water.

Physics is the study of the interaction of energy and matter. Many topics that physicists study overlap with what chemists study. Physicists investigate such topics as forces, motion, and different types of energy. They study particles that are far tinier than an atom and systems larger than a galaxy. Physicists use mathematics to quantify how systems work. They develop principles, theories, and laws that predict how objects move. For example the great English scientist and mathematician Isaac Newton conceived of a law of motion that explains the motion of rockets that drive objects into space, although in Newton's time no such rockets existed.

Other Sciences That Use Physical Science

Just as chemistry and physics are interrelated, other branches of science overlap with physical science.

Astronomy is the study of the objects and energy beyond Earth's atmosphere. For example, astronomers use physics to understand how objects such as Earth's moon stay in orbit (see the illustration below). They also study the lives of stars and how stars change over time. They investigate star systems called galaxies. Astronomers also investigate the chemical composition and paths of planets, comets, asteroids, and moons. On the basis of scientific observations, astronomers have even developed theories of how all the matter and energy in the universe came to be.

Geology is the study of the structure of Earth and the processes that shape it. Geologists may investigate the forces that cause the continents to move or the chemistry of different soils.

Meteorology is the study of weather in Earth's atmosphere. Meteorologists study such phenomena as the physics of tornadoes and hurricanes, how pressure and temperature affect weather conditions, and the ways that water and other substances move between Earth and its atmosphere.

Oceanography is the study of the Earth's oceans. Oceanographers investigate such topics as the chemistry of the ocean, ocean waves, the formation of structures on the ocean floor, ocean currents, and ocean life. In their work, oceanographers employ surface research vessels as well as submersibles that can dive thousands of meters beneath the surface.

Biology is the study of living things. Biologists study both the largest systems of living things, such as biomes that cover huge areas of Earth, to the smallest, such as the molecules that make living things what they are. These molecules include DNA, the substance that passes on traits from one generation to the next.

DISCUSSION QUESTION

How do different branches of science differ? What branches of science employ mathematics and physical science?

LESSON REVIEW

1. What kind of scientist might look at how the temperature of ocean water affects the movement of an ocean current?

   A. biologist

   B. biochemist

   C. astronomer

   D. oceanographer

2. What science deals with systems beyond Earth's atmosphere?

   A. meteorology

   B. astronomy

   C. chemistry

   D. oceanography

3. How might understanding the chemistry of living systems on Earth be useful to an astronomer?

   A. It might help the astronomer look for clues of life on other planets.

   B. It might help the astronomer understand the physics of star systems.

   C. It might help the astronomer better understand the movement of a comet.

   D. It might help the astronomer understand the nuclear reactions that take place in the sun.

4. Which of the following might a chemist study?

   A. how weather systems develop and move

   B. how ocean waves interact with a sea cliff

   C. how forces affect the movement of planets

   D. how molecules in living systems interact with energy

11 Reading Scientific Materials

SCSh9.a-d

Getting the Idea

Key Words
scientific journal
affiliation
editorial
sources

Because scientific knowledge is always changing, scientists must keep up with current trends and discoveries. One way scientists stay informed in their field of study is by reading scientific journals and science news publications. Knowing how to read and understand scientific materials is a valuable skill. A new finding in a related scientific field can give scientists insight into their own work. Reading scientific materials can even help non-scientists make informed decisions about purchases, voting, and health.

Types of Scientific Reading Materials

Just as science is all around you, scientific ideas can pop up in many different types of reading materials. Scientists who want to stay informed about science might read from the following types of publications:

- **Scientific journals**—These are weekly or monthly publications that print scientific papers and reports of experiments. They are often peer reviewed and represent the latest scientific findings. You usually have to go to the library or have a subscription to read scientific journals. Some scientists post their articles online.

- **Science magazines**—Many popular weekly or monthly magazines print feature articles about science and technology topics. They often include science related news stories and reviews of new products and new technologies that are of interest to a broad segment of the population. You can find science magazines at a library, bookstore, or other store that sells magazines.

- **Newspapers**—Daily newspapers often have a weekly section that highlights science, health, and technology topics. In addition, newspapers publish arcticles on breaking scientific news.

- **Web sites**—Many newspapers and magazines have web sites that feature articles from their print versions. They may also have new content that appears only online. In addition, you can use various search engines to access scientific information.

- **Nonfiction books**—At any given time, there are dozens of popular nonfiction books that make the bestseller lists. These may include biographies of famous scientists, political commentary about science and technology policies, or in-depth examinations of interesting science topics.

Building a Scientific Vocabulary

You may have a favorite hobby or sport that uses special words to describe equipment or procedures specific to that activity. Science is the same way. Scientists have their own vocabulary for discussing scientific issues. Although many of these words may be unfamiliar to you at first, practice using and looking up scientific terms. Regular exposure to scientific reading materials can help you better understand how scientists express themselves.

When you come across an unfamiliar word, try looking at the sentence or paragraph around it to figure out what it means. Then look it up in the dictionary or online. If you don't have access to a dictionary, jot it down on a piece of paper and look it up later. Once you learn a new word, try using it in a sentence as practice.

Evaluating Reading Materials

An important part of science is discussing ideas with other scientists. An interesting part of staying informed on science news is finding out what other scientists think about a news topic. You may find that reading an article on your own is boring or difficult, but discussing it with a friend can be more fun. Your friend may have insights that may not have occurred to you, and sharing your own insights can give you practice in scientific communication.

Remember that not all reading materials are reliable sources of scientific information. It is especially important in science to question the source of information. Scientific journals are the most reliable sources of information. Advertisements and commercial are among the least reliable sources.

First, when evaluating a scientific article, you should look at who is printing the article. Many publications have reputations for printing reliable information about science, while others may not. For example, you would probably trust the scientific information in an article about health in your local newspaper before you would trust information in a fashion magazine advertisement about a beauty product. Also, you should question why someone is printing the information you are reading. Look at the authors' **affiliation**, where they work or who they work for. Are they scientists at a large university? Or are they spokespeople for a business that wants to sell you something?

Next, consider the authors' purpose in writing. As mentioned above, think about whether the authors will make money off of the ideas that they are promoting. Consider whether the article is an unbiased report or whether it is an editorial. An **editorial** is an article that expresses an opinion. It can be informative to read editorials, because they can help you form your own opinion about science topics. However, you must keep in mind that they represent a biased point of view, and there may be many other and contradictory opinions.

Finally, look at the data. Does the article give numbers to back up its claims? Evaluate those data just as you would the data in a lab report. Consider whether the author is leaving out any important information. Ask yourself whether the data match your own experience. Also, look at how the data compare to those in similar reports in other articles.

DISCUSSION QUESTION

How might you go about building a better scientific vocabulary?

LESSON REVIEW

1. Which of the following is NOT a reliable source for scientific information?

   A. newspaper

   B. scientific journal

   C. science news website

   D. advertisement

2. What is an affiliation?

   A. where someone works

   B. an opinion someone holds

   C. an article that expresses an opinion

   D. a publication that comes out weekly

3. A newspaper prints an editorial about a science-related issue in the news. Why might you question the claims in this article?

   A. Editorials do not contain data to back up any claims.

   B. Editorials present opinions that may or may not be valid.

   C. Newspapers are not a good source for scientific information.

   D. Scientists rarely read newspaper editorials about science topics.

4. Which of the following is the MOST effective way to improve your scientific vocabulary?

A. read science fiction novels and memorize the words that look technical

B. look for science words in newspaper articles that are about non-science topics

C. read scientific materials regularly and look up any words that you do not know

D. carry a science textbook with you at all times in case you need to look up a word

1. **What is a universal principle?**

   A. a theory about how galaxies form
   B. a rule that is true anywhere in the universe
   C. a hypothesis that has been tested several times
   D. a possible explanation or tentative answer to a scientific question

2. **Which of the following is NOT an activity in which scientists participate?**

   A. accepting all long-standing theories
   B. revising theories in the face of new data
   C. testing theories as new ideas are formed
   D. developing new hypotheses from old data

3. **How can you identify the independent variable in an experiment?**

   A. Its measured value does not change during the experiment.
   B. It is the variable that is manipulated or changed in an experiment.
   C. It changes in response to some other variable in the experiment.
   D. It is part of the control group but not part of the experimental group.

4. **A scientist is increasing the concentration of reactants in a chemical reaction in order to find out how concentration affects the rate of the reaction. In this experiment, what is the rate of the reaction?**

   A. hypothesis
   B. independent variable
   C. dependent variable
   D. conclusion

5. **Which of the following is a source of bias in a scientific investigation?**

   A. observing patterns in nature
   B. overcoming personal prejudice
   C. letting opinions color observations
   D. conducting controlled experiments

6. **How is the merit of a new theory judged by scientists?**

   A. by how well it explains scientific data
   B. by how well it convinces important scientists
   C. by how many experiments were used to develop it
   D. by how many details are included in its description

7. **What branch of science deals MOSTLY with interactions among different substances and energy?**

   A. astronomy
   B. chemistry
   C. meteorology
   D. oceanography

8. **How might understanding the physics of fluids be useful to an oceanographer?**

   A. It might help the oceanographer study ways to protect ocean life.
   B. It might help the oceanographer predict the movement of ocean currents.
   C. It might help the oceanographer understand the chemistry of ocean water.
   D. It might help the oceanographer understand the interactions of different ocean animals.

9. **Where would you go to find papers written by scientists discussing the methods and results of their experiments?**

   A. newspaper
   B. nonfiction book
   C. scientific journal
   D. science news website

10. **Which of the following is NOT a way to evaluate reading material for scientific reliability?**

    A. look at the data
    B. check the author's affiliation
    C. consider the reputation of the publication
    D. decide whether you agree with the conclusions

CHAPTER

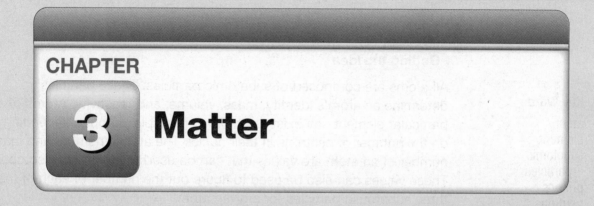

3 Matter

12 Atomic Structure

 SPS1.b

Getting the Idea

Key Words

atom
element
subatomic
  particles
protons
neutrons
electrons
electron cloud
atomic mass units
isotopes
stable
unstable
atomic number
atomic mass
mass number

All atoms are composed of subatomic particles. These particles determine an atom's identity, mass, volume, and reactivity. Atoms of a particular element can exist as stable or unstable isotopes depending on the number of neutrons in their nuclei. The atomic number and mass number of an atom are values that can be used to identify the isotopes. These values can also be used to figure out the number of each of the three subatomic particles for a given atom.

Subatomic Particles and Atomic Structure

The basic building block of all matter is the **atom**; it is the smallest unit of an **element** that still has the chemical properties of that element. An element is any substance made up of only one type of atom. Currently, there are 117 known elements.

Atoms are composed of three major **subatomic particles—protons, neutrons**, and **electrons**. Subatomic particles are classified based on their location within the atom, their relative mass, and their charge. Protons and neutrons are located in the center of the atom and make up the atom's nucleus. Electrons are found in a much larger region surrounding the nucleus called the **electron cloud.**

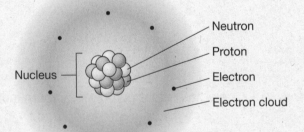

The mass of the proton and the mass of the neutron are about the same. The mass of the electron is so much smaller than the masses of protons and neutrons that it is insignificant to the total mass of an atom. When comparing the masses of the particles, protons and neutrons are assigned a relative mass of 1 **atomic mass unit** (abbreviated amu), and electrons are assigned a relative mass of 0 amu.

The table below summarizes the characteristics of the three major subatomic particles. Note their charges.

Subatomic Particles

Particle	Electrical Charge	Mass (amu)	Location
Protons	Positive (+1)	1	nucleus
Neutrons	Neutral (0)	1	nucleus
Electrons	Negative (-1)	0	electron cloud

The nucleus of an atom has a positive charge equal to the number of protons it contains. The electron cloud has a negative charge equal to the number of electrons it contains. The number of protons and electrons in an atom are equal. This means that the total positive and total negative charge is also equal, making the atom neutral (having no charge).

Opposite electrical charges attract. Like charges repel one another. The opposite charges of protons and electrons result in an attractive force between the nucleus and the electron cloud region of atoms. This attractive force is stronger than the repulsive force between like-charged particles. Without this attractive force between protons and electrons, the repulsive force between electrons and electrons and between protons and protons would make it impossible for an atom to exist. The attractive force between the nucleus and electron cloud holds atoms together. Within the nucleus, the neutrons keep the repulsive forces between positively charged protons from splitting the nucleus apart.

The protons and neutrons are tightly bound in the nucleus. This region is very tiny compared to the electron cloud region. Scientists used to believe that electrons orbited the nucleus in the same way that planets orbit the sun. Electrons actually move erratically far away from the nucleus within areas of space called energy levels. Electrons that have high energy are found in energy levels farther away from the nucleus. Electrons with less energy are found in energy levels closest to the nucleus. Each energy level can hold a specific number of electrons. As the energy levels move farther away from the nucleus, the number of electrons that can occupy them increases. Because the volume of the nucleus is so small compared to the volume of the electron cloud, the volume of the electron cloud is what determines the volume of an atom.

Subatomic Particles and Chemical Properties

The identity of an element is determined by the number of protons in the nucleus of its atoms. Atoms of the same element have the same number of protons in each of their nuclei. For example, every single atom of the element gold has 79 protons in its nucleus. Each atom of silver has 47 protons in its nucleus. Every element has atoms with a number of protons that is different from the number of protons in atoms of any other element. Although atoms of the same element must have the same number of protons, their number of neutrons can vary. Atoms with the same number of protons but different numbers of neutrons are called **isotopes**.

When an atom gains or loses electrons, it remains the same element because the number of protons has not changed. Atoms of the same element may gain or lose electrons in order to react with different elements and form chemical compounds, such as water and carbon dioxide. Chemical reactions between different elements occur in the electron cloud because that is where the electrons are located. Electrons located in the energy level farthest from the nucleus are the electrons that will form chemical bonds with other elements to make chemical compounds.

Isotopes, Atomic Number, and Mass Number

Many elements have two or more isotopes. For most elements, only one isotope is stable. A **stable** isotope is an element whose nucleus does not spontaneously give off particles or energy. An **unstable** isotope is an element whose nucleus decomposes, or decays, by losing particles and energy. Such isotopes are said to be radioactive. The energy or particles that are emitted from the nucleus is called radiation.

Since all isotopes of an element have the same number of protons, their atomic number is always the same. The **atomic number** of an element is equal to the number of protons in its atoms. The atomic number of an element is printed near the symbol of the element in the periodic table of the elements.

The periodic table also provides the atomic mass of elements. The **atomic mass** of an element, or its mass number, is the weighted averages of the masses of the naturally occurring isotopes of an element. For most elements, the atomic mass is represented by the decimal number found near its symbol in the periodic table.

The mass number of an atom is an important number when comparing isotopes of elements to determine how many neutrons their atoms have. The mass number is equal to the total number of protons and neutrons in the atom. To determine the number of neutrons in an atom of an element, the following formula is used:

number of neutrons = mass number – number of protons

Unlike atomic number and atomic mass, the mass number is generally not printed in the periodic table. A common misconception is that the mass number can be determined by rounding off the atomic mass in the periodic table. This is not true. Each isotope has its own mass number. The mass number must be given to determine the number of neutrons in a particular isotope of an element.

Two ways in which isotopes are written are shown below. In the first example, the mass number (upper left), the atomic number (lower left), and the element's symbol are given. In the second example, only the mass number and the element's symbol are provided.

$$^{27}_{13}Al \text{ or } Al\text{-}27$$

The symbol Al can be found in the periodic table of elements. Its name is aluminum. The mass number is given in both examples for aluminum. It is 27. The atomic number is given in the first example. It is 13. Remember that the atomic number on the periodic table is the whole number equal to the number of protons in an atom's nucleus. So the nucleus of this isotope of aluminum contains 13 protons. The following formula can be used to determine the number of neutrons in this isotope of aluminum.

number of neutrons = *mass number – number of protons*

number of neutrons = 27 – 13

The nucleus of this isotope contains 14 neutrons.

When enough information is provided, the symbols for the isotope can be constructed The symbol for uranium is U. All uranium atoms have 92 protons. One isotope of uranium has a mass number of 238. The mass number for this uranium isotope is 238, and the atomic number is equal to the number of protons which is 92. The two ways to write the symbols for this isotope are:

$$^{238}_{92}U \text{ or } U\text{-}238$$

DISCUSSION QUESTION

When the element sodium reacts with the element chlorine, sodium loses an electron and chlorine gains an electron to make a common chemical compound called table salt, or sodium chloride. Use subatomic particles to explain why the elements sodium and chlorine can still be identified in the new compound sodium chloride.

LESSON REVIEW

1. Why do atoms of elements have neutral charges?

   A. All atoms contain neutrons which have no charge.

   B. The number of protons and the number of neutrons are equal.

   C. The number of protons and the number of electrons are equal.

   D. The number of neutrons and the number of electrons are equal.

2. What region of the atom determines the volume of the atom?

   A. the nucleus because it is extremely dense

   B. the nucleus because almost all of the mass of the atom is located here

   C. the electron cloud because it is extremely dense

   D. the electron cloud because the volume of the nucleus is insignificant compared to the volume of the electron cloud

Has the same # of protons but a different # of NEUTRONS

same Atomic# → different form of element

mass changes

3. An isotope of chlorine has 17 protons and 19 neutrons. What is the mass number for that isotope of chlorine?

   A. 2

   B. 17

   C. 19

   D. 36

4. The most commonly occurring isotope of argon is Ar-40. The atomic number of argon is 18. Which symbol below represents another way to illustrate Ar-40?

   A. $_{18}^{40}$Ar

   B. $_{22}^{40}$Ar

   C. $_{40}^{18}$Ar

   D. $_{40}^{22}$Ar

13 Atomic Bonds

 SPS1.b

Getting the Idea

There are approximately 117 known chemical elements, as indicated in a current periodic table, and there are countless substances that can be formed by these elements. Substances are formed by various combinations of atoms held together by forces of attraction. This joining together of atoms is called **chemical bonding**.

Bonding and Stability

To understand chemical bonding, it is important to know that the electrons in an atom are organized in energy levels. The electrons closest to the nucleus of an atom have less energy than those electrons located in the levels farthest from the atom. The organization of electrons in energy levels is known as **electron configuration**.

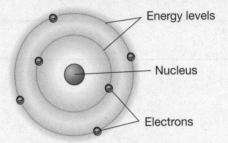

When each energy level contains the maximum number of electrons, then it is considered to be full and therefore less likely to react or combine with another element. Such is the case of the Group 18 elements (the farthest right-hand column of the periodic table), known as the noble gases. The electron configuration of the noble gases is very stable. Helium has two electrons in the outside energy level, thus composing a stable **helium structure**, and the remaining noble gases all have eight electrons in the outside energy level, resulting in stable structures. These stable structures are the reason why the noble gases exist in the air as single atoms. They tend not to react with other elements.

Key Words

chemical bonding
electron
   configuration
helium structure
stability
noble gas electron
   configuration
nonmetals
metals
covalent bond
ionic bond
ion
positive ion
negative ion
ionic crystal

Test Tips . . .

Remember to refer to the reference materials provided with the exam. The periodic table gives you a lot of information and can be useful when determining when an atom is likely to gain or lose one or more electrons to achieve stability. The formula sheet can assist you in problem-solving.

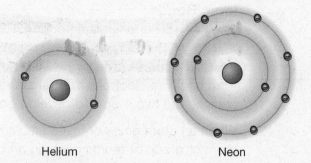

Helium   Neon

For all of the other atoms that do not have full energy levels, if they bond chemically with another atom and fill up the vacant spot in the energy level, they will be achieve **stability**. More simply stated, atoms will become more stable if they achieve a **noble gas** electron configuration.

Achieving Chemical Stability

Chemical bonding occurs when atoms gain, lose, or share electrons. **Nonmetals**, those elements grouped on the right side of the periodic table, have less than the number of electrons that they need in order to have a stable arrangement. So in order to become more stable, nonmetals can:

- gain electrons, or

- share electrons with another nonmetal.

Metals, those elements grouped on the left side of the periodic table, have one, two, or three more than the number of electrons that they need in order to have a stable arrangement. So in order to become more stable, metals can:

- lose electrons, or

- combine electrons with another metal.

Covalent Bonds

Covalent bonds are formed by atoms sharing electrons to form molecules. Covalent bonding is caused by the force of the attraction between the two positive nuclei of the two atoms of the bond and the electrons between them. This type of bond is usually formed between two non-metallic elements.

Example of sharing electrons:

Two chlorine atoms form the stable molecule chlorine Cl_2. A covalent bond is formed between the atoms.

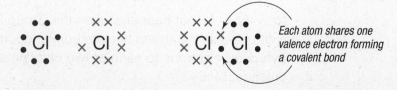

Each atom shares one valence electron forming a covalent bond

Ionic Bonds

Another type of chemical bond that can occur between atoms is called an ionic bond. **Ionic bonds** typically occur between the atoms of metals and non-metals to form binary ionic compounds. These compounds form because electrons are transferred from one atom to the other, causing the two atoms to develop opposite charges.

When an atom gains or loses an electron, an ion is formed. An **ion** is an atom or group of atoms carrying an overall positive or negative charge.

When electrons are removed from an atom, the excess charge from the protons produces an overall **positive ion**, such as Na+.

When an atom gains an electron, there is an excess of negative charge, so a **negative ion** is formed, such as Cl–. Basically, the charge on an ion is numerically related to the number of electrons gained or lost.

The metallic elements, specifically those in Groups 1 and 2 in the periodic table, readily lose electrons from their outer shell. Conversely, the atoms of elements in Groups 16 and 17 tend to gain electrons and therefore pick up "stray" electrons to achieve a stable electron configuration. When a metal loses an electron, it forms a positive ion. When a non-metal gains an electron, it forms a negative ion. These two ions are held together as an electrically neutral compound.

Consider the Group 1 metal sodium and the Group 17 nonmetal chlorine. When the two are combined, the sodium atom donates its outer electron to the chlorine atom to form one positive sodium ion and one negative chloride ion. The resulting compound is called sodium chloride. This compound is an electrically neutral, or stable, ionic compound.

Example of gaining electrons:

A chlorine atom gains an electron from a sodium atom. An ionic bond is formed between the atoms.

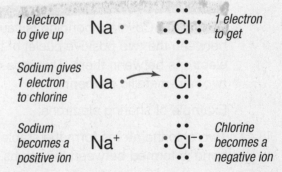

Now look at what happens when the Group 2 metal magnesium reacts with chlorine. When the two are combined, magnesium transfers its two outer electrons to each of two chlorine atoms to form magnesium chloride, $MgCl_2$.

Knowing the positions of two elements in the periodic table helps to predict the ratio that the elements will combine. The table below shows the ratios of common binary ionic compounds.

Metals Positive Ion	Non-Metals Negative Ion		
	Group 15 (X^{-3})	Group 16 (X^{-2})	Group 17 (X^{-1})
Group 1 (M^{+1})	3:1	2:1	1:1
Group 2 (M^{+2})	3:2	1:1	1:2

The positively and negatively charged ions that make up an ionic compound, such as those in sodium chloride, are bonded tightly together in a three-dimensional crystal lattice, as shown in the illustration. This structure is known as an ionic crystal.

Sodium Chloride Lattice Structure

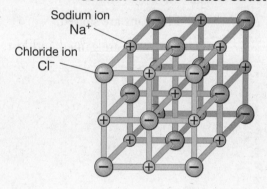

Sodium ion
Na^+

Chloride ion
Cl^-

DISCUSSION QUESTION
Explain how nonmetals in Groups 16 and 17 tend to gain electrons in order to achieve stability.

LESSON REVIEW

1. Which element is stable, exists as a single atom in air, and has a full outer energy level?

   A. helium

   B. hydrogen

   C. gold

   D. oxygen

2. What type of element typically loses electrons to form a bond?

   A. metal

   B. metalloid

   C. noble gas

   D. nonmetal

3. At what ratio will potassium and sulfur form a binary ionic compound?

   A. 1:1

   B. 1:2

   C. 2:1

   D. 3:1

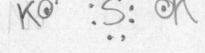

4. Which of the following occurs during covalent bonding?

   A. Electrons are gained only.

   B. Electrons are lost only.

   C. Electrons are shared.

   D. Electrons are gained and lost.

14 Physical Properties of Matter

 SPS2.a

Getting the Idea

All matter has both physical and chemical properties; those characteristics that classify the matter. These properties allow and direct certain physical and chemical changes to occur. Different types of matter behave differently based on their unique properties. Density is a physical property of matter that represents the ratio of mass to volume of a substance. The density of a substance determines whether that substance will float or sink in a certain fluid.

Key Words

matter
physical property
physical change
chemical property
chemical change
density
mass
volume
solubility
viscosity
conductivity

Identifying Matter

Matter is anything that takes up space and has mass. Physical and chemical properties are used to describe different behaviors of matter. A **physical property** is a characteristic of a substance that can be observed directly or measured with a tool without changing the composition of the substance. Physical properties result in physical changes. A **physical change** is any change in a substance in which the composition of the substance does not change. A **chemical property** is a description of the potential that a substance has to undergo a change that alters the composition of the substance. Chemical properties result in chemical changes. A **chemical change** is any change that results in the formation of new substances. Substances can be identified by their physical and chemical properties.

Physical Properties and Physical Changes

Some examples of physical properties include boiling point, freezing/melting point, density, solubility, viscosity, and electrical conductivity. As each of these properties is observed or measured for a substance, its composition does not change. Examples of physical changes include phase changes, size changes, and shape changes.

Evaporating, condensing, freezing, and melting are physical changes that result in a phase change, changing from one state of matter into another. All phase changes are physical changes because the composition of a substance does not change during phase changes. Boiling point and freezing (or melting) point refer to the temperature at which each phase change occurs.

Test Tips . . .

Completing word problems in science is just like completing word problems in math. Following these steps will ensure success in solving word problems.

1. Write down the "known(s)."

2. Write down the "unknown(s)."

3. Choose an equation that relates the "known(s)" and "unknown(s)."

4. Substitute the known numbers in the equation and solve.

Always check that the answer has the correct units.

A substance can change size due to expansion or contraction because of a change in temperature. This is a physical change because the composition of the substance has not changed A substance can also change size by being broken into smaller pieces. For example, hammering metals into thin sheets is a physical change. Metals can be hammered into thin sheets because they are malleable, a physical property unique to metals. A substance may change shape by being stretched or pulled Another property of metals is that they can be drawn into thin wires, a physical property known as ductility.

Density

Density, the mass of a substance per unit volume, is another physical property of matter. **Mass** is the amount of matter in an object, and **volume** is the amount of space an object occupies. Density cannot be measured directly but it is the ratio of two direct measurements: mass over volume. The following equation is used to calculate density:

$$\text{density} = \text{mass} / \text{volume}$$
$$D = m / V$$

Example 1: What is the density of a sample of gold that has a mass of 386.4 g and a volume of 20.0 cm^3?

Knowns: $m = 386.4$ g, $V = 20.0$ cm^3

Unknown: D

Equation: $D = m / V$

Solve: $D = 386.4$ g $/ 20.0$ cm^3

             $D = 19.3$ g $/$ cm^3

The density of gold is 19.3 g $/$ cm^3.

Example 2: What volume of mercury has a mass of 54 g? The density of mercury is 13.53 g $/$ cm^3.

Knowns: $m = 54$ g, $D = 13.53$ g $/$ cm^3

Unknown: V

Equation: $D = m / V$

Solve: 13.53 g $/$ cm$^3 = 54$ g $/ V$

             $V = 54$ g $/ 13.53$ g $/$ cm^3

             $V = 4.0$ cm^3

The volume of mercury that has a mass of 54 g is 4.0 cm^3.

The density of a substance at a certain temperature and pressure never changes under normal conditions. Because the formula for density is a ratio of mass to volume, as the mass of a substance increases, its volume also increases.

The density of a substance determines whether or not it will float in a surrounding fluid Denser substances tend to sink in a fluid that is less dense. For example, gold has a density of 19.3 g/cm³. Water has a density of 1.0 g/cm³. A piece of gold will sink in a tank of water. A piece of wood that has a density of 0.5 g/cm3 will float in a tank of water. Ice is the solid form of water. Ice is also less dense than water, so it will float in water.

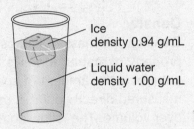

Ice
density 0.94 g/mL

Liquid water
density 1.00 g/mL

When poured into the same container, liquids that do not mix will form layers. These layers will sit in order from densest at the bottom to least dense at the top.

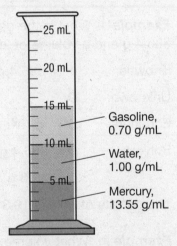

25 mL

20 mL

15 mL

Gasoline,
0.70 g/mL

10 mL

Water,
1.00 g/mL

5 mL

Mercury,
13.55 g/mL

Other Physical Properties

Solubility is the maximum amount of solute that will dissolve in a given solvent at a particular temperature and pressure. The solute is the substance that dissolves, and the solvent is the substance that does the dissolving. Together, the solute and solvent make up a solution, which is a mixture. The solute and solvent do not chemically combine during the dissolving process. Each substance retains its own properties. Therefore, solubility is a physical property.

Viscosity is a physical property of fluids. It is a measure of a fluid's resistance to flow. Fluids with high viscosity take longer to pour than fluids with low viscosity. As the temperature changes, a fluid's viscosity may also change. Because the composition of a fluid does not change when it is poured, viscosity is a physical property.

Electrical **conductivity** is a measure of a material's ability to conduct electrical current, or allow the movement of electrical changes through it. It is a physical property because the conduction of electrical current does not change the composition of matter. In general, metals have high conductivity and are good conductors because they allow electrical charges to flow. Nonmetals have low conductivity and are good insulators because they inhibit the flow of electrical charges.

The table below summarizes several physical properties and physical changes of matter.

Physical Properties		Physical Changes	
temperature	phase	freezing	cutting
color	density	melting	breaking
mass	viscosity	condensing	conducting
volume	solubility	evaporating	separating
shape	conductivity	expanding	mixing
boiling point	freezing point	contracting	dissolving

Chemical Changes versus Physical Changes

Some examples of chemical properties include the potential to combust (burn) and to corrode (rust). When substances undergo such changes they undergo chemical changes because new substances are formed. During a chemical change, there is a change in the arrangement of atoms involved, so a different substance with different properties is produced.

In a chemical change, chemical bonds between atoms break and reform between different atoms, which produces new substances. During a physical change, on the other hand, chemical bonds are not affected by the change, so no new substances are formed. Many of the clues that indicate a physical change are also clues that indicate a chemical change. Both kinds of changes can result in substances with new physical properties, such as color, density, and phase. For example, when water freezes (a physical change), its density decreases, and its phase changes from liquid to solid; but it is still water. However, when water (H_2O) breaks down into hydrogen (H_2) and oxygen (O_2), a chemical change takes place that produces new substances with both different physical and chemical properties. The only way to know for certain whether a chemical change or a physical change has taken place is to determine the chemical compositions of the substances before and after the change occurs. If they are alike, the change is a physical change. If they are different, the change is a chemical change.

DISCUSSION QUESTION

How would you determine the density of a solid object?

LESSON REVIEW

1. The density of aluminum is 2.70 g/cm³. A piece of aluminum foil has a volume of 54.0 cm³. What is the mass of this piece of aluminum foil?

   A. 146 g

   B. 20.0 g

   C. 14.6 g

   D. 0.050 g

$$D = \frac{M}{V}$$

$$2.7 = \frac{x}{54}$$

2. Which of the following is an example of a physical change?

   A. burning of methane gas produces water and carbon dioxide

   B. vinegar and baking soda combining to form a salt and water

   C. condensation of water vapor on the outside of a cold can of soda

   D. formation of silver sulfide when silver reacts with sulfur in the air

3. When copper reacts with oxygen in the air, a color change takes place, and the metal changes color from reddish brown to green. This green color is called a patina, and it has a different chemical composition from copper. What type of change occurs to produce a patina?

   A. dissolving

   B. conductivity

   C. physical change

   D. chemical change

4. Examine the diagram below.

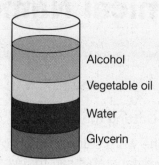

Alcohol

Vegetable oil

Water

Glycerin

Which substance is the densest?

A. alcohol

B. vegetable oil

C. water

D. glycerin

Chemical Names and Formulas

Getting the Idea

The word salt can refer to several different chemicals. Salt can mean the ordinary table salt that you put on your food, a household remedy called Epsom salt, and also a variety of ionic compounds that can be very dangerous if swallowed. In the laboratory, if you ask someone to pass the salt, they could hand you one of dozens of different chemicals. For this reason, chemists use a naming system that is much more specific.

Compounds

Compounds are pure substances composed of more than one type of element chemically combined in a fixed proportion. For example, every molecule of water has two hydrogen atoms and one oxygen atom. The ratio of hydrogen to oxygen in a sample of water is always 2 to 1.

Compounds have different properties than the component elements that form them. For example, sodium chloride is the chemical name for table salt. It is a solid at room temperature, soluble in water, and not combustible. The elements that make up sodium chloride are sodium and chlorine. Sodium is a very reactive metal that explodes when exposed to air. Chlorine is a poisonous gas at room temperature. The elements in compounds can be separated only by chemical reactions; they cannot be separated by physical means.

Compounds can be categorized into two groups based on the type of bonds formed between atoms. Covalent bonds form covalent compounds (molecular substances) and ionic bonds form ionic compounds. In a covalent compound, atoms share electrons. In an ionic compound, atoms gain or lose electrons.

Chemical Formulas

A **chemical formula** is a shorthand notation for identifying a compound. Chemical formulas consist of the symbols of the elements that make up the compound. These symbols can be found on the periodic table. Each symbol in a chemical formula may be followed by **subscripts**, small numbers that tell how many atoms (or ions) of that element are in each molecule (or unit) of the compound. When there is only one atom of an element in a compound, no subscript is used. For example, a water molecule has two atoms of hydrogen and one atom of oxygen. The chemical formula for water is shown on the next page:

Key Words
compound
chemical formula
subscript
binary compound

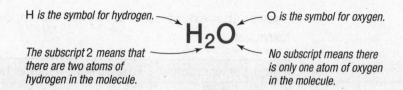

H *is the symbol for hydrogen.* → H_2O ← O *is the symbol for oxygen.*

The subscript 2 means that there are two atoms of hydrogen in the molecule.

No subscript means there is only one atom of oxygen in the molecule.

The chart below shows the chemical formulas for oxygen gas, glucose (a sugar), and table salt. Notice how the subscripts indicate how many atoms of each element are in an individual molecule of the compound.

Chemical Formula	Identify Elements	Number of Atoms of Each Element
O_2	oxygen	oxygen = 2
$C_6H_{12}O_6$	carbon hydrogen oxygen	carbon = 6 hydrogen = 12 oxygen = 6
$NaCl$	sodium chlorine	sodium = 1 chlorine = 1

Chemical Formulas for Ionic Compounds

Knowing the charge of the ions in an ionic compound can help you predict the ratios of the ions in the compound and therefore the chemical formula for the compound. In order for an ionic compound to be stable, the charges of the ions in the compound must be balanced. That means that there must be equal numbers of positive and negative charges in the ionic crystal.

Binary compounds are compounds that consist of only two elements. For binary compounds consisting only of ions that have +1 and −1 charges, there are equal numbers of each type of ion. The chemical formula for such a compound is simply the chemical symbols of the two elements. For example, table salt, sodium chloride, consists of Na^+ and Cl^- ions in equal amounts, or a 1:1 ratio. Thus, the chemical formula for sodium chloride is $NaCl$.

For binary compounds consisting of ions that have +2 and −2 charges, there are also equal numbers of each type of ion. That's because the ions have opposite charges of the same magnitude, so they balance each other out when in equal proportions. An example of such a compound is calcium oxide, CaO, which consists of Ca^{2+} ions and O^{2-} ions in a 1:1 ratio.

When the charges on the ions differ in magnitude, then the ratio of ions is no longer 1:1. For example, a binary ionic compound made up of Ca^{2+} ions and Cl^- ions would have to have a ratio of 1:2. So for every Ca^{2+} ion, there would have to be two Cl^- ions to balance the charges. Thus, the chemical formula for calcium chloride is $CaCl_2$. The chart below shows other examples of binary ionic compounds and their chemical formulas.

Name of Ionic Compound	Positive Ion	Negative Ion	Ratio of Ions (+ to −)	Chemical Formula
magnesium fluoride	Mg^{2+}	F^-	1:2	MgF_2
zincchloride	Zn^{2+}	Cl^-	1:2	$ZnCl_2$
potassium nitride	K^+	N^{3-}	3:1	K_3N
potassium oxide	K^+	O^{2-}	2:1	K_2O
aluminum sulfide	Al^{3+}	S^{2-}	2:3	Al_2S_3

Naming Ionic Compounds

When given the chemical formula for a binary ionic compound, you can figure out the name of the compound. To write the name, begin with the name of the element for the positive ion spelled normally. Then write the first part of the name of the second element (the negative ion), only end with the suffix -ide. For example, the name for NaCl uses the full name of the positive ion's element, sodium, followed by the first part of the name for the negative ion's element and the suffix -ide. Chlorine becomes chloride. The name for NaCl is sodium chloride.

When there is more than one type of positive ion for an element, the name also includes a roman numeral to indicate the charge of the ion. For example, iron has two stable positive ions. Fe^{2+} is called iron(II), and Fe^{3+} is called iron(III). Thus, the compound Fe_2O_3 is named iron(III) oxide, and the compound FeO is named iron(II) oxide.

Naming Covalent Compounds

As with binary ionic compounds, binary covalent compounds begin with the name of the first element spelled normally. The second element begins with the first part of the element's name and ends with the suffix -ide. However, in covalent compounds, both element names also include a prefix that shows the number of atoms of that element in each molecule. The chart below shows the prefixes used for different numbers of atoms in a molecule.

Prefix	Number of Atoms	Prefix	Number of Atoms
mono-	1	hexa-	6
di-	2	hepta-	7
tri-	3	octa-	8
tetra-	4	nona-	9
penta-	5	deca-	10

For example, NO_2 is nitrogen dioxide, N_2O is dinitrogen oxide, N_2O_3 is dinitrogen trioxide, and N_2O4 is dinitrogen tetroxide. The prefix *mono-* is usually omitted, unless there is a reason that similar compounds may be confused For example, molecules of carbon dioxide, CO_2, and carbon monoxide, CO, differ by only one atom of oxygen, so the prefix mono- is included for clarity; carbon dioxide vs. carbon monoxide.

DISCUSSION QUESTION

Why is it important for chemists to use the proper chemical name and chemical formula for identifying a compound?

LESSON REVIEW

1. Which of the following is the correct chemical formula for an ionic compound consisting of Ca^{2+} ions and I^- ions?

    A. CaI

    B. Ca_2I

    C. CaI_2

    D. CaI_3

2. Which of the following is the correct chemical formula for the covalent compound carbon tetrachloride?

    A. CCl

    B. C_4Cl

    C. CCl_4

    D. C_4Cl_4

3. What is the name for the ionic compound $AlCl_3$?

    A. aluminum chloride

    B. trialuminum chloride

    C. aluminum dichloride

    D. aluminum chloride(III)

4. What does the name copper(II) oxide tell you about the copper ions in the compound?

    A. Each copper ion in the compound has a +2 charge.

    B. There is only one type of stable positive copper ion.

    C. There are two copper ions for every O^{2-} ion in the compound.

    D. The formula for the compound has a subscript after the symbol for copper.

Conservation of Matter

SPS2.d-e

Getting the Idea

Numerous **chemical reactions** occur constantly in everyday life, and they all have two things in common: chemical reactions involve change, and no mass is lost during the change. The change occurring in a chemical reaction is represented by a **chemical equation**—a shorthand description, using symbols and formulas, depicting the reactants and products involved in a reaction. Reactants, the starting substances, appear to the left of the reaction arrow. Products, the resulting substances, appear to the right of the reaction arrow.

Reactants → Products

Important information can be obtained from a chemical equation, which is why there is a systematic approach for writing chemical equations.

Conservation of Mass

In any equation, the products contain the same atoms as the reactants, but the atoms are usually arranged in different ways. Basically, an equation shows that a chemical reaction involves changing the ways atoms are grouped, or arranged. So atoms that existed before the reaction have to exist after the reaction. This important principle is known as the **law of conservation of mass.**

> *Law of Conservation of Mass:*
> *Mass is neither created nor destroyed*

Balancing Chemical Equations

In order to verify that a chemical equation for a reaction obeys the law of conservation of mass, the equation has to be **balanced.** That is, each side of the equation has the same number of atoms of each element and mass is conserved.

Example of an unbalanced equation:

$$H_2 + O_2 \rightarrow H_2O$$
$$\downarrow \quad \downarrow \qquad \qquad \downarrow$$

2 H atoms 2 O atoms $\neq$ 2 H atoms and 1 O atom

Example of a balanced equation:

$$2H_2 + O_2 \quad \rightarrow \quad 2H_2O$$

$$\downarrow \qquad \downarrow \qquad \qquad \downarrow$$

4 H atoms 2 O atoms = 4 H atoms and 2 O atom

Consider the following scenario to understand how to identify an unbalanced equation and how to balance it.

By experimentation it was discovered that the combination of sodium molecules and oxygen molecules produce sodium peroxide molecules. The formulas of these substances are Na, O_2, and Na_2O_2. The chemical equation is shown.	$Na + O_2 \rightarrow Na_2O_2$
The chemical equation is a representation of the atoms in the reactants and products. However, in a chemical reaction, atoms can neither be created nor destroyed. But it appears, in the chemical equation, that a sodium atom has been destroyed. Since the formulas are correct, then the problem must be with the coefficients.	1 Na atom + 2 O atoms $\neq$ 2 Na atoms + 2 O atoms
To balance an equation is to simply adjust the coefficients so that no atoms are created or destroyed. The formulas cannot be altered, so do not ever change the subscripts. Sodium is Na, not Na_2 . By counting atoms, it appears that the oxygen atoms are already balanced, but the sodium atoms are not. Balance the sodium atoms by placing a "2" before the Na reactant.	$2Na + O_2 \rightarrow Na_2O_2$ 2 Na atoms + 2 O atoms = 2 Na atoms + 2 O atoms
Since no atoms may be created or destroyed in a chemical reaction, all that can happen is regrouping or rearrangement. The diagram illustrates how this chemical reaction results from bonds breaking and forming.	Reactants Products Na—Na. Na Na O=O O=O

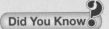

Did You Know?

A subscript in a chemical formula is an important indicator of the compound. If you change the subscript, you actually change the compound. When balancing a chemical equation, you cannot change subscripts. You can, however, change the coefficients—because it is only an indicator of the number of atoms or molecules of each reactant and product.

Follow these steps to balance a given chemical equation:

Step 1 Count the number of atoms of each element in the reactants and products.

Step 2 Balance the elements, one at a time, by using coefficients.

- When no coefficient is written, it is assumed to be 1.

- Never balance an equation by changing subscripts.

- Make sure all coefficients are in the lowest possible ratio.

Types of Chemical Reactions

Four types of chemical reactions that are easy to balance following the above steps are synthesis reactions, decomposition reactions, single replacement reactions, and double replacement reactions.

A **synthesis reaction** is when there is a combination of two or more substances that form a new compound, usually written in the form: $A + B \rightarrow AB$

Example: $S + O_2 \rightarrow SO_2$

A **decomposition reaction** is the opposite of synthesis. In a decomposition reaction, a single compound is broken down into two or more simpler substances, usually written in the form: $AB \rightarrow A + B$

Example: $PbO_2 \rightarrow Pb + O_2$

A **single replacement reaction** is a reaction in which an element replaces an ion in a compound, usually written in the form: $A + BC \rightarrow AB + C$

Example: $Zn + 2HCl \rightarrow ZnCl_2 + H_2$

A **double replacement reaction** is a reaction in which the ions in two compounds exchange bonding partners, usually written in the form: $AB + CD \rightarrow AC + BD$

Example: $NaCl + AgF \rightarrow NaF + AgCl$

DISCUSSION QUESTION

Explain how the conservation of mass is related to the balancing of a chemical equation.

LESSON REVIEW

1. Which chemical equation is properly balanced?

    A. $4Ba(s) + S8(s) \rightarrow 2BaS(s)$

    B. $4HgO(s) \rightarrow 4Hg(l) \rightarrow 3O_2(g)$

    C. $2FeO(s) + 4C(s) \rightarrow Fe(l) + S_8CO_2(g)$

    D. $SiI_4(s) + 2Mg(s) \rightarrow Si(s) + 2MgI_2(s)$

2. Which chemical equation represents a decomposition reaction?

    A. $8Ba(s) + S8(s) \rightarrow 8BaS(s)$

    B. $6HgO(s) \rightarrow 6Hg(l) + 3O_2(g)$

    C. $2FeO(s) + C(s) \rightarrow 2Fe(s) + CO_2(g)$

    D. $SiI_4(s) + 2Mg(s) \rightarrow Si(s) + 2MgI_2(s)$

3. What is the coefficient on Al_2O_3 when the equation describing the following synthesis reaction is balanced?

    $$Al + O_2 \rightarrow Al_2O_3$$

    A. 1

    B. 2

    C. 3

    D. 6

4. What is true in every balanced chemical equation?

    A. Mass has to be conserved.

    B. The reaction does not give off any energy.

    C. All coefficients have to be an even number.

    D. Atoms are created when products are formed.

Nuclear Reactions and Radioactivity

 SPS3.a-d

Getting the Idea

Nuclear reactions involve changes in the nucleus of atoms. Three types of nuclear reactions are nuclear decay, nuclear fission, and nuclear fusion. These reactions have many practical applications in the fields of medicine, weaponry, and production of electricity. Nuclear technologies have many benefits but also some significant drawbacks.

Key Words
nuclear reactions
nuclear decay
radiation
alpha particle
beta particle
gamma ray
half-life
nuclear fission
chain reaction
critical mass
nuclear fusion

Nuclear Reactions versus Chemical Reactions

Nuclear reactions take place in the nucleus of atoms and involve changes in the number of protons and neutrons. The products of nuclear reactions contain different elements from the reactants. Chemical reactions take place in the electron cloud of atoms and only involve valence electrons. The products of chemical reactions contain the same elements as the reactants. During nuclear reactions, the mass of the reactants is greater than the mass of the products. The "lost mass" is converted into huge amounts of energy. The amount of mass in chemical reactions is the same before and after chemical reactions. The amount of energy released during chemical reactions is much less than in nuclear reactions. The table below summarizes the major differences between nuclear and chemical reactions.

	Nuclear Reaction	**Chemical Reaction**
Location in the Atom	nucleus	electron cloud
Subatomic Particles Involved	protons and neutrons	valence electrons
Elements	products are *different* elements from reactants	products are *the same* elements as reactants
Mass Changes	mass of products *less than* mass of reactants	mass of products *equal to* mass of reactants
Energy Changes	huge amounts of energy released	small amounts of energy (released or absorbed)

Three types of nuclear reactions are nuclear decay, nuclear fission, and nuclear fusion. These reactions differ in the number of nuclei involved, how the nuclei change, and the type of particles or energy that are emitted during the change.

Nuclear Decay

Many elements have one or more unstable isotopes. An unstable isotope is radioactive. Radioactive isotopes undergo **nuclear decay**, which means that the nuclei in their atoms will change and emit energy or particles to produce a more stable nucleus. The energy or particles that are emitted from the decaying nucleus are called **radiation**. There are many different ways that an unstable nucleus can decay. Three common types of radiation are alpha decay, beta decay, and gamma radiation. In all three types of radiation, a change in the number of protons in a nucleus results in an atom of a different element.

In alpha decay, a nucleus spontaneously emits an alpha particle. An **alpha particle** consists of two protons and two neutrons, which are the equivalent of a helium nucleus. In alpha decay, the mass number (or number of protons and neutrons) of the unstable nucleus decreases by four, and the atomic number (or number of protons) decreases by two. The result is a helium nucleus and the nucleus of an atom of a different element. Consider as an example the alpha decay of uranium-238.

Alpha Decay

$$^{238}_{92}\text{U} \quad \rightarrow \quad ^{234}_{90}\text{Th} \quad + \quad ^{4}_{2}\text{He}$$
$$\text{alpha particle}$$

In beta decay, a neutron spontaneously becomes a proton and emits a **beta particle**. A beta particle is an electron. In beta decay, the mass number of the unstable nucleus stays the same, and the atomic number increases by one. The result is an electron and the nucleus of an atom of a different element. Consider as an example the beta decay of carbon-14.

Beta Decay

$$^{14}_{6}\text{C} \quad \rightarrow \quad ^{14}_{7}\text{N} \quad + \quad ^{0}_{-1}e$$
$$\text{beta particle}$$

In gamma decay, a particle of high energy called a gamma ray is released. In this type of decay, the mass number and atomic number of the atom undergoing decay does not change. Consider as an example the gamma decay of barium-137.

Gamma Decay

$$^{137}_{56}\text{Ba} \quad \rightarrow \quad ^{137}_{56}\text{Ba} \quad + \quad \gamma \text{ (gamma ray)}$$

The table below summarizes these three types of nuclear decay and the types of changes that occur in each.

Types of Nuclear Decay

Nuclear Decay	Emission	Change in Mass Number	Change in Atomic Number
Alpha decay	alpha particle	decreases by 4	decreases by 2
Beta decay	beta particle	no change	increases by 1
Gamma radiation	gamma ray	no change	no change

Different radioactive elements decay at different rates. Some radioactive elements decay rapidly. The atoms in a sample of such an element will quickly change from the unstable radioactive element to the stable, non-radioactive product in a short amount of time. Other radioactive elements take a very long time to undergo nuclear decay. These different rates of nuclear decay are described using the term half-life. A **half-life** is the amount of time it takes for half of the nuclei in a sample of radioactive atoms to undergo nuclear decay. The table below gives the half-lives of several different radioactive isotopes.

Isotope	Half-life
Polonium-214	0.164 second
Oxygen-15	2 minutes
Bismuth-212	60.5 minutes
Sodium-24	15 hours
Iodine-131	8 days
Phosphorus-32	14.3 days
Cobalt-60	5.3 years
Carbon-14	5,730 years
Plutonium-239	24,110 years
Uranium-238	4.5 billion years

To understand the concept of half-life, consider a sample of 1,000 atoms of carbon-14. Carbon-14 spontaneously undergoes beta decay to become nitrogen-14. The half-life of carbon-14 is 5,730 years. This means that after 5,730 years—one half-life—half the atoms of carbon-14 will have decayed to nitrogen-14 atoms. After a second half-life, another 5,730 years, half of the remaining carbon-14 atoms will have decayed to nitrogen-14 atoms. Only one quarter of the atoms in the original sample will still be carbon-14 atoms. The graph below illustrates how many atoms of carbon-14 remain after 1, 2, 3, 4, and 5 half-lives have passed.

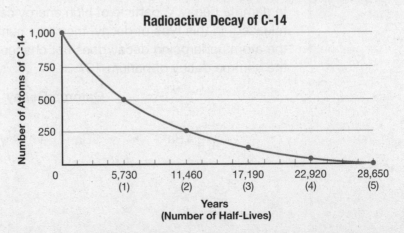

Chemists can use the concept of half-life to determine the age of samples. By looking at the fraction of radioactive atoms that remain in a sample and knowing the half-life of that isotope, scientists can determine how old the sample is. For example, if only one sixteenth of a sample of polonium-214 has not undergone nuclear decay, then the chemist knows that only four half-lives have passed (1\2 × 1\2 ×1\2 ×1\2 = 1\16). This means that a period of time equal to four times the half-life of polonium-214 (4 × 0.164 seconds, or 0.656 seconds) has passed.

Nuclear Fission

A second type of nuclear reaction is nuclear fission. **Nuclear fission** is the splitting of a heavy nucleus into two lighter nuclei, releasing a tremendous amount of energy. Notice that the single large nucleus is the reactant and the two smaller nuclei are products.

Nuclear Fission

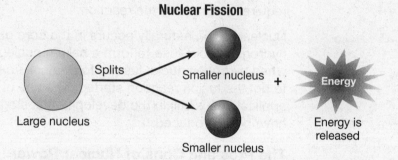

Splits   Smaller nucleus   +   **Energy**

Large nucleus   Smaller nucleus   Energy is released

A nuclear fission reaction can be started by penetrating a large nucleus such as U-235 (a uranium isotope) with a neutron. The neutron penetrates the uranium nucleus and splits it apart into two smaller nuclei. In the process of the fission reaction, some of uranium's neutrons are ejected. If the ejected neutrons penetrate another U-235 nucleus, another fission reaction occurs. The continuation of this process is called a **chain reaction**. In order for this nuclear fission reaction to continue, at least one ejected neutron from the fission of each U-235 isotope must penetrate another U-235 nucleus and cause fission. The mass of U-235 required for the chain reaction to occur is called the **critical mass**. The mass of the products in fission reactions is less than the mass of reactants. The "lost mass" is converted into the tremendous amounts of energy that nuclear fission produces.

Nuclear Fusion

A third type of nuclear reaction is nuclear fusion. **Nuclear fusion** occurs when small nuclei fuse, or combine, to form a larger, single nucleus. Notice that the two small nuclei are reactants and the single, large nucleus is the product.

Nuclear Fusion

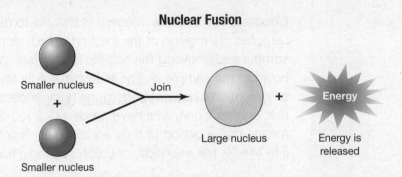

The mass of the products in fusion is less than the mass of the reactants. The "lost mass" is again converted to large amounts of energy. Nuclear fusion is difficult to produce at low temperatures. The fusing of small nuclei requires a huge input of energy. However, more energy is released during fusion reactions than the amount of energy required to produce the reaction.

Nuclear fusion naturally occurs in the core of stars like our sun. Two hydrogen nuclei fuse to form a helium nucleus. More energy is released when hydrogen nuclei fuse to form a helium nucleus than is required to get the fusion reaction started. The use of nuclear fusion for human applications is still in the developmental stage, although fusion bombs have been produced.

The Pros and Cons of Nuclear Power

Nuclear reactions can be used to produce electricity. Nuclear-power plants use controlled nuclear fission to convert heat energy into electricity. The difference between a coal-powered electric generating plant and a nuclear-powered electric generating plant is in the method of heating water. The burning of coal, a fossil fuel, is used in coal-powered electric generating plants. The fission of nuclear material is used in nuclear-powered electric generating plants. The advantages of nuclear-powered plants include tremendous amounts of energy produced from little fuel, the lack of air pollution that is produced from fossil fuel burning, and the abundant amounts of fuel that are available.

However, there are some drawbacks of nuclear-power plants. The cooling of the nuclear core results in thermal (heat) pollution of water systems such as rivers. Nuclear-power plants have the potential to fail causing dangerous radioactive leaks. Nuclear wastes must be stored in special ways for long periods of time. If leaks occur in the storage of nuclear wastes, the environment can become contaminated, causing long-term health problems to living things, including people.

DISCUSSION QUESTION

Imagine that your town is considering building a nuclear-powered electric generating plant to replace the current coal-burning electric generating plant. Assume the role of the general manager of the nuclear-powered electric generating plant. How would you defend the construction of the plant to members of the town that are against the use of nuclear power?

LESSON REVIEW

1. Nuclear reactions produce tremendous amounts of energy. Where does this energy originate?

    A. the conversion of mass into energy

    B. the valence electrons during chemical bonding

    C. the conversion of thermal energy into nuclear energy

    D. the extreme temperatures produced during nuclear reactions

2. During nuclear fission, how does the mass of the reactants compare to the mass of the products?

    A. The mass of the reactants is equal to the mass of the products.

    B. The mass of the reactants is less than the mass of the products.

    C. The mass of the reactants is greater than the mass of the products.

    D. The mass of the reactants can be greater than or less than the mass of the products.

3. What type of nuclear reaction results in a single nucleus undergoing a decrease in mass number, a decrease in atomic number, and the release of a helium nucleus?

    A. alpha decay

    B. beta decay

    C. gamma radiation

    D. nuclear fusion

4. Look at the reaction below.

    neutron + U-235 → Kr-92 + Ba-142 + 2 neutrons + ENERGY

    How do you know this reaction is a nuclear fission reaction?

    A. Energy is released.

    B. One large nucleus is split into two smaller nuclei.

    C. There are more neutrons in the products than in the reactants.

    D. The mass of the reactants is greater than the mass of the products.

18 The Periodic Table of Elements

 SPS4.a-b

Getting the Idea

Key Words

period
group
family
atomic number
metals
nonmetals
metalloids
energy level
valence electrons

The periodic table provides information about the elements, including name, symbol, atomic number, and atomic mass. Elements are classified as metals, nonmetals, and metalloids based on their positions on the periodic table and their physical and chemical properties. The structure of the periodic table includes periods and groups. Elements found within the same periods have the same number of energy levels, and elements within the same groups have the same number of valence electrons. The number of energy levels increases from top to bottom within all groups. The number of valence electrons increases from left to right across periods 1–3 and 13–18.

Periodic Table Structure

The periodic table of elements is a chart that contains extensive information about every element currently known. As you read this lesson, use the periodic table below to locate all information as it is described.

Periodic Table

IA 1	IIA 2										IIIA 13	IVA 14	VA 15	VIA 16
1 **H** 1.0														
3 **Li** 6.9	4 **Be** 9.0										5 **B** 10.8	6 **C** 12.0	7 **N** 14.0	8 **O** 16.0
11 **Na** 23.0	12 **Mg** 24.3	IIIB 3	IVB 4	VB 5	VIB 6	VIIB 7	VIIIB 8	9	10	IB 11	IIB 12	13 **Al** 27.0	14 **Si** 28.1	15 **P** 31.0	16 **S** 32.1

19 **K** 39.1	20 **Ca** 40.1	21 **Sc** 45.0	22 **Ti** 48.0	23 **V** 50.9	24 **Cr** 52.0	25 **Mn** 54.9	26 **Fe** 55.8	27 **Co** 58.9	28 **Ni** 58.7	29 **Cu** 63.5	30 **Zn** 65.4	31 **Ga** 69.7	32 **Ge** 72.6	33 **As** 74.9	34 **Se** 79.0
37 **Rb** 85.5	38 **Sr** 87.6	39 **Y** 88.9	40 **Zr** 91.2	41 **Nb** 92.9	42 **Mo** 95.9	43 **Tc** 98.0	44 **Ru** 101.1	45 **Rh** 102.9	46 **Pd** 106.4	47 **Ag** 107.9	48 **Cd** 112.4	49 **In** 114.8	50 **Sn** 118.7	51 **Sb** 121.8	52 **Te** 127.6
55 **Cs** 132.9	56 **Ba** 137.3	57-71	72 **Hf** 178.5	73 **Ta** 181.0	74 **W** 183.9	75 **Re** 186.2	76 **Os** 190.2	77 **Ir** 192.2	78 **Pt** 195.1	79 **Au** 197.0	80 **Hg** 200.6	81 **Tl** 204.4	82 **Pb** 207.2	83 **Bi** 209.0	84 **Po** 209.0
87 **Fr** 223.0	88 **Ra** 226.0	89-103	104 **Rf** 261	105 **Db** 262	106 **Sg** 263	107 **Bh** 262	108 **Hs** 265	109 **Mt** 266							

57 **La** 138.9	58 **Ce** 140.1	59 **Pr** 140.9	60 **Nd** 144.2	61 **Pm** 145.0	62 **Sm** 150.4	63 **Eu** 152.0	64 **Gd** 157.3	65 **Tb** 158.9	66 **Dy** 162.5	67 **Ho** 164.9	68 **Er** 167.3	69 **Tm** 168.9	70 **Yb** 173.0
89 **Ac** 227.0	90 **Th** 232.0	91 **Pa** 231.0	92 **U** 238.0	93 **Np** 237.0	94 **Pu** 244.0	95 **Am** 243.0	96 **Cm** 247.0	97 **Bk** 247.0	98 **Cf** 251.0	99 **Es** 252.0	100 **Fm** 257.0	101 **Md** 258.0	102 **No** 259.0

A **period** is a horizontal row of elements on the periodic table. There are seven periods. A **group** is a vertical column of elements on the periodic table. A group is also called a **family** because the elements in a group have similar chemical properties. Groups are given numbers and some are even given names. Group 2 elements are assigned the name alkaline earth metals. Group 17 elements are called halogens. The table on the last page of this lesson shows other group names. There are 18 groups on the periodic table.

Each element's box on the periodic table includes information specific to that element. The key below shows how to interpret the information in the periodic table for the element silicon.

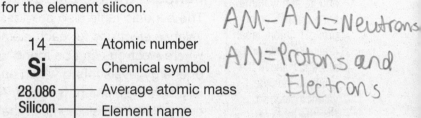

14	Atomic number
Si	Chemical symbol
28.086	Average atomic mass
Silicon	Element name

AM - AN = Neutrons
AN = Protons and Electrons

Notice that an element's name is abbreviated with a symbol. Silicon's symbol is Si. In many periodic tables, the name of the element is also given. This leaves two very important numbers: the atomic number and the average atomic mass. The **atomic number** is always a whole number. It equals the number of protons in an element's nucleus, and it is different for each element. Silicon's atomic number is 14, so a silicon atom contains 14 protons. Since atoms are neutral, the number of protons also equals the number of electrons in an atom. For silicon, the number of electrons is 14 since the number of protons is 14. The remaining number is the average atomic mass. It is always the larger number and usually is a decimal number. The average atomic mass is the weighted average of the masses of the naturally occurring isotopes of an element. Silicon's atomic mass is 28.086.

Metals, Nonmetals, and Metalloids

The elements on the periodic table are placed into one of three categories based on their physical and chemical properties. These categories are metals, nonmetals, and metalloids.

Over 75 percent of the elements in the periodic table are metals. **Metals** are generally shiny, malleable (can be hammered into thin sheets), ductile (can be drawn into thin wires), solid at room temperature (except for mercury which is a liquid at room temperature), and good conductors of heat and electricity. They are located on the left side and the middle of the periodic table. All of the elements in groups 1–12, many of the elements in groups 13, and a few elements in groups 14 and 15 are metals.

Nonmetals are generally dull in appearance, nonmalleable, nonductile, and are poor conductors of heat and electricity. Many are gases at room temperature, while others are solids. One, bromine, is a liquid at room temperature. The nonmetals are located on the right side of the periodic table. All of the elements in groups 17 and 18 and most of the elements in group 16 are nonmetals.

Metalloids have characteristics of metals and nonmetals and are known for being good semiconductors of electricity. The metalloids border an imaginary stair-step line near the right side of the periodic table in groups 13, 14, 15, and 16. The elements that are categorized as metalloids, also called semimetals, are boron, silicon, germanium, arsenic, antimony, tellurium, and astatine.

Periodic Trends: Energy Levels and Valence Electrons

The periodic table also provides information about energy levels and valence electrons for each element. **Energy levels** are general locations where electrons can be found within an atom of an element. The number of energy levels found within an element is equal to the period number in which the element is found. All elements in the first period have one energy level. All elements in the second period have two energy levels. All elements in the third period have three energy levels, and so on. Within a period, the number of energy levels is the same. From top to bottom within a group, the number of energy levels increases. Atoms of each subsequent element (from top to bottom) in any given group contain one more energy level than the atoms of the element above.

Only electrons that are found in the outermost energy level form chemical bonds. These bonding electrons are called **valence electrons**. All elements within a group have the same number of valence electrons. In periods 1–3, atoms of each element in a period contain one more valence electron than the atoms of the previous element within the same period This trend does not apply to elements in periods 4–7. The table below summarizes the group number, family name, and number of valence electrons for groups 1, 2 and 13–18.

Group or Family Number	Group or Family Name	# of valence electrons
1	Alkali Metals	1
2	Alkaline Earth Metals	2
13		3
14		4
15		5
16	Oxygen Group	6
17	Halogens	7
18	Nobel Gases	8 (except He, 2)

In general, the type of ion formed by atoms of an element can be predicted by its place on the periodic table. Metals on the far left side of the periodic table that have only one or two valence electrons (Groups 1 and 2), tend to give up electrons when forming a chemical bond. Thus, these elements form positive ions. For example, potassium forms K$^+$ ions and calcium forms Ca^{2+} ions. Nonmetals on the far right side of the periodic table tend to gain electrons when forming a chemical bond. Thus, these elements form negative ions. For example, chlorine forms Cl$^-$ ions and sulfur forms S^{2-} ions.

DISCUSSION QUESTION

Fluorine is located in period 2 and group 17. Magnesium is located in period 3 and group 2. How can this information be used to determine which element has the higher number of valence electrons and which element contains the most energy levels?

LESSON REVIEW

1. Look at the element in the picture.

| 19 |
| **K** |
| 39.098 |
| Potassium |

What is the element's name, atomic number, and number of electrons?

   A. K, 19, 19

   B. K, 39.098, 19

   C. Potassium, 19, 19

   D. Potassium, 39.098, 39

2. Francium is an element found in group 1 and period 7. How many valence electrons does an atom of francium contain?

   A. 1

   B. 6

   C. 7

   D. 8

3. Sodium is an element found in group 1 and period 3. What kind of ion is sodium most likely to form?

   A. −7

   B. −1

   C. +1

   D. +7

4. Iodine is a halogen found in group 17 and period 5. How many valence electrons does iodine have?

   A. 6

   B. 7

   C. 11

   D. 17

19 Phases of Matter

SPS5.a

Getting the Idea

Matter can be classified by its state, or phase. The four states of matter are solid, liquid, gas, and plasma. The way in which particles move and the attractive force between particles determine into which state matter is classified. When matter transitions between states, making what is known as a "phase change," temperature remains constant as energy is added or removed.

States of Matter

All matter is composed of small particles (atoms, ions, and molecules), which are in constant, random motion. These particles are constantly colliding with each other and with the sides of any container that holds them. Given this constant motion, all matter can be categorized as solids, liquids, gases, or plasma based on the specific ways their particles behave.

A **solid** has a definite shape and a definite volume. The particles in a solid are closely packed together because there is an attractive force between all particles of matter. They are constantly vibrating, but they do not slip past one another because of the attractive force that holds them together. Since particles in a solid cannot slip past one another, solids cannot be poured but instead maintain a definite shape.

A **liquid** has an indefinite shape but a definite volume. The particles in a liquid are in contact with one another because of the attractive force that holds them together. This force gives liquids their definite volume. The particles in liquids are moving quickly enough to partially overcome the attractive force of surrounding particles, which allows the particles to slip past one another. Because the particles can slip past one another, liquids can be poured so that they take the shape of the container that holds them.

A **gas** has both indefinite shape and indefinite volume. The particles in gases are not in contact with one another because they are moving quickly enough to overcome the attractive force between particles. Gas particles move randomly, in straight lines until they bump into other gas particles or the walls of the container. When a gas particle hits another particle or the wall of the container, it bounces off and continues to move. Gases take the shape and fill the volume of the container that holds them because gas particles move independently of one another.

Key Words
solid
liquid
gas
plasma
temperature
phase change
sublimation

The following picture illustrates solids, liquids, and gases. Note which states have particles that do not overcome the attractive force holding them together.

Molecules in Solids, Liquids, and Gases

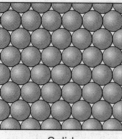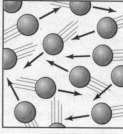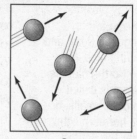

| Solid
(low energy) | Liquid
(moderate energy) | Gas
(high energy) |

Plasma, the fourth state of matter, consists of positively and negatively charged particles. Plasma is the most common state of matter in the universe because it is found at extremely high temperatures such as those found in stars. It is also found on Earth in lightning bolts, neon and fluorescent light bulbs, and auroras. A gas is converted into plasma at extremely high temperatures. Because the temperatures are so high, the particles in plasma are moving at great speeds. Collisions between particles at these speeds result in the electrons being stripped from the atoms. The electrons are negatively charged, and the remaining atom becomes positively charged.

Phase Changes

Temperature is a measure of the average kinetic energy of the particles in a substance. The faster that particles move, the higher the temperature of a substance, and conversely, the slower that particles move, the lower the temperature. The temperature of a substance increases or decreases until the temperature reaches the melting/freezing point or the boiling point. Once the temperature reaches the melting/freezing point or the boiling point, a phase change occurs. A **phase change** is the physical change that occurs when a substance changes state.

During phase changes, the temperature remains constant, but the amount of heat increases or decreases in the substance. When heat is added, the particles are able to overcome the attractive forces between them. When heat is taken away, the attractive forces between the particles become more significant and cause the particles to stay together.

Examples of phase changes include freezing and melting, evaporating and condensing, and subliming. During the process of freezing, a liquid changes into a solid. The temperature, called the freezing point, remains constant. Heat is taken away, and the attractive forces between the particles start to cause them to stay in place. During the process of melting, a solid changes into a liquid. The temperature, called melting point, remains constant. Heat is added, and the particles are no longer

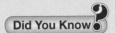
held together by the attractive forces between them. The freezing point and melting point are the same temperature for any given substance.

Evaporating and condensing are opposite phase changes. Evaporation is the change of state from a liquid to a gas. When heat is added to a liquid, the temperature of the liquid increases until the temperature reaches the boiling point. When the temperature of the liquid is equal to the boiling point, additional heat is used to overcome the attractive forces between the molecules in the liquid and change the substance to a gas. Condensation is the change of state from a gas to a liquid. When heat is taken away from a gas, its temperature decreases. When the temperature reaches the condensation point (the same temperature as the boiling point), the attractive forces between gas particles become comparatively more significant until the particles are pulled together and liquid forms.

Sublimation occurs when a solid changes directly into a gas without going through the liquid state. Dry ice, which is solid carbon dioxide, will sublime to carbon dioxide gas because its melting point is nearly equal to its boiling point.

Phase Change Diagram

A phase change diagram relates temperature and heat energy as a substance changes state from a solid to a liquid to a gas. The graph below shows a typical phase change diagram. Note that the line of the graph has a positive slope until a phase change occurs. The positive slope indicates an increase in temperature. During the phase change, the slope is flat or zero. This flat slope indicates that the temperature remains constant during a phase change even as heat is added After a phase change, the slope becomes positive again, indicating an increase in temperature.

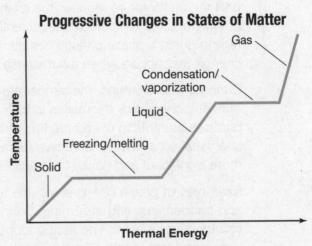

Progressive Changes in States of Matter

DISCUSSION QUESTION

A substance changes from a solid to a liquid. During the process of melting, what happens to the temperature, heat, and arrangement of the particles in the substance?

LESSON REVIEW

1. What type of arrangement and motion do particles in a liquid have?

    A. Particles in liquid are closely packed together and vibrating.

    B. Particles in liquid are not in contact with each other and are moving very quickly.

    C. Particles in liquid are in contact with each other, but they are able to slip past one another.

    D. Particles in liquid are not in contact with one another and are moving at extreme speeds.

2. What phase change occurs when a solid changes directly into a gas?

    A. freezing

    B. melting

    C. evaporation

    D. sublimation

3. Which state of matter is characterized by neutral particles that have no definite volume and take the shape of the container in which they are placed?

    A. solid

    B. liquid

    C. gas

    D. plasma

4. During the process of melting, what happens to the temperature of the substance?

    A. It stays constant.

    B. It increases.

    C. It decreases.

    D. It increases and then decreases.

20 Gas Laws

 SPS5.b

Getting the Idea

Gas particles are constantly moving. They move so quickly that they are not bound by the forces that hold the particles of liquids and solids together. Unlike solids and liquids, gases are highly compressible, which means that they can be squeezed into small spaces or expand to fill very large spaces. These behaviors give gases several unique properties. Their pressure, temperature, and volume are interrelated and can be predicted by three gas laws: Boyle's Law, Charles's Law, and Gay-Lussac's Law.

Key Words

pressure
atmosphere (atm)
compressible
Boyle's Law
temperature
Charles's Law
Gay-Lussac's Law

Pressure

Gas particles move randomly, in straight lines until they bump into other gas particles or the walls of the container. When a gas particle hits another particle or the wall of the container, it bounces off and continues to move. This bouncing exerts a force on the sides of the container. The collective force that all of the gas particles exert on the sides of their container exerts pressure. **Pressure** is an amount of force exerted over a certain area. The more often the particles hit the walls of the container, the higher the pressure.

Pressure is often described in units called **atmospheres** (atm). One atmosphere, 1 atm, is equal to the pressure of air at sea level. The air around you exerts pressure on you, and on everything around you. When you blow up a balloon, the balloon expands so that the air pressure inside the balloon matches the air pressure outside the balloon.

Recall that the particles in gases are not in contact with one another because they are moving quickly enough to overcome the attractive force between them. Thus, there is a lot of space between gas particles. This means that gases are **compressible**, or easily pushed into a smaller space. If you cap off a tire pump, you can push down on the pump handle and compress the gas that is trapped inside. The more you compress it, the harder it is to hold the pump handle down. This is because the gas inside is at a higher pressure. It is exerting more force on the walls of the pump. The gas particles are also much closer together.

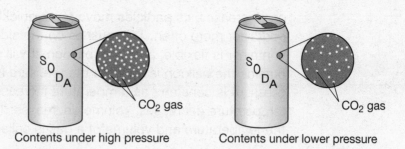

Contents under high pressure   Contents under lower pressure

Boyle's Law

When the gas particles are compressed into a smaller space, they have a shorter distance to move before they hit the walls of their container again. This means that they hit the walls of their container more often. When temperature does not change, decreasing the volume of a gas will cause the pressure to increase. Increasing the volume will cause the pressure to decrease. This relationship between the volume and pressure of a gas is called **Boyle's law**.

Boyle's Law
For a fixed amount of gas at constant temperature, the volume of the gas increases as the pressure decreases.

The graph below shows the relationship between pressure and volume at a fixed temperature. It is an inverse relationship, meaning the line has a slope of -1 (slopes downward from left to right at a 45° angle).

Boyle's Law

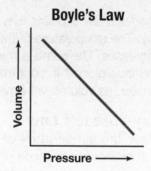

Boyle's law explains in part why scientists who study the weather using equipment attached to large weather balloons will only partially inflate them. At ground level, air pressure is much greater than it is higher up in the atmosphere. As the weather balloon rises and the surrounding pressure decreases, the balloon's volume will expand. The weather balloon is still sealed and has the same amount of gas in it. It just has a larger volume at the lower pressure of the upper atmosphere.

Charles's Law

Recall that **temperature** is a measure of the average kinetic energy of the particles in a substance. The faster that particles move, the higher the temperature of a substance. And conversely, the slower that particles move, the lower the temperature. When the temperature of a gas increases, its particles move more quickly and hit the sides of their container more often. This pushes on the sides of the container. If the container is flexible, as with a balloon, it will expand until the pressure outside the balloon is equal to the pressure inside the balloon. So when pressure is constant, as temperature increases, volume increases. As temperature decreases, volume decreases. This relationship between the temperature and volume of a gas is called Charles's law.

Charles's Law

For a fixed amount of gas at constant pressure, the volume of the gas increases as the temperature increases.

The graph below shows the relationship between temperature and volume at a fixed pressure. It is a direct relationship, meaning the line has a slope of 1 (slopes upward from left to right at a 45° angle).

Charles's Law

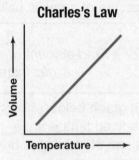

Charles's law explains why tires inflated on a warm day will look flat on a cold day. The temperature of the gas inside decreases, so the volume of the tire decreases. The same is true for a balloon. If you blow up and tie off a balloon and then place it in your freezer, you will notice that the balloon will get smaller. Its volume will have decreased with a decrease in temperature.

Gay-Lussac's Law
When the temperature of a gas increases, its particles hit the sides of their container more often. In a container with sides that are rigid (do not move), the volume is fixed As temperature increases and thus particle collision increases, this means that pressure increases. So as temperature increases, pressure increases. As temperature decreases, pressure decreases. This relationship between the pressure and temperature of a gas is called **Gay-Lussac's law**.

Gay-Lussac's Law

For a fixed amount of gas at constant volume, the pressure of the gas increases as the temperature increases.

The graph below shows the relationship between pressure and temperature at a fixed volume. It is also a direct relationship.

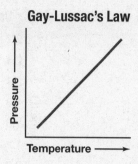

Gay-Lussac's Law

Have you ever seen aerosol cans that warn you not to overheat them? Because of Gay-Lussac's law, if you heat a sealed can containing a gas, the pressure inside the can will increase. Heating the can too much may result in an explosion when the can is no longer able to contain the increased pressure within the fixed volume of the can.

DISCUSSION QUESTION

Why might it be difficult to demonstrate Guy-Lussac's law with a balloon?

LESSON REVIEW

1. What law relates the temperature and pressure of a gas at a fixed volume?

    A. Boyle's law

    B. Charles's law

    C. Gay-Lussac's law

    D. Newton's First law

2. Rita constructed the following graph during an investigation. What law does her data illustrate?

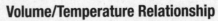

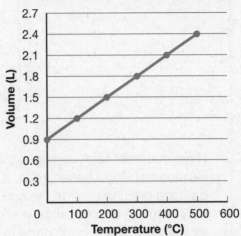

A. Boyle's law

B. Charles's law

C. Gay-Lussac's law

D. Newton's First law

3. Xavier filled up a balloon to its maximum capacity inside his air-conditioned home. He walked outside into the intense summer heat. According to Charles's Law, what could happen to his balloon?

A. It could pop because the increase in temperature would cause an increase in volume.

B. It could pop because the increase in temperature would cause a decrease in pressure.

C. It could get smaller because the increase in temperature would cause a decrease in pressure.

D. It could get smaller because the increase in temperature would cause a decrease in volume.

4. Which of the following graphs BEST illustrates Boyle's law?

A.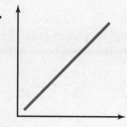

C.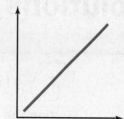

B.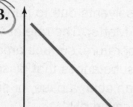

D.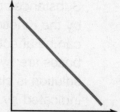

21 Solutions

3.1.spi.1–3

Getting the Idea

Substances dissolve in solvents due to particle movements described by the Kinetic Theory of Matter. The rate at which substances dissolve can be affected by temperature, surface area, and agitation. Acids and bases are two types of substances that dissolve in water. Whether a solution is classified as an acid, a base, or simply a neutral substance is indicated by a measure called pH.

Kinetic Theory and Dissolving

The Kinetic Theory of Matter describes the motion of particles of matter. This theory has three basic assumptions:

1. All matter is composed of small particles (atoms, ions, and molecules).

2. The particles in matter are in constant, random motion.

3. The particles in matter are constantly colliding with each other and any container that holds them.

These assumptions can be used to describe the behavior of particles in a solution. A **solution** is an evenly distributed mixture of two or more substances. The particles in the solution can be atoms, ions, or molecules. Solutions involving two substances include a solute and a solvent. The **solute** is the substance that dissolves, and the **solvent** is the substance that does the dissolving. The most familiar solution is between a solid solute and a liquid solvent, such as sugar and water. However, solutions can form between all phases of matter: solid/solid, solid/liquid, liquid/liquid, liquid/gas, and gas/gas.

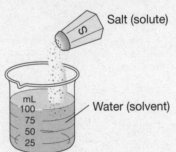

Salt (solute)

Water (solvent)

A saturated solution is a solution in which the maximum mass of solute is dissolved in a solvent. Water is a unique solvent because so many substances readily dissolve in it. Water is able to dissolve solid solutes such as salt and sugar, liquid solutes such as ethyl alcohol, and gas solutes such as oxygen and carbon dioxide.

Key Words

solution
solute
solvent
conductivity
concentration
acid
base
pH scale
neutralization

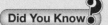

Not only can an increase in temperature increase the rate that a solute dissolves, it can also increase the amount of solute that dissolves. At room temperature, only 91 g of glucose will dissolve in 100 ml of water. At 90°C, 556 g of glucose will dissolve in water, and the solution will become super-saturated. Slowly cooling a super-saturated solution of sugar and water is the technique that is used to make rock candy.

In a solution of sugar water, water is the solvent, and sugar is the solute. In water, individual water molecules are close enough to be touching each other even though they are in constant motion, moving over, under, and past one another. A crystal of sugar is composed of millions of sugar molecules. The individual molecules are attracted to one another, but they are not chemically bonded to one another. Only the atoms that make up a single sugar molecule are chemically bonded. The sugar molecules are also in constant motion. Because sugar is a solid, the molecules vibrate back and forth. They do not move past one another.

When sugar is placed in water, the sugar molecules on the surface of the sugar crystals are pulled away from each other by the water molecules. As the surface sugar molecules dissolve, they expose more sugar molecules to water, and more dissolving takes place until the sugar is completely dissolved or the solution is saturated (or cannot dissolve any more solute). The sugar molecules that have dissolved are surrounded by water molecules. They are not chemically bonded to the water molecules. These water molecules block the attractive forces between sugar molecules. Because of the constant, random motion of particles, the sugar molecules become evenly distributed throughout the water. The sugar and water are not chemically bonded, so they can still be separated by physical means. For example, the water can be evaporated, allowing the attraction between sugar molecules to reform sugar crystals.

Factors That Affect the Dissolving Rate of Solids in Liquids

Three factors can affect the rate at which a solid solute dissolves in a liquid solvent: temperature, amount of surface area, and agitation. Increasing temperature will increase the rate of dissolving. At higher temperatures, the particles are moving faster and colliding more often. For a sugar-water solution, the water molecules collide more frequently with the sugar molecules, and dissolving takes place more quickly. The sugar molecules also vibrate more rapidly, which allows them to overcome their attractive forces more easily. The picture illustrates the effect that temperature has on the dissolving of sugar. Note how much more sugar has dissolved in the solution that was heated.

Sugar cube in water

Sugar cube in solution

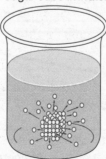
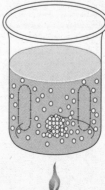

As particle size decreases, the rate of dissolving increases. The smaller the size of solute particles, the faster they dissolve. In the case of the sugar-water solution, finely-ground sugar would have more surface area than granulated sugar. So it follows that finely-ground sugar would dissolve more quickly than granulated sugar when placed in water. With more surface area to contact, the water molecules have more opportunities to pull the finely-grained solute molecules away from the solute's surface, dissolving it faster.

The more a solution is agitated or stirred, the faster the rate of dissolving for a solid in a liquid. When a solution is stirred, the water molecules collide with the surface of the solute molecules more frequently, and the dissolving process occurs more quickly.

Although these three factors increase the rate at which dissolving takes place, they are not necessary for a substance to dissolve. As long as a substance is soluble in a solvent, it will eventually dissolve no matter how large the particle size is, how low the temperature is, and how little agitation takes place.

Properties of Solutions

Solubility is the maximum amount of solute that will dissolve in a given solvent at a particular temperature and pressure. At a given temperature and pressure, solubility is a physical property that can be used to identify a substance, because solubility is often unique to a specific solute.

A solubility curve is a graph of solubility as temperature increases. The solubility curves below show how increasing temperature increases the solubility of various solutes.

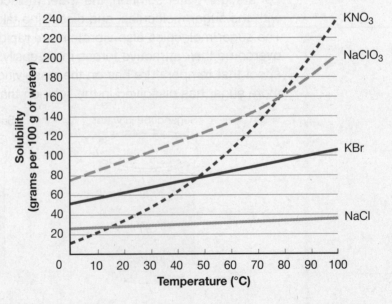

Concentration is a measure of the mass of solute dissolved in a certain volume of solvent. The more solute dissolved in the solvent, the greater is the concentration of the solution. A dilute solution has very little solute dissolved in it. A concentrated solution has a lot of solute dissolved in it. A saturated solution is a solution in which the maximum mass of solute is dissolved in the solvent at a particular temperature. No more solute can dissolve in a saturated solution. In an unsaturated solution, more solute can dissolve in the solvent at a given temperature.

Electrical **conductivity** is a measure of a material's ability to conduct electrical current, or allow the movement of electrical changes through it. Some solutions can conduct electrical current depending on the properties of the solute. Solutes that form ions in solution allow the solutions to conduct electricity. Such solutes are called electrolytes. Table salt, sodium chloride, is an electrolyte. Salt water conducts electric current.

Properties of Acids and Bases in Solution

There are a variety of different types of solutions, and based on their physical and chemical properties, some can be classified as acids or bases. An **acid** is any substance that releases hydrogen ions (H^+) in solution. Acids can easily be recognized by their chemical formulas. Many acids have formulas whose first element is H. For example, HCl, is hydrochloric acid, the acid found in the human stomach. H_2SO_4 is sulfuric acid, an acid found in batteries. A **base** is any substance that releases hydroxide ions (OH^-) in solution. Many bases have chemical formulas that end in OH. For example, NaOH is sodium hydroxide, a base used in drain cleaner. $Ca(OH)_2$ is calcium hydroxide, a base used in fertilizer.

The **pH scale** is a way to measure the concentration of hydrogen ions in solution. The pH range is from 0 to 14. The pH of a solution can be measured using litmus paper, pH paper, or a pH meter. The pH of an acid is less than 7. In acids, the concentration of H^+ is greater than the concentration of OH^-. The lower the pH value, the stronger the acid The pH of bases is greater than 7. In bases, the concentration of OH^- is greater than the concentration H^+. The higher the pH value, the stronger the base. Any substance that has a pH of 7 is neutral which means the concentration of H^+ ions equals the concentration of OH^- ions. Pure water, H_2O, has a pH of 7 and is neutral. The diagram on page 140 shows the pH of various common substances.

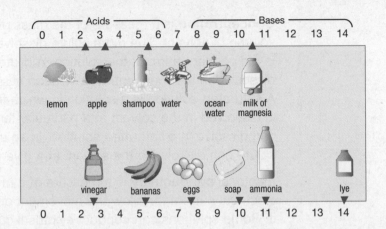

A **neutralization reaction** is a chemical reaction in which an acid and a base react to form a salt and water. During a neutralization reaction, the concentration of H^+ ions is equal to the concentration of OH^- ions, so the pH is 7.

The properties of acids and bases are summarized in the table below.

Properties of Acids	Properties of Bases
conduct electricity	conduct electricity
taste sour	taste bitter
turn blue litmus paper red	turn red litmus paper blue
pH < 7	pH > 7
react with metals such as zinc and magnesium	feel slippery
release H^+ ions in solution	release OH^- ion in solution
react with bases to produce water and salt	react with acids to produce water and salt

DISCUSSION QUESTION

Explain why the process of dissolving is considered an example of a physical change.

LESSON REVIEW

1. An unknown solution is tested using blue litmus paper. The blue litmus paper remains blue. What can be determined about the pH using this test?

   A. The pH is greater than 7.

   B. The pH is less than 7.

   C. The pH could be 7 or greater.

   D. The pH could be 7 or less.

2. Four solutions are prepared in beakers. In all solutions, 20 g of sugar are added to 100 ml of water. Beaker A is placed on the lab table at room temperature (25°C). Beaker B is placed in the refrigerator. Beaker C is placed on a hot plate set at 40°C. In what order would the beakers be arranged to show the dissolving of sugar from fastest to slowest?

   A. A, B, C

   B. C, B, A

   C. C, A, B

   D. B, A, C

3. An unknown substance is dissolved in water. The solution is corrosive, conducts electricity, and has a higher concentration of H^+ ions than OH^- ions. What kind of solution does this unknown substance form?

   A. an acidic solution

   B. a basic solution

   C. a neutral solution

   D. a non-electrolyte solution

4. What happens to the solubility of a typical solid solute as temperature increases?

   A. The solubility decreases.

   B. The solubility increases.

   C. The solubility remains the same.

   D. There is no way to know without knowing which exact solute.

EOCT Review

1. Sulfur has three common isotopes. One of the isotopes of sulfur has 18 neutrons. Its atomic number is 16. Which of the following symbols correctly identifies this isotope of sulfur?

   A. S-2
   B. S-16
   C. S-18
   D. S-34

2. How many electrons must barium lose to achieve a noble gas electron configuration?

   A. 0
   B. 1
   C. 2
   D. 4

3. What is the density of a piece of silver that has a mass of 210 g and a volume of 20.0 cm³?

   A. 10.5 g/cm³
   B. 190 g/cm³
   C. 230 g/cm³
   D. 4200 g/cm³

4. Two ions, a calcium ion (Ca^{+2}) and nitride (N^{-3}) react to form a binary ionic compound, calcium nitride. Which of the following formulas correctly shows the ratio that these ions combine?

   A. CaN
   B. Ca^2N
   C. Ca^2N^3
   D. Ca^3N^2

5. What is the coefficient on Hg when the following equation is balanced?

$$HgO \rightarrow Hg + O_2$$

   A. 1
   B. 2
   C. 3
   D. 4

6. What type of nuclear reaction results in a single nucleus undergoing an increase in atomic number, no change in mass number, and the release of an electron?

   A. alpha decay
   B. beta decay
   C. gamma radiation
   D. nuclear fusion

7. Cesium is a Group I alkali metal. It is found in Period 6 of the periodic table. What kind of ion will a cesium atom form to reach chemical stability?

   A. +1
   B. −1
   C. +6
   D. −2

8. Which state of matter is characterized by a definite volume and an indefinite shape?

   A. solid
   B. liquid
   C. gas
   D. plasma

9. What law relates the volume and pressure of a gas at a constant temperature?

   A. Boyle's law
   B. Charles's law
   C. Gay-Lussac's law
   D. Newton's First law

10. Which of the following processes would increase the rate of dissolving?

   A. decrease the amount of solvent
   B. increase the amount of solvent
   C. decrease the size of solute particles
   D. increase the size of solute particles

CHAPTER 4

Force, Mass, and Motion

22 Velocity and Acceleration

 SPS8.a

Getting the Idea

Have you ever been on a Ferris wheel? This and other amusement park rides are examples of physics in action. Many of these rides involve **motion**, or the change in position of an object with respect to time. In order to make sense of motion a reference point is used. A reference point is a stationary object, such as a tree, a street sign, or a line on the road. Once a reference point has been established, motion can be defined in terms of speed, position, and direction. In this lesson, you will also discover two formulas relating to velocity and acceleration that will help you further understand the concept of motion.

Distance versus Displacement

When something moves, it changes position. **Distance** is a measure of how far an object has moved after leaving a reference point. If a truck exits a loading station and travels 30 miles east to its first stop and then another 20 miles east to its second stop, the total distance it traveled is 50 miles. Distance does not involve direction but only magnitude.

Displacement, on the other hand, is a measure of how far the object traveled and its direction. Making the statement "140 miles west" is a description of displacement. Total (or final) displacement is defined as a change in position relative to the starting point or origin. In the example above, the truck first traveled 30 miles east. If it then turns around and travels 20 miles west, based on its starting point, it has a total displacement of 10 miles east. If the truck drives 30 miles east and then another 20 miles east, the total displacement would be 50 miles east because both measures are in the same direction.

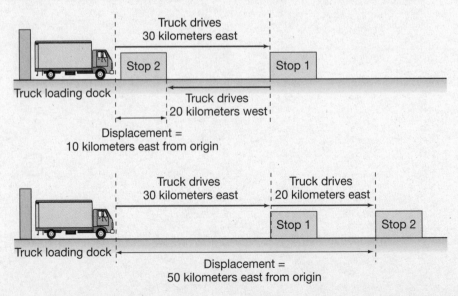

Key Words

motion
distance
displacement
speed
instantaneous speed
average speed
velocity
instantaneous velocity
average velocity
acceleration
positive acceleration
negative acceleration

 **Did You Know**

The Peregrine Falcon is believed to be able to fly at speeds of 100–200 miles/hour!

Speed versus Velocity

A roller coaster is a very exciting amusement park ride for some because it involves speed. **Speed** is a measure of how fast something is moving. It is a measure of the distance traveled per unit of time. For example, if a car travels a total of 120 miles in 2 hours it has a speed of 120 miles per 2 hours, or 60 miles per hour. Like distance, speed does not involve direction. It is considered a rate because it involves a change in distance over a certain period of time.

There are different ways to describe speed. **Instantaneous speed** is a measure of speed at a given moment. A car's initial (starting) speed and its final speed are examples of instantaneous speed. A speedometer in a car measures instantaneous speed. Speed can also be described as average speed. **Average speed** is a measure of the total distance covered in a particular time period. If an object is traveling at a constant speed, its instantaneous speed will be the same at each point. This means that its average speed will equal the instantaneous speed. If it travels at varying speeds, an average will be taken whereby the total distance traveled is divided by the total time traveled.

Velocity refers to both the speed of an object and the direction of its motion. It should have both speed units and direction units. For example, while the speed of a particular object is 25 miles/hour, the velocity of that object would be, for example, 25 miles/hour north. To illustrate the difference further, imagine a motorcycle traveling at 50 miles/hour. It passes another motorcycle traveling 50 miles/hour in the opposite direction. While both motorcycles have the same speed, their velocities are different. Just as speed is a rate, so too is velocity because it shows change in displacement over a certain period of time.

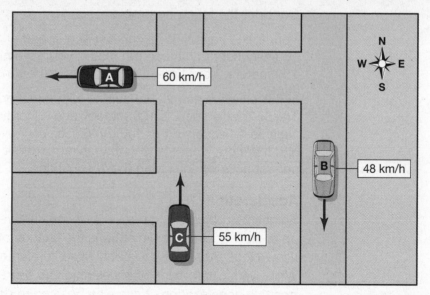

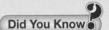
Velocity can be changed in two ways:

- The speed of an object can change by slowing down or speeding up.
- The direction of an object can change.

There are several different ways to describe velocity. Instantaneous velocity is a measure of velocity at a given moment. A car's initial velocity and its final velocity are examples of instantaneous velocity.

Average velocity is a measure of the total displacement in a particular time period and is similar to average speed. If an object is traveling at a constant velocity, its instantaneous velocity will equal the average velocity. If it travels at varying velocities (by changing speed or direction), an average will be taken whereby the total displacement from the point of origin is divided by the total time traveled.

Determining Speed and Velocity

There is one basic equation that is used to calculate (average) speed or (average) velocity:

$$v = d/t$$

The variable "v" equals the variable "d" divided by the variable "t." This equation can also be arranged to solve for "d" ($d = vt$) or "t" ($t = d/v$). In this equation, "v" equals either velocity or speed, and "t" equals time. When speed is being determined "d" equals total distance, and when velocity is being determined "d" equals total displacement.

The most important thing to remember is that velocity requires distance and direction (displacement) while speed only requires distance.

Consider the following problem:

Your friend says that he can run at a speed of 3 meters/second (m/sec). To see whether you can run faster, you have him time you while you run 100 meters. Your time is 40 seconds. Who runs faster?

In this case we are not concerned with direction, so we solve for speed. The "d," or distance, is 100 meters, and "t," or time, is 40 seconds. The variable "v" equals d/t or 100 m/40 sec. Your average speed is 2.5 m/sec and therefore, your friend is the faster runner. It is important to use the correct units when solving these equations.

Acceleration

Sometimes objects don't travel at a constant velocity but rather speed. up or slow down. **Acceleration** is the change of an object's velocity over time. (Note: Acceleration is only used in reference to velocity, not speed.) While we typically think of acceleration as something speeding up, or **positive acceleration**, it can also be used to describe something slowing down, or **negative acceleration**. Consider the following diagrams:

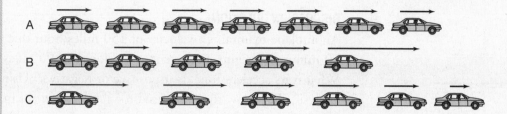

In diagram A each car represents the position of an object at a different time. They are equal distances apart, and therefore traveling at a constant velocity. Since the velocity is not changing, the acceleration is zero. In diagram B the cars are becoming farther apart. This suggests that because they are covering more distance in the same time period, the velocity is increasing. The acceleration is positive because the displacement to the right is increasing. In diagram C the cars become closer together as time passes. This shows that because they are covering less distance in the same time period, the velocity is decreasing. The acceleration is negative because the displacement to the right is decreasing.

Like velocity, the acceleration of an object can change in two ways. Either the speed can increase or decrease, or the direction can change.

Determining Acceleration

To calculate acceleration, the following equation is used:

$$a = (v_f - v_i)/t$$

To solve for acceleration a, the initial velocity v_i is subtracted from the final velocity v_f. This quantity is then divided by the total time t. In order to find the final units for acceleration, dimensional analysis can be used In this example, the units for velocity are m/sec while the units for time are sec: (m/sec − m/sec) / sec = (m/sec) / sec or m/sec^2.

Consider the following example:

Along a north straightaway a racecar's velocity changes from 0 m/s to 50 m/s in 5 seconds. What is the car's acceleration?

In this problem the initial velocity v_i is 0 m/s while the final velocity v_f is 50 m/s. The time t is 5 seconds.

a = (50 m/sec − 0 m/sec) / 5 sec

a = 50 m/sec / 5 sec or 10 m/sec^2 north

Since this equation involves velocity, the direction should be included in the final answer.

DISCUSSION QUESTION

An airplane maintains a velocity of 150 miles/hour due east. After 10 minutes it begins its descent at a velocity of 90 miles/hour due southeast. What is its acceleration? Is it positive or negative? Using dimensional analysis, show how the units used for acceleration are miles / hour².

LESSON REVIEW

1. Which of the following BEST describes the difference between speed and velocity?

    A. Speed includes distance and direction while velocity includes only distance.

    B. Speed includes distance and direction while velocity includes only direction

    C. Velocity includes distance and direction while speed includes only direction.

    D. Velocity includes distance and direction while speed includes only distance.

2. The diagram below shows three cars traveling.

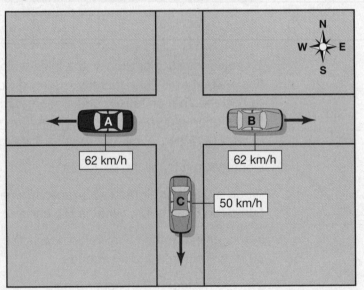

Which car has a velocity of 62 km/hour going west?

    A. car A

    B. car B

    C. car C

    D. cars A and B

3. Sound travels at a speed of 330 meters/second. If John hears a police siren 165 meters away, how <u>long</u> did it take for the sound to travel from the police siren to his ear?

    A. 0.5 second

    B. 2 seconds

    C. 5 seconds

    D. 20 seconds

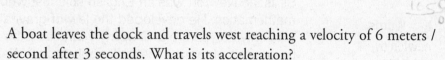

$$t = \frac{d}{s} = \frac{165}{330}$$

4. A boat leaves the dock and travels west reaching a velocity of 6 meters / second after 3 seconds. What is its acceleration?

    A. 0.5 meters/second²

    B. 2 meters/second²

    C. 6 meters/second²

    D. 18 meters/second²

$$\frac{6-0}{3-1} = \frac{6}{2} = 3$$

Newton's Laws of Motion

 SPS8.b

Getting the Idea

Sir Isaac Newton was an English scientist who worked in physics and mathematics. He developed the law of gravitation in 1666, when he was only 23 years old! Twenty years later, he gave the world three basic laws of motion that still apply today. We call them Newton's laws. These laws explain how and why objects move. They examine common forces we sometimes take for granted and how they interact to produce motion.

Key Words

newton (N)
net force
inertia
friction
law of action and
   reaction

Newton's First Law of Motion

Forces are defined as pushes and pulls that one object exerts on another object. Thanks to Newton's contributions to the world of physical science, force is measured in units called **newtons** (N). Sometimes an object has more than one force acting upon it. In these cases it is necessary to find the **net force**, or unbalanced force. In the first diagram the forces are balanced because both teams are pulling on the rope equally. This causes them to remain stationary. In the second diagram the forces are unbalanced because the team on the left is exerting a stronger "pulling" force. This causes the rope to move to the left.

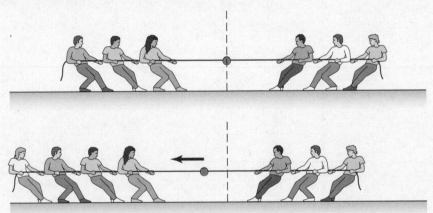

All objects have a natural tendency to resist changes in motion. This tendency, called **inertia**, causes objects to remain constant in terms of speed and direction. Newton's first law of motion, also referred to as the law of inertia, states that the velocity of an object will remain constant unless a net force acts on it. If an object is moving, it will continue to move in a straight line with a constant velocity unless a net force acts on it. Likewise, if an object is at rest, it will remain at rest until a net force acts on it.

An object's inertia depends on its mass, the amount of matter it has. The greater the mass of an object, the greater the inertia it has. A greater inertia means that something is harder to slow down, speed up, or change direction if it is moving. It also makes it more difficult to make something start moving if it is at rest. Because inertia depends on an object's mass, which is the same no matter where that object is in the universe, it is not affected by gravity or the lack of gravity. In other words, even out in the middle of empty space objects have inertia.

An example of how a moving object is affected by inertia is a person inside in a car that stops suddenly. The car is moving at a constant velocity. When the brakes are applied, a net force is exerted on the car in the direction opposite to its motion. This causes the car to slow down or stop. Because of inertia, the person inside the car however tends to continue moving forward in the direction of the motion. If the person is wearing a seatbelt, the seatbelt will exert a force to stop the person from continuing to move forward. If the person is not wearing a seatbelt, the person will continue to move forward until something (like a windshield) exerts an opposite force on the person.

Seatbelt or windshield

If all objects experience constant inertia, why do objects eventually stop moving? According to Newton's first law of motion, if you slide a box across the floor, it should move forever unless another force acts on it. This force is called friction. **Friction** is a net force that slows or stops an object. In other words, friction is a force that opposes motion.

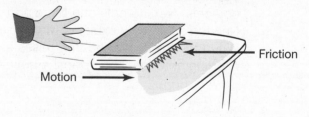

Friction

Motion

Newton's Second Law of Motion

As you will recall from Lesson 22, acceleration can cause an object to speed up, slow down, or change direction. Newton's second law of motion states that when a net force acts on an object, the object will accelerate in the direction of the net force. The net force acting on an object and the object's acceleration are directly related: the larger the net force, the greater the rate of acceleration. On the other hand, an object's mass and its acceleration are inversely related: the larger the mass of the object, the smaller the rate of acceleration. When comparing two objects acted on by the same net force such as a bowling ball and a volley ball, the one with the smaller mass (the volley ball) will accelerate at the greater rate.

Consider a stationary soccer ball. If someone kicks the ball, it will accelerate from rest to some speed depending on the magnitude of the force. If the soccer ball is already moving and someone kicks it in the same direction in which it's traveling, the ball will accelerate from its initial speed to a greater speed in the same direction.

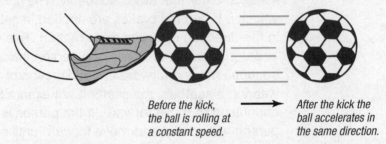

Before the kick, the ball is rolling at a constant speed.

After the kick the ball accelerates in the same direction.

If the soccer ball is traveling in one direction and someone kicks it in the opposite direction, it will have a negative acceleration and slow down. Once it slows down from its initial speed, it will either continue to slow down, stop, or begin to move in the opposite direction.

Newton's Third Law of Motion

Have you ever noticed what happens when an ice skater pushes against a wall? The ice skater begins to move backwards because just as the skater exerts a force on the wall, the wall exerts a force on the skater. Newton's third law of motion states that when one object exerts a force on a second object, the second object exerts a force on the first that is equal in magnitude and opposite in direction. The third law is also referred to as the **law of action and reaction**.

In the case of the ice skater, the forces are equal in magnitude but opposite in direction. Although there are two objects involved, each object is exerting only one force and experiencing only one force. Newton's third law explains why rockets are pushed upward into space. When the fuel is burned, the gases exert a downward force, thereby exerting an equal and opposite upward force on the rocket.

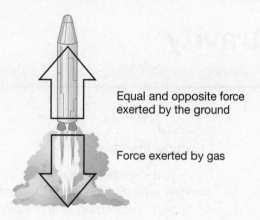

Equal and opposite force
exerted by the ground

Force exerted by gas

DISCUSSION QUESTION

Explain what happens to an uncovered cup of coffee in a car that stops suddenly in terms of Newton's first law of motion.

LESSON REVIEW

1. In order to move a wheelbarrow a constant force is exerted. Which of the following will increase its acceleration?

    A. increasing the mass of the wheelbarrow

    B. decreasing the mass of the wheelbarrow

    C. reversing the direction of the wheelbarrow

    D. changing the color of the wheelbarrow

2. Inertia is the tendency of an object to continue its current state of motion. Which of the following BEST describes the relationship between inertia and mass?

    A. A greater mass means that something is easier to slow down or speed up.

    B. The amount of inertia of an object is equal to its mass.

    C. The greater the mass of an object, the greater the inertia it has.

    D. The greater the mass of an object, the less inertia it has.

3. When a teacher is standing at the front of the class, the force of gravity is pulling her down toward the ground. The ground is pushing back with an equal and opposite force. This is an example of

    A. Newton's first law of motion

    B. Newton's second law of motion

    C. Newton's third law of motion

    D. The law of gravitation

24 Gravity

SPS8.d

Getting the Idea

Key Words

force
gravity
acceleration of
   gravity (ag)
law of universal
   gravitation

Have you ever heard the story in which a scientist named Sir Isaac Newton was sitting under an apple tree when he got hit on the head by an apple? According to the story, the apple falling from the tree inspired Newton to wonder, "Why did it fall downward instead of flying off into space?" He realized that a **force**, a push or pull in some direction, was pulling downward on the apple. He later stated that this attractive force, called **gravity**, was everywhere in the universe and not just on Earth. Scientists have used Newton's theory to explain the motions of the planets and other phenomena in the universe.

Gravity and Acceleration

According to Newton, Earth exerts a force that pulls every object toward its center. This downward force is referred to as gravity. When the apple fell from the tree, Newton realized that the apple was actually accelerating toward Earth. Acceleration is defined as the rate at which an object changes its velocity. Since the apple started at zero velocity or 0.0 meters/second (m/sec), and then started moving toward the ground, it was accelerating. (Note: Just as the force of gravity acts in a downward direction, objects will also accelerate in a downward direction.) Consider the following diagram:

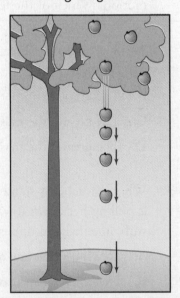

The diagram shows an apple in freefall at equal time intervals. As the apple approaches the ground, it appears that the distance it travels between each time interval increases. This suggests that the apple is

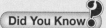
speeding up. Since Earth continually exerts a gravitational force on all objects, all objects must therefore accelerate as they fall.

The rate at which objects accelerate toward the earth is 9.8 meters/second per second. This value is called the **acceleration of gravity** (a_g). It means that for every second of freefall, the object's velocity increases by 9.8 m/sec.

Acceleration Due to Gravity

Time	Changing Velocities
0 seconds	0.0 meters/second
1 second	9.8 meters/second
2 seconds	19.6 meters/second
3 seconds	29.4 meters/second
4 seconds	39.2 meters/second

Initially, the object has a velocity of 0.0 m/sec because it is at rest. After one second, it is traveling at a velocity of 9.8 m/sec. Finally, after four seconds, it is traveling at a velocity of 39.2 m/sec. The velocity of the object will tend to continue to increase in a downward direction until it hits the ground.

Law of Universal Gravitation

In general, gravity is an attractive force that works to pull objects together. Newton's **law of universal gravitation** states that this force is not only limited to Earth, but also acts between all objects in the universe. Therefore, any two objects, from the smallest particle of an atom to the largest star, experience a gravitational attraction. Just as you are attracted to Earth, Earth is also attracted to you! You also share an attractive force with all the other objects around you. You tend to notice only the force that Earth exerts on you because the other attractive forces are smaller compared to Earth's.

The Effects of Mass on Gravity

The force of gravity between two objects depends on two factors. The first factor is the combined amount of mass the objects have. Mass is the amount of matter in an object. The force of gravity is directly related to mass. Therefore, the more mass something has, the greater its force of gravity. For something like two apples, it is barely measurable. However, because Earth's mass is so great, it exerts a strong gravitational force on objects such as the moon. This is why the moon and other objects in space, such as weather satellites, tend to remain in orbit around Earth and not fly away from Earth.

The Effects of Distance on Gravity

The second factor that determines the force of gravity between two objects is their distance from each other. The force of gravity (Fg) is inversely proportional to the square of the distance (d²) between them.

$$F_g = 1/d^2$$

This means that as the distance increases between two objects, the force of gravity between them decreases dramatically. Likewise, as the distance decreases, the force of gravity increases dramatically. In other words, as objects move closer together, their pull on one another grows rapidly. As objects move farther apart, their pull on one another weakens rapidly. A good example is a spacecraft traveling toward another planet. As the spacecraft moves away from Earth, Earth's pull on it lessens. Meanwhile, as it moves closer to another planet, that planet's pull on it strengthens.

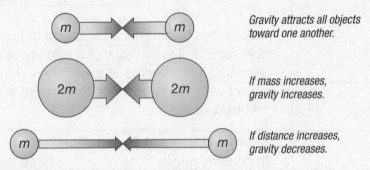

Gravity attracts all objects toward one another.

If mass increases, gravity increases.

If distance increases, gravity decreases.

DISCUSSION QUESTION

According to Newton's law of gravitational force, all objects in the universe exert an attractive force on all other objects. And that force increases with increasing mass. If this is true, why don't we float off toward the sun, which has a much greater mass than the Earth?

LESSON REVIEW

1. Which of the following BEST describes an object's velocity during freefall?

    A. An object travels at a constant velocity throughout the fall.

    B. An object's velocity increases as it falls.

    C. An object's velocity decreases as it falls.

    D. An object during freefall does not have a measurable velocity.

2. Maddie drops a baseball from a window on the tenth floor of her apartment building. What is the baseball's velocity after two seconds?

    A. 2.0 m/sec

    B. 9.8 m/sec

    C. 19.6 m/sec

    D. 96.0 m/sec

3. The mass of two objects is an important factor in determining the force of gravity between them. What is the second most important factor?

    A. their volume

    B. the distance between them

    C. their diameters

    D. their densities

4. What is the BEST explanation for why the moon orbits Earth rather than Earth orbiting the Moon?

    A. Earth has less mass than the moon.

    B. Earth rotates faster than the moon rotates.

    C. The moon has no gravitational pull on anything.

    D. Earth has more mass than the moon.

5. Suppose you roll a basketball and a baseball toward each other. How does this affect the force of gravity they exert on one another?

    A. It increases.

    B. It decreases.

    C. It stays the same.

    D. It disappears.

25 Mass versus Weight

 SPS8.d

Getting the Idea

Key Words

weight (F_w)

According to Newton's law of universal gravitation, all objects that have mass have an attractive force toward other objects. In other words, everything around us is pulling on everything else. When two objects are pulling on each other, the object that has the greater mass exerts the greater attractive force, or a net force. Lesson 24 discussed the fact that on Earth, objects accelerate as they fall because a net force is acting on them. This net force is caused by Earth's gravity. Scientists are able to calculate how the force of gravity acts on various objects using their masses.

Mass versus Weight

Mass is the amount of matter in an object. The amount doesn't change when the object's location changes. For example, an apple has a specific amount of material in it. Its mass doesn't change whether the apple is on a table, under water, or even on another planet. Since an object's force of gravity depends on its mass, the more mass an object has, the stronger the force of gravity it exerts. Because the sun has more mass than the planets, the sun's gravitational force is stronger than that of the planets. Therefore it pulls on them, and they revolve around it.

The force of gravity acting on an object's mass is called **weight (F_w)**. Unlike mass, it can change depending on an object's location. In order to calculate an object's net force, its mass and acceleration are multiplied (F = ma). A similar equation is used to calculate an object's weight.

$$Force\ of\ weight = mass \times acceleration\ due\ to\ gravity$$
$$(F_w = ma_g)$$

In this case, weight is a measure of force. While gravity is also a force, in this equation a_g refers to acceleration caused by gravity.

The units used for weight are newtons (N). On Earth, the force of gravity is a constant, with an approximate value of 9.8 meters per second per second (9.8 m/sec^2). Let's calculate the weight of an apple on a table on Earth.

Mass of an apple = 0.1 kg

Force of gravity on Earth = 9.8 m/sec^2

Weight of the apple on Earth = 0.1 kg $\times$ 9.8 m/sec^2 = 0.98 N

Just as the apple exerts a downward force of gravity on the table, its weight is balanced by the same force exerted upward by the table. According to Newton's third law of motion, when one object exerts a force on a second object, the second object exerts a force on the first that is equal in magnitude and opposite in direction. In the case of the apple and the table, the forces are equal in magnitude but opposite in direction.

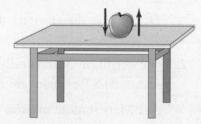

Let's calculate the weight of the same apple on the moon.

Mass of an apple = 0.1 kg

Force of gravity on the moon = 1.6 m/sec^2

Weight of the apple on the moon = 0.1 kg $\times$ 1.6 m/sec^2 = 0.16 N

Why are the weights different? The mass of the apple remains the same whether the apple is on Earth or on the moon. The force of gravity is different however, and this affects the weight of the apple. The apple weighs more on Earth. This is because the moon is less massive than Earth, so it has a weaker force of gravity. The force of gravity on the moon is about 1/6 that of Earth. Therefore, on the moon, you would weigh about 1/6 what you weigh on Earth. Each planet in the solar system has a different force of gravity based on its mass. Therefore, your weight would change depending on the planet you were on. The table below shows how gravity compares among the planets.

Planet	Gravity (× Earth's)
Mercury	0.38
Venus	0.91
Earth	1.00
Mars	0.38
Jupiter	2.53
Saturn	1.14
Uranus	0.9
Neptune	1.14

DISCUSSION QUESTION

Look at the table above. How does Jupiter's force of gravity compare to Earth's? What might be the reason for this?

LESSON REVIEW

1. Which statement is correct?

    A. Weight is the amount of material in an object.

    B. Mass is the physical dimensions of an object.

    C. Weight is the gravitational pull on an object.

    D. Mass is the gravitational pull on an object.

2. Your weight on Mars is only about 1/3 your weight on Earth. Which reason BEST explains this?

    A. Mars is more massive than Earth.

    B. Mars has a smaller force of gravity than Earth.

    C. Mars has a greater force of gravity than Earth.

    D. An object on Mars has less mass than the same object on Earth.

3. The Moon has 1/6 the gravity of Earth, which is approximately 9.8 m/sec^2. If something has a mass of 120 g, what will be its approximately weight on the moon?

    A. 0.2 g

    B. 120 g

    C. 120 N

    D. 0.2 N

4. If F equals force and a_g equals acceleration due to gravity, which of the following equations could be used to calculate an object's mass?

    A. $m = F/a_g$

    B. $m = a_g/F$

    C. $m = F \times a_g$

    D. $m = F + a_g$

5. A farmer brings his prize pumpkin to the annual country fair. If the mass of the pumpkin is 140 kg, what is its weight?

    A. 14 g

    B. 140 N

    C. 1400 kg

    D. 1372 N

26 Simple Machines

SPS8.e

Getting the Idea

A tire on a car goes flat and must be changed. A jack is used to lift and support the heavy car so the repair can be completed. A jack is one of six kinds of **simple machines**, devices with *few* moving parts that make work easier to do. Simple machines can increase the amount of force that is needed to move objects too resistant to be moved by hand. They can also be used to move objects faster. Common tools such as hammers and pliers, sports equipment such as racquets and fishing rods, and even door handles are simple machines. **Compound machines**, such as bicycles, are combinations of two or more simple machines. A bicycle is able to change speeds, directions, and the force needed to turn its pedals. In this lesson, you will review how to calculate the work a simple machine does and the mechanical advantage it provides.

Key Words

simple machines
compound machines
work
power
effort force
effort distance
work input
resistance force
resistance distance
work output
mechanical advantage
efficiency

Force, Work, and Power

If you simply hold a backpack, you are not doing work since the backpack is not moving. **Work** requires a force to push or pull an object in the same direction as the force. If you lift the backpack, then you do work because you are moving the backpack in the direction of the applied force, that is, upward. The amount of work is calculated using this equation:

$$W = F_d$$

The work (W) is found by multiplying the applied force (F) times the distance (d) moved.

The units of force are newtons (N). The units of distance are meters (m). The product of the two gives the units of work, newton-meters, normally called joules (j). Since work is the use of energy to move objects, its unit, the joule, is also a unit of energy.

Power is the rate at which work is done. The ability of a machine to work faster depends on its power. Machines that can do more joules of work per second have more power. The amount of power used to do some work is found by using this equation:

$$P = \frac{W}{t}$$

In this equation, work (W) is measured in joules (J) and time in seconds (sec). Therefore, the units of power (P) are joules per second, also known as watts (W). One watt is equal to one joule per second. Watt ratings indicate the brightness of incandescent bulbs. A 100-watt bulb is brighter than a 75-watt bulb, but it takes an additional 25 watts of power to produce the extra light.

You need to use both the work and power equations to solve this power question. How much power is used to hoist a load of shingles with a weight of 500 N to a roof 10 m above the ground in 40 s? First calculate the work done in joules (J). Then calculate the watts (W) of power used by entering the work answer in the power equation.

$$W = Fd = (500 \text{ N}) (1 \text{ m}) = 5000J$$

$$P = \frac{W}{t} = \frac{500J}{40 \text{ sec}} = 125\text{W}$$

It takes 125 watts of power to do 5000 joules of work in 40 seconds.

Simple Machines

There are six simple machines, as shown in the illustration on page 166. A simple machine, such as a lever, can increase the force you apply to it and change its direction. You can apply an **effort force** (F_e) to the longer lever arm section by pushing it down through an **effort distance** (d_e). The effort force moving through the effort distance produces a **work input** (W_i) to the machine. You can calculate the work input of the lever using this equation:

$$W_i = F_e \times d_e$$

Note the equation is similar to $W = F \times d$, except that it names F and d as effort factors.

As the longer end of the lever moves down, the shorter end applies a resistance force (F_r) through a resistance distance (d_r) as it moves up. The **resistance force** moving through the **resistance distance** results in a work output (W_o). The work output of the lever is found using this equation:

$$W_o = F_r \times d_r$$

Remember that work is energy, so it cannot be created or destroyed The work output of the lever cannot be greater than the work input. A machine cannot increase the amount of work. In theory, work input equals work output so $F_e \times d_e = F_r \times d_r$. This equation can be arranged to calculate any of its factors. For example, to find F_r, rearrange the equation to $F_r = F_e \times \frac{d_e}{d_r}$.

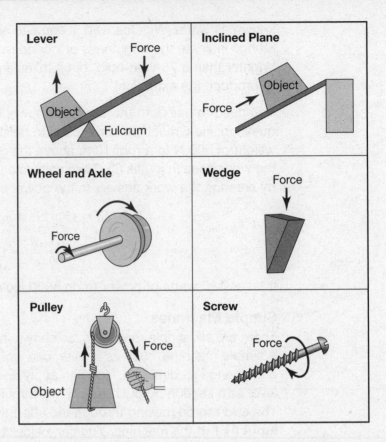

You can use the equations to calculate the resistance force a machine can produce. In the diagram below, a lever is set on a fulcrum so that its effort arm is 10 times longer than its resistance arm. An effort force of 100 N pushes the effort arm down 0.1 m. What is the resistance force produced when the resistance arm pushes up a distance of 0.01 m?

$$F_r = F_e \times \frac{d_e}{d_r} = (100 \text{ N}) \frac{(0.1 \text{ m})}{(0.01 \text{ m})} = 1000 \text{ N}.$$

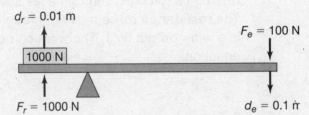

$d_r = 0.01$ m

$F_e = 100$ N

1000 N

$F_r = 1000$ N

$d_e = 0.1$ m

In the above problem, the lever multiplies the effort force 10 times from 100 N to 1000 N in the resistance force. The number of times a machine increases the effort force is termed the machine's **mechanical advantage** (*MA*). It is calculated by using either of these equations:

$$MA = \frac{F_r}{F_e} \text{ or } MA = \frac{d_e}{d_r}$$

A machine multiplies effort force if its effort arm is longer than its resistance arm. In the previous problem, the effort arm was 10 times longer than the resistance arm. The smaller effort force moves 10 times more than the resistance force. This produces more work and a greater resistance force. All machines use this concept.

Every machine, simple or compound, has to overcome frictional forces. These use up some of the work input. As a result, the work output of every machine is less than its work input. The efficiency (e) of a machine is determined by the ratio of its work output (Wo) to its work input (Wi). Efficiency is calculated and expressed as a percentage by using this equation:

$$e = \frac{W_o}{W_i} \times 100\%$$

For example, what is the **efficiency** of a machine which has a work output (W_o) of 500 joules and a work input (W_i) of 800 joules? Substituting the given values in the equation, we obtain:

$$e = \frac{500 \text{ joules}}{800} \text{ joules} \times 100\% = 62.5\%$$

Engineers can design compound machines in ways that reduce friction and increase efficiency. When possible, they use ball bearings that only have to overcome rolling friction. They also install lubrication systems in vehicles to minimize sliding friction.

DISCUSSION QUESTION

A company claims its washing machine produces 4000 joules of work output for every 3000 joules of work input. What would make you skeptical about this claim?

LESSON REVIEW

1. Which student is doing work?
    A. Rebecca is leaning against the classroom wall.
    B. Marcus is lifting his backpack onto his shoulders.
    C. Starr is carrying her lunch tray to the table.
    D. Louis is studying the science chart on the wall.

2. It takes 8 seconds for a pulley system to lift a load that weighs 400 N to a height of 10 m. How much power is required?
    A. 4000 watts
    B. 3200 watts
    C. 500 watts
    D. 80 watts

3. Which one of the following is NOT a simple machine?

   A. wheel and axle

   B. inclined plane

   C. lever

   D. bicycle

4. In order for a lever to multiply its effort force,

   A. its effort arm must equal its resistance arm.

   B. its resistance arm must be longer than its effort arm.

   C. its resistance arm should be one meter in length.

   D. its effort arm should be longer than its resistance arm.

5. What is the definition of power?

   A. the ability to do work

   B. the rate of doing work

   C. the amount of work done

   D. work output divided by work input

EOCT Review

1. Which of the following statements BEST describes the definition of speed?

    A. Speed is the same as velocity.
    B. Speed is the distance traveled.
    C. The distance traveled is never a factor in determining speed.
    D. Speed is the distance traveled per unit of time.

2. Use the table below to answer the following question. The table shows changes in velocity over a period of time.

    Time–Velocity Data

Time (s)	Velocity (m/s)
0	2
1	1.5
2	1
3	0.5
4	0

    When the traffic light changed from green to yellow, Mr. Jefferson, the mathematics teacher stepped on the brake. The car eventually came to a stop as the light turned red. What was the car's rate of acceleration?

    A. -0.5 m/sec^2
    B. 0.5 m/sec^2
    C. 1 m/sec^2
    D. 1.5 m/sec^2

3. A car travels 150 kilometers west in 3 hours? What is its average velocity?

    A. 150 km/h
    B. 50 km/h
    C. 50 km/h west
    D. 150 km/h west

4. Newton's first law of motion describes the tendency of objects in motion to continue in motion and objects at rest to remain at rest. What term is used to describe this behavior?

    A. velocity
    B. acceleration
    C. displacement
    D. inertia

5. Four racing cars are equipped with equally powerful engines. Which one of the racing cars described below will accelerate the fastest under the same net force?

    A. the racing car with a mass of 1000 kg
    B. the racing car with a mass of 900 kg
    C. the race car with a mass of 800 kg
    D. the race car with a mass of 700 kg

6. One student in a tug of war is pulling with a force of 21 N east. A second student is pulling with a force of 18 N west. What is the net force in the contest?

    A. 39 N north
    B. 3 N east
    C. 3 N west
    D. 3 N south

7. Which statement describes an object's velocity during freefall?

    A. An object travels at a constant velocity throughout the fall.
    B. An object's velocity increases as it falls.
    C. An object's velocity decreases as it falls.
    D. An object during freefall does not have a measurable velocity.

8. **An acorn falls from a tall oak tree to the ground. What is the acorn's final velocity if it falls for 3 seconds?**

   A. 9.8 m/sec
   B. 19.6 m/sec
   C. 29.4 m/sec
   D. 96.0 m/sec

9. **What factor in addition to distance determines the force of gravity between two objects?**

   A. the volumes of the objects
   B. the diameters of the objects
   C. the masses of the objects
   D. the density of the objects

10. **Lucius calculated that his weight on Venus would be about 90 percent of his weight on Earth. Which one of the following explanations is BEST?**

    A. Venus is closer to the Sun than Earth.
    B. The force of gravity is lower on Venus.
    C. The force of gravity is higher on Venus.
    D. The surface temperature is higher on Venus.

11. **Which statement about the mass of an object is FALSE?**

    A. Mass is the amount of matter in an object.
    B. An object's mass may be expressed in kilograms.
    C. An object's mass does not change with location.
    D. An object's mass increases in stronger gravity fields.

12. **Which statement about the weight of an object is correct?**

    A. The force of gravity determines an object's weight.
    B. Weight is an unchanging measure of an object's mass.
    C. The weight and mass of an object are the same.
    D. An object's weight is not related to its mass.

13. **A heavy box is pushed up an inclined plane as shown in the diagram below.**

    1.5 m   4.5 m

    What is the mechanical advantage of the inclined plane?

    A. 1.5
    B. 3
    C. 4.5
    D. 6

14. **Which one of the following is a simple machine?**

    A. wedge
    B. meat grinder
    C. car
    D. bicycle

CHAPTER

5 Energy

27 Energy Transformations

 SPS7.a

Getting the Idea

Key Words

energy
work
kinetic energy
potential energy

Energy exists in different forms—electrical, mechanical, chemical, heat, light, sound, and nuclear. It can move among different substances, and it can change from one form to another. For example, a car moves because of a series of energy conversions: electrical energy produces a spark that converts stored chemical energy in gasoline to heat energy when the gasoline burns. The energy of heat is then converted into mechanical energy when expanding gases move pistons. This movement is eventually transmitted to the car's wheels, which makes the car move.

What Is Energy?

Energy is the ability to do work. **Work** is a scientific term. Work is the product of a force applied to an object and the distance through which the force is applied.

$$\text{work} = \text{force} \times \text{distance, or } W = F \times d$$

In simple terms, work results in the movement of an object. So energy can be thought of as the ability to move objects. The objects may be as large as a giant cruise ship or as small as an atom.

Kinetic Energy

Energy is classified into two broad categories: kinetic energy and potential energy. **Kinetic energy** is energy due to the motion of an object. The amount of kinetic energy an object has depends on two factors: the object's mass and its velocity.

The amount of kinetic energy an object has can be calculated Kinetic energy is equal to one half an object's mass multiplied by its velocity (speed) squared. Thus, the formula for calculating kinetic energy is:

$$\text{Kinetic energy} = \tfrac{1}{2} \times \text{mass} \times (\text{velocity})^2$$

$$KE = \tfrac{1}{2}\, mv^2$$

The kinetic energy of an object changes if either its mass or its velocity changes. However, a change in velocity results in a greater change in kinetic energy because this value is squared. The example below illustrates this point using two cars of equal mass traveling at different speeds.

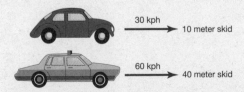

Potential Energy

Potential energy is the energy an object has because of its position or composition. Potential energy is stored energy that can become kinetic energy under the appropriate conditions. For example, a rock at the edge of a cliff has potential energy due to its position. This potential energy changes to kinetic energy when the rock falls. A stick of dynamite that is not in use also has potential energy. In this case, the potential energy is stored in the chemical composition of the dynamite. The potential energy is converted to kinetic energy when the dynamite explodes.

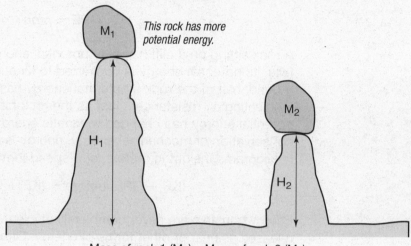

Mass of rock 1 (M_1) = Mass of rock 2 (M_2)
Height 1 (H_1) > Height 2 (H_2)

The rocks shown above have potential energy because of their position above the ground The amount of potential energy each rock has can be calculated by multiplying the mass of each rock by its height above the ground. Thus, the formula for calculating potential energy (PE) is:

$$\text{Potential energy} = \text{mass} \times \text{height}$$
$$PE = m \times h$$

In this example, both rocks have the same mass. However, the height of the first rock is greater than that of the second. Because it is higher off the ground, the potential energy of the first rock is greater than that of the second rock.

Energy Conversions and Conservation

An object can have both potential energy and kinetic energy. For example, a roller coaster car has its greatest potential energy when it is at the top of its tallest hill. As the roller coaster moves over the hill, some of its potential energy is converted to kinetic energy. The kinetic energy is greatest just as the roller coaster races through the bottom of the hill. As the roller coaster moves through the entire track, its energy changes form many times. However, no energy is created or destroyed

Mechanical energy is equal to the sum of an object's kinetic energy plus its potential energy. Potential energy that results from the position of an object is called gravitational potential energy (GPE). If the rock falls, its potential energy changes to kinetic energy as it falls.

The amount of gravitational potential energy, GPE, in an object can be calculated by multiplying the mass, m, of the object by the force of gravity (9.8 m/sec^2), g, pulling on the object by the height, h, of the object above the ground. Thus, the formula for calculating gravitational potential energy (GPE) is:

$$GPE = mgh$$

A rock sitting on a cliff has only potential energy. However, as the rock falls, its potential energy is converted to kinetic energy. Halfway to the ground, half of the rock's potential energy has changed to kinetic energy (neglecting air resistance). Just as the rock hits the ground, all of its potential energy has changed to kinetic energy. In calculations related to conservation of mechanical energy, energy is expressed in joules, mass in kilograms, height in meters, and speed in meters per second:

$$(KE + GPE) \text{ before} = (KE + GPE) \text{ after}$$

Energy transfers are never completely efficient. Some energy is always released as heat or other forms of energy. Often this loss of efficiency occurs because of **friction**—a force that opposes the motion of an object.

When an object moves through air, for example, air resistance is a form of friction. A swinging pendulum eventually stops because some of its kinetic energy is transformed into heat due to friction. If you drop a ball, some of the ball's energy is changed to heat, and the ball doesn't bounce back to its original height. Because the energy that is changed to heat is not useful energy, it is sometimes described as "lost" energy. However, the energy is not truly "lost"; it is simply converted to a form of energy that is no longer immediately useful.

DISCUSSION QUESTION

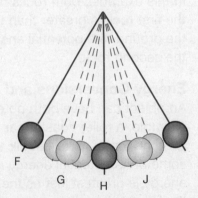

As a pendulum swings, its energy is constantly converted between kinetic energy and potential energy. At which point in its swing does a pendulum have the least potential energy and the greatest kinetic energy? Explain your answer.

LESSON REVIEW

1. A book sits on a desk that is 1 meter (m) high. The book's gravitational potential energy is 10 joules (J). If the book falls from the desk, what is the sum, in joules, of its gravitational potential energy and kinetic energy when the book is 0.5 m from the ground?

   A. 5

   B. 10

   C. 15

   D. 20

2. An orange is hanging from the tip of a branch that is 2 meters (m) above the ground. A gust of wind blows the tree, and the orange begins to fall to the ground. Which of the following describes the orange's energy just as the orange hits the ground?

   A. Its gravitational energy is zero.

   B. Its kinetic energy is zero.

   C. Its kinetic energy is twice its gravitational energy.

   D. Its kinetic energy equals its gravitational energy.

3. Which of the following is an example of gravitational potential energy changing to kinetic energy?

   A. a person riding a bicycle along a level road

   B. rocks falling down a mountainside

   C. sunlight heating the water in a lake

   D. a plant producing food by photosynthesis

28 Heat Transfer

 SPS7.b

Getting the Idea

Key Words
heat transfer
conduction
conductors
insulators
convection
radiation

Thermal energy, also called heat energy, always flows from a warmer object to a cooler object. This is called heat transfer. The process continues until both objects reach the same temperature. For example, you blow on a hot slice of pizza. Thermal energy flows out of the pizza slice to the cooler air. The pizza slice cools. In winter, the heating system in your home transfers thermal energy from the furnace to warm the colder rooms. When objects reach the same temperature, **heat transfer** occurs equally in both directions. There is no net change in this state of equilibrium.

Some materials readily transfer thermal energy. Pots and pans are made of such materials in order to do cooking. Other materials do just the opposite and impede the flow of thermal energy. When you go outside in the winter, you wear clothing made from such materials in order to keep warm. Another example of slowing the flow of thermal energy is the thermos bottle. It can keep hot liquids hot or cold liquids cold for many hours.

Heat Transfer

There are three ways in which heat transfer can happen: conduction, convection, and radiation. **Conduction** is the transfer of heat energy from one solid object to another when they are in direct contact. The particles in the warmer solid vibrate more rapidly. The vibrations pass heat energy along the particles and transfer to the cooler object at the point of contact. The diagram below shows how conduction transfers heat energy. The spoon in the pot of hot water is too hot to touch. The metal pot conducts heat energy from the burner flame to the water. The water gets hot and transfers heat energy to the spoon, which then transfers the heat energy to the handle. Metals and other materials that readily transfer heat energy through themselves are called **conductors**. Materials that transfer heat energy poorly are called **insulators**.

Conduction

Convection is the process of heat transfer in fluids by means of rising and falling currents of liquid or gas. When a region of liquid or gas absorbs heat energy, its molecules move faster, and the distance between them increases. The region of fluid expands as a result and becomes less dense than its surroundings. The warm fluid floats upward as cooler denser fluids sink beneath it. This process creates rising convection currents of warmer fluid and falling currents of cooler fluid The rising warm fluids gradually cool as they mix with cooler ones. The process repeats itself as shown in the diagram below. A pot of hot water on a burner forms convection currents that transfer heat energy throughout the mass of liquid

Heating systems apply convection currents produced by the radiators, convectors, and air vents to circulate warm air and heat rooms. On hot summer days, you can see the process in action in the atmosphere as huge cumulonimbus clouds form. Rising columns of hot humid air cool off when they reach lower temperature air at higher altitudes. The water vapor condenses into fine droplets of mist that form the changing shape of the cloud. Convection currents also affect the oceans of Earth. The Gulf Stream is a warm current of water that forms in the Gulf of Mexico. It then flows into the Atlantic Ocean, turns north past Georgia as it brings warm water to Canada and Europe. Many other convection currents in the oceans transfer heat energy from warmer regions to colder ones.

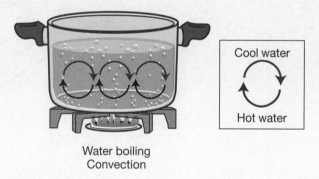

Water boiling
Convection

Radiation is the transfer of heat energy in the form of electromagnetic waves. The same kinds of energy waves transfer heat and light energy from the Sun as it radiates energy to Earth.

Space is filled with electromagnetic force fields produced by electrically charged subatomic particles. Disturbances in these force fields produce electromagnetic vibrations and waves. The process is analogous to a pebble tossed in a pond making ripples. Electromagnetic waves travel through the emptiness of space. They can also pass through many types of matter.

Electromagnetic waves are invisible to the eye, but their energy is often able to affect matter in various ways. Certain electromagnetic waves that we call visible light, even though invisible, illuminate objects

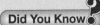
Did You Know?

Every warm object or body emits infrared radiation. Security lights and night vision systems detect the invisible infrared. The night vision systems transform the infrared into visible images.

and make them visible to the eye. In daylight, the air glows with light reflecting off particles in the atmosphere. On the airless moon, the daytime sky is as black as if it were night.

Infrared electromagnetic waves are sensed by nerves in the skin as heat. All warm bodies radiate heat energy in the form of infrared electromagnetic waves. When you sit near a fireplace, you can feel the effect of these waves warming you. Toaster ovens heat and toast bread and other food products by radiation.

Unlike conduction and convection, radiation does not require the presence of particles of matter in order to transfer heat energy. You may wonder how radiation transfers heat energy to an object. Particles of matter can absorb some of the energy in the wave as it passes through them. This increases the kinetic energy of the particles and their rate of motion. At this point, heat energy transfer takes place within the object by either conduction, if the object is a solid, or convection, if it is a liquid

If you bring a case of cold soda cans to the beach, you need to shield them from the sun's rays if you want to enjoy a cold drink. The diagram below illustrates how the sun's radiation warms a can of soda that is left in its rays to absorb the electromagnetic energy.

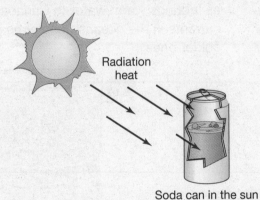

Soda can in the sun

Preventing heat transfer is also important. A thermos bottle does this very well. Its design prevents most conduction, convection, and radiation. The thermos is built of two containers, one usually made of glass sitting inside the other made of plastic or metal. In the sealed space between the two is a vacuum. The lack of particles in the vacuum slows conduction and convection. The surfaces facing the vacuum are coated with a reflective metal that acts like mirror. It reflects much of the infrared radiation to minimize loss of heat by radiation.

DISCUSSION QUESTION

Explain how molecular motion affects heat transfer in conduction, convection, and radiation.

LESSON REVIEW

1. Why is it very dangerous to leave a child or animal in a locked car with the windows closed in bright sunlight?

    A. The air in a car with closed windows will soon run out of oxygen and asphyxiate the living things inside.

    B. The car becomes dangerously cold as it transfers heat energy to the air by radiation.

    C. The car's temperature remains equal to the air temperature outside due to a state of equilibrium that could be dangerous.

    D. The car can absorb and hold enough radiant heat energy from the sun to make its temperature hot enough to be dangerous.

2. The metal handle of a pot cooking on a stove soon becomes too hot to touch. What type of heat transfer causes this?

    A. conduction

    B. radiation

    C. convection

    D. no heat transfer takes place

3. Heat transfer always results in a change of temperature when it flows

    A. between equally cold objects.

    B. between equally warm objects.

    C. from a colder object to a warmer object.

    D. from a warmer object to a colder object.

4. The type of heat transfer that takes place in fluids is

    A. conduction.

    B. convection.

    C. radiation.

    D. electromagnetic waves.

5. Materials that prevent heat flow are

    A. usually metals.

    B. conductors.

    C. insulators.

    D. radiators.

29 Heat Capacity and Phase Diagrams

 SPS7.c-d

Getting the Idea

A metal pot heats up and cools down quickly. Water in the same pot heats up and cools down slowly. The heat capacity of metals is low, while that of water is high. **Heat capacity** is the number of joules of heat energy needed to change the temperature of a mass of substance one degree Celsius. If mass is measured in kilograms instead of grams, then heat capacity is measured in kilojoules instead of joules. **Heat energy** is the total kinetic energy of all the molecular particles in an object. Objects that gain heat energy usually rise in temperature.

When you heat or cool an object, it absorbs or loses heat energy. Its temperature usually goes up or down. There are times when the temperature of the object remains unchanged as it gains or loses energy. Those times are when it changes phase. The term **phase** refers to an object's state, whether it is in the solid, liquid, or gas phase. A **phase change** can occur when heating a substance. Solid ice melts into water, a liquid. Boiling water changes into steam, a gas. The reverse of these phase changes can occur during cooling, when steam condenses into water, or water freezes into ice.

Heat Capacity

Substances with high heat capacities can store more heat energy. From spring through summer, cool ocean waters slowly warm as they absorb heat energy from the sun. The oceans during the winter release the energy into the atmosphere warming it. This moderates coastal climates by making summers cooler and winters warmer. Inland, the ground has low heat capacity, summers are hotter, and winters are colder.

The definition of heat capacity does not specify the amount of mass. If you double the mass, you double the heat capacity. The **specific heat**, also called specific heat capacity, of a substance is the number of kilojoules of heat energy needed to raise the temperature of 1 kilogram of substance one degree Celsius. **Temperature** (T) is a measure of the average kinetic energy of the particles. A thermometer scaled in units of degrees Celsius (°C) is commonly used to measure temperature.

The number of kilojoules of heat energy (Q) a substance gains or loses is directly related to three factors: the change in its temperature (ΔT) or ($T_f - T_i$), the specific heat (c) of the substance, and the mass (m) in

Key Words

heat capacity
heat energy
phase
phase change
specific heat
temperature
phase diagram

kilograms of the substance. Heat energy is gained if ΔT is positive or lost if ΔT is negative. This is expressed by the equation:

$$Q = cm\ (\Delta T)\ \ \text{or}\ \ Q = cm\ (T_f - T_i)$$

The specific heat of the substance is a measured quantity that has been accurately determined by many experiments. Specific heat is measured in kilojoules per kilogram·degree Celsius (kJ/kg·°C). Tables of specific heat data provide this information for most substances. Subtract the initial temperature (T_i) from the final temperature (T_f) to find the change in temperature ($\Delta T = T_f - T_i$). The units of mass of the substance are kilograms (kg).

You may be asked to determine the heat capacity of a certain mass of substance. Here is a typical problem. How much heat energy is needed to raise the temperature of 100 kg of water (specific heat = 4.19 kJ/kg·°C) from 15°C to 25°C? Substituting the given values in the equation, we obtain:

$$Q = cm\ (T_f - T_i) = (4.19\ \text{kJ/kg·°C})\ (100\ \text{kg})\ (25°C - 15°C) =$$
$$4190\ \text{kilojoules}$$

Note that the kilogram and degree Celsius units cancel out, leaving kilojoules, a unit of heat energy, as the remainder. You may be asked to solve for any factor in the equation. For example, to find the final temperature of a substance, rearrange the equation to

$$T_f = Q/cm + T_i$$

Phase Changes

Whether a substance is in the solid, liquid, or gas phase depends on the temperature at standard pressure (1 atmosphere). In the diagram below, the models indicate how the particles of matter are arranged in the solid, liquid, and gas phases.

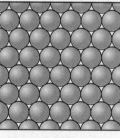
Solid

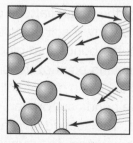
Liquid

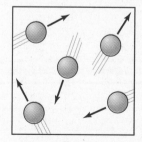
Gas

What happens to the solid phase if the temperature rises enough? The particles absorb heat energy. This raises their average kinetic energy. They move more rapidly. The average distance between the particles increases, weakening the bonds binding them. The particles separate just enough to slide around each other. For clarity, the diagram exaggerates the degree of separation. The substance changes phase from a solid to a liquid. An example of this is an ice cube melting into a puddle of liquid water. At still higher temperatures, the particles completely break their bonds and fly off in random directions. At that point, the substance changes to the gas phase. An example is boiling water changing to steam.

Phase Diagrams

Suppose you heat a substance and record its temperature over time as it changes from a solid to a liquid. You observe that the temperature rises steadily as the substance absorbs heat energy. But you note that the temperature stops rising when the substance begins the phase change and that it remains constant until the phase change is completed. You summarize and communicate the data on a graph as shown in the diagram below.

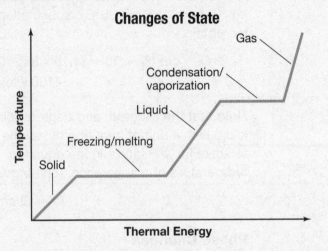

A phase diagram shows the change in temperature of a heated substance over time as it undergoes phase changes. Under the slope of the graph as it rises to the first horizontal portion, the substance is in the solid phase. The change from the solid to liquid phase takes place where the graph flattens out. The temperature stops rising even though heat energy is still being absorbed. All of the heat energy is used up to break the bonds that bind the particles into a solid. This temperature is the melting point of the substance. Under this segment of the graph, the substance is a mix of solid and liquid. The temperature rises again after all the bonds are broken. The substance under this part of the graph is liquid. The second leveling of the graph occurs at the boiling point of the substance. The remaining bonds that hold the particles in the liquid phase are broken, and they change to gas. The temperature of the particles in the gas phase can rise.

The phase diagram also shows the phase changes that occur during cooling. Just follow the graph back to its starting point. In the reverse direction, the slope traces a decrease in the temperature. The flat portions of the graph indicate condensation when particles change

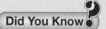
from gas to liquid and freezing when the change is from liquid to solid During these phase changes, the bonds reestablish themselves as the particles transfer energy to their surroundings. The same amount of heat energy absorbed by the particles during boiling and melting is released by them when condensing or freezing. The released energy keeps the temperature constant during the phase changes and is further proof of the law of conservation of energy.

DISCUSSION QUESTION

Geraldo and Jill are heating a beaker containing a mixture of ice cubes and water. They use a thermometer to measure the temperature of the mixture. They record the temperature data once every minute until all the ice cubes are melted. Describe and explain what a graph of their data would look like.

LESSON REVIEW

1. A material that heats up and cools down quickly

   A. is useful for storing heat energy.

   B. has a high specific heat.

   C. is most likely water.

   D. has a low heat capacity.

2. Samantha decides to use her new aluminum pan to scramble eggs. She wants to determine how much heat energy will be needed to heat her aluminum pan from 20°C to 220°C. Samantha obtains the specific heat of aluminum from the reference table. It lists the specific heat of aluminum as 0.90 kJ/kg·°C. The pan has a mass of 0.5 kg. She does the calculation correctly. Which one of the following is her answer?

   A. 0.45 joules of heat energy

   B. 0.9 kilojoules of heat energy

   C. 90 kilojoules of heat energy

   D. 180 joules of heat energy

3. You are asked to find the specific heat of a substance. You will have to rearrange the terms of the equation in order to solve the problem. Which one of the following is the correct rearrangement?

    A. $c = Q/m \, (\Delta T)$

    B. $\Delta T = Q/cm$

    C. $Q = cm \, (\Delta T)$

    D. $Q = cm \, (T_f - T_i)$

4. How does a phase diagram indicate when a substance is changing phase?

    A. The temperature rises during a phase change.

    B. The temperature is constant during a phase change.

    C. The temperature falls during a phase change.

    D. The temperature changes 20 degrees Celsius during a phase change.

5. In which phase do the particles of a substance have the greatest freedom of motion?

    A. All phases have the same freedom of motion.

    B. the gas phase

    C. the solid phase

    D. the liquid phase

30 Transfer of Energy by Waves

SPS9.a

Getting the Idea

Though usually not obvious, waves are all around us. The sounds that we hear, the light that we see, an X-ray in the hospital, the ripples from a rock thrown into the water—all are different manifestations of energy traveling in waves. Waves transfer energy, and it's that property that makes them a central component of our physical world.

Key Words

wave
medium
electromagnetic
   wave
mechanical wave
longitudinal wave
compressional
   wave
transverse wave
surface wave
rest position/
   equilibrium
crest
trough
compression
rarefaction

Transferring Energy but Not Matter

Simply put, a **wave** is a disturbance that carries energy while traveling from one location to another. Most often, the wave is traveling through some kind of medium. A **medium** is a substance that waves utilize to transport the wave's energy. This medium can be almost anything, such as water, a metal, or air. While traveling, a wave displaces matter, however temporarily, in order to transfer its energy. Once the wave passes, the matter returns close to its original position. An example that anyone can duplicate is to tie one end of a long rope to a tree and quickly "snap" the free end up and down, thereby creating a wave that travels along the rope to the tree.

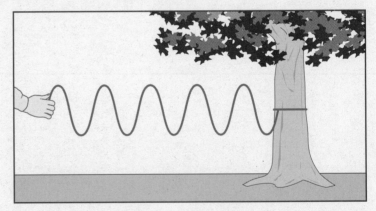

You'll notice that the physical makeup of the rope did not change. Instead, the rope was the medium through which the wave traveled to the tree.

Types of Waves

There are two main types of waves, **electromagnetic** and **mechanical**. Mechanical waves always utilize a medium to transfer their energy. Mechanical waves can be further classified as either being **longitudinal** or **transverse** waves. A longitudinal wave, also known as a **compressional** wave, is a wave in which the particles in the medium move in a direction parallel to the direction of the wave itself. Sound waves are an excellent example of a longitudinal wave.

A coil models what a compressional wave looks like.

A rope models what a transverse wave looks like.

As a sound emerges from its source toward the ear of a listener, particles of air move forward in all directions away from the source. Each air particle pushes toward an adjacent particle, causing the first particle to return to its original position and the other to then push toward another neighboring particle. This back and forth oscillation among the particles creates areas where the particles are compacted and other areas where they are spread apart. Another way of stating the above is that no one particle travels the entire distance of the sound wave. Instead, the particle simply pushes its neighbor in the direction of the wave. Other examples of longitudinal waves include primary earthquake waves and shock waves from an explosion.

For transverse waves, the particles of the medium move in a direction perpendicular to the direction of the wave. A classic and readily observable example of a transverse waves is that of the ripples created when a stone is thrown into still water. As the water ripples radiate out, the water particles are oscillating up and down, while the energy of the ripples is moving out. Other examples of transverse waves include the rope tied to the tree in the example above, secondary earthquake waves, and the motion of a plucked guitar string.

Light waves are another example of a transverse wave. However, light waves belong to a class of waves called electromagnetic waves. Electromagnetic waves are unique in that while they can transfer energy through a medium, more commonly they transfer energy in a vacuum. For example, light energy from the sun travels through the vacuum of space before reaching earth.

There are some waves that are neither transverse nor longitudinal. Waves that travel along the surface of the ocean or Earth's surface are termed **surface waves**, whereby the particles of the medium undergo a circular motion.

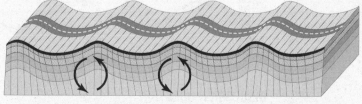

Direction of surface wave ⟶

Earthquakes produce waves. There are two main types of earthquake waves: body waves and surface waves. Body waves can be broken down into P-waves, which are longitudinal waves, and S-waves, which are transverse waves. P-waves, which stands for "primary," are the fastest waves and are the first tremors felt during an earthquake. S-waves, for "secondary," follow next. The other main type of wave, surface waves, are, as their name states, waves that roll along just under Earth's surface. Surface waves are usually the most destructive of the earthquake waves.

Properties of a Wave

As shown in the examples above, a transverse wave is a series of peaks and valleys. In the diagram below, the dashed line through the middle of the wave is its **rest position** or **equilibrium**. This represents the medium without a wave acting upon it. The peak of the wave is known as its crest while the valley is its trough. The **crest** and the **trough** represent points of maximum displacement of the particles in a medium from the equilibrium position. For the crest, it's the maximum positive displacement from the rest position, and for the trough it's the maximum negative displacement.

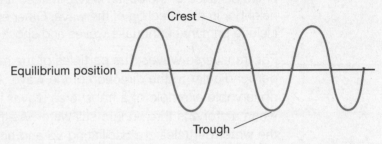

In longitudinal waves, the movement or displacement of particles of the medium results in alternate regions of high particle density, resulting in high pressure and regions of low particle density, resulting in low pressure. In the high particle density area, the particles are tightly compacted, while in the low pressure region, the particles are spread apart. Regions of high particle density are called **compressions**. Regions of low particle density are called **rarefactions**.

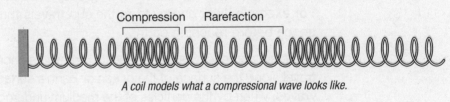

A coil models what a compressional wave looks like.

A rope models what a transverse wave looks like.

DISCUSSION QUESTION

Give examples of the types of various waves that one might experience every day. Which waves do you think are the most common? Give examples of various mediums.

LESSON REVIEW

1. What kind of wave does NOT require a medium for its propagation?

    A. a mechanical transverse wave

    B. an electromagnetic mechanical wave

    C. an electromagnetic transverse wave

    D. a mechanical longitudinal wave

Use the following illustration of a wave to answer questions 2 and 3.

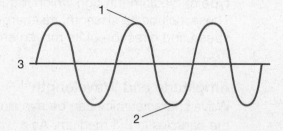

2. Which answer correctly names the parts of the wave numbered 1–3?

    A. compression, rarefaction, equilibrium

    B. trough, crest, equilibrium

    C. equilibrium, crest, compression

    D. crest, trough, equilibrium

3. Which statement MOST accurately describes a characteristic of this type of wave?

    A. The direction of the back and forth motion of the particles is perpendicular to the direction in which the wave is moving.

    B. The point of minimum displacement of the particles in a medium from the equilibrium position is called a crest or trough.

    C. The direction of the back and forth motion of the particles is parallel to the direction in which the wave is moving.

    D. The high pressure area is called a compression, and the lower pressure area is called a rarefaction.

4. A wave is propagating energy from left to right. The particles of the medium are moving back and forth from left to right. What is this type of wave?

    A. surface wave

    B. longitudinal

    C. transverse

    D. electromagnetic

31 Characteristics of Waves

SPS9.b-c

Getting the Idea

In order to understand how waves behave, you need to learn the different parts of a wave. The components of the wave together with the type of medium through which it travels determine the wave's actions. These include its strength, its energy, its periodic behavior, and the speed and direction of its movements.

Key Words

displacement
polarized light
amplitude
wavelength
frequency
hertz (hz)
period
speed
electromagnetic
   spectrum

Amplitude and Wavelength

Wave characteristics can be explained in relation to the behavior of the particles in the medium. As a wave travels, it causes a vibratory **displacement** of the particles in the medium. The direction of displacement varies. In longitudinal waves, it is in the same direction as the wave's motion. In transverse light waves that are unpolarized, it is at right angles to the wave's direction, but in all directions outwards, which causes glare. Some sunglasses have lenses that reduce glare by limiting the vibrations to one direction only, called **polarized light**. In surface waves, a circular motion combines parallel and perpendicular movements. The amount of displacement is the maximum distance of the particle from the movement's midpoint. The displacement of the particles is a quantity that can be measured.

In the analysis of a transverse wave, there are key properties that describe the state of the particles in the medium.

The **amplitude** of a wave is the maximum amount of displacement of the particles from the wave's rest position. In a transverse wave, that is the distance from the equilibrium point (rest position) to either the top of the crest or the bottom of the trough. In a longitudinal wave such as sound, there are no crests or troughs. The amplitude there is the difference between the pressures of the compressions and the rarefactions.

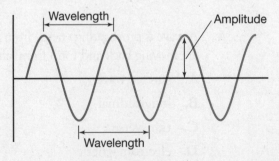

Duplicating any part of this book is prohibited by law.

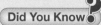
The amplitude of the wave is proportional to its energy. The greater the amplitude of a sound wave, the louder the sound In transverse light waves, the greater the amplitude, the brighter the light.

The wavelength is another property of a wave. Observe the repeating pattern of crests and troughs. The **wavelength** is the distance from mid-crest to mid-crest or from mid-trough to mid-trough. For longitudinal waves, the wavelength can be measured from a point in one compression to a similar point in the next. The wavelength is inversely proportional to the wave's energy. At double the energy, the wavelength is half as long. In the visible light spectrum, as wavelengths shorten you see colors with increasingly higher energy: red, orange, yellow, green, blue, indigo, and violet. Students use the acronym ROYGBIV to remember the order of the colors.

Frequency, Period, and Speed

Other key components of waves are quantifiable attributes such as frequency, period, and velocity. A wave's **frequency** is the number of wave cycles the particles go through per second. One wave cycle is equal to one wavelength. Frequency is measured in **hertz** (hz). One hertz equals one wave cycle per second. The frequency and the wavelength are inversely related. When the frequency increases, the wavelength decreases. In the visible light spectrum, red has the lowest frequency, violet has the highest frequency.

The period is a term that often gets confused with frequency. The **period** of a wave is the time for a complete cycle to pass a particular point. A period is measured by time, such as seconds, minutes, or hours. The frequency, measured in cycles/second, contrasts with a period measured in seconds/cycle. If a drum is banged 2 times in one second, its frequency is 2 Hz, but its period is one cycle per 0.5 second. Frequency and period are inversely related. As the frequency increases, the period decreases.

The **speed** or velocity of a wave is determined by the medium the wave passes through and by the type of wave itself. The velocity of a wave is constant in any medium at standard conditions. This means that if the wave's frequency changes, its wavelength must change inversely in order to keep the velocity constant. When the frequency gets greater, the wavelength gets shorter. One way to picture this is to think of two people walking side by side. The taller person takes longer strides but fewer steps per minute. The smaller person maintains the same velocity with shorter steps but takes more steps per minute. The length of each person's stride times the frequency of their steps produces the same velocity or speed of walking for each.

The Electromagnetic Spectrum

The energy of both mechanical and electromagnetic waves increases as their wavelengths become shorter and their frequency increases. High frequency sound waves have short wavelengths. Their energy can shatter glass. In the full range of the **electromagnetic spectrum**, the highest frequency X-rays and gamma rays have enough energy to penetrate solids and damage living tissue. In the opposite direction, although wave energy decreases, ultraviolet rays are still strong enough to cause sunburn and the risk of skin cancer. Lower frequency infrared rays transfer heat, microwaves can carry data or cook food, and the longest waves transfer data to TV, FM, shortwave, and AM sets.

Electromagnetic Spectrum

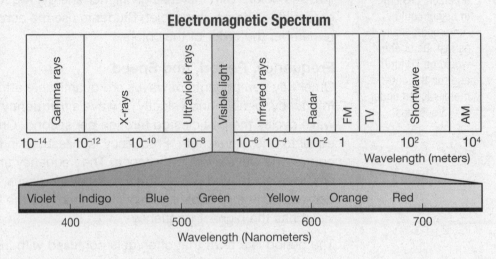

Wave Speed and the Wave Equation

Waves have speed (velocity). The distance a wave travels per unit of time is its speed or velocity (v). When driving a car, the units for speed are miles or kilometers per hour. In equation form, the following is used to illustrate wave velocity:

$$v = \text{distance/time or } v = d/t$$

Problem: What is the speed of a wave that travels 100 meters in 20 seconds?

Solution: $v = d/t$ or $v = 100\text{m}/20\text{sec} = 5$ m/sec

You may have to rearrange the equation if the problem asks for the value of the distance a wave travels or the time it takes.

Problem: How far has a wave traveled after 30 seconds at a velocity of 4 m/sec?

Solution: $d = vt$ or $d = (4$ m/sec$)(30$ sec$) = 120$ meters

A wave's velocity or speed is proportional to its frequency and its wavelength. The wave equation relating these factors is speed equals frequency (f) $\times$ wavelength (λ), or $v = f \times \lambda$.

When measuring λ, the length of a wave, select two periodic points on the wave, such as mid-crest to mid-crest to use for the measurement. The velocity units will be meters per second (m/sec) if frequency is measured in hertz (cycles/sec) and λ is in meters.

As an example, if a wave has a frequency of 2.0 Hz and its wavelength is measured at 1.5 meters, then the wave equation will be:

$$v = (2.0 \text{ Hz}) (1.5 \text{ m}) = 3 \text{ m/sec}$$

In another example, if a wave has a velocity of 25 m/sec and a wavelength of 2.5 meters, then the wave equation will be rearranged to determine its frequency:

$$25 \text{ m/sec} = f (2.5 \text{ m}) \text{ or } f = 25 \text{ m/sec} / 2.5 \text{ m} = 10 \text{ Hz (cycles/sec)}$$

DISCUSSION QUESTION

Discuss the relationship between wave frequency and wavelength. For example, why does an increase in wavelength equate to a decrease in frequency?

LESSON REVIEW

Use the following illustration of a wave to answer questions 1 and 2.

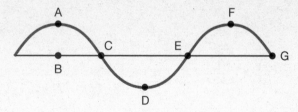

1. Which two letters when connected with a straight line show the size of one wavelength?

    A. AB

    B. AF

    C. BC

    D. EG

2. Which two letters when connected with a straight line show the size of the amplitude?

A. AB

B. AF

C. CE

D. EG

3. Light waves travel at the speed of light 3×108 m/sec. What is the frequency of a light wave with a wavelength of 5×10^{-9} m?

A. 15×10^{-1} Hz

B. 0.6×10^{16} Hz

C. 1.67×10^{17} Hz

D. 6.0×10^{16} Hz

4. How long does it take a wave to travel 1,200 meters with a speed of 3×108 m/sec?

A. 4.0×10^{6} sec

B. 400 sec

C. $.04 \times 10^{-8}$ sec

D. 4.0×10^{-6} sec

32 Reflection, Refraction, Interference, and Diffraction of Waves

 3.1.spi.1–3

Getting the Idea

What happens if a traveling wave and the energy it carries run into another wave or reaches a new medium? Does the wave stop, does it turn around and head back, does it keep on traveling, or does it go off in a different direction? All of these actions can occur. It depends on the characteristics of the medium and any new medium that the wave may encounter.

Key Words

interference
constructive
    interference
destructive
    interference
reflection
diffraction
refraction

Interference and Reflection

Many sound and light waves may travel through a medium at the same time. When these waves meet or contact objects, interactions occur that affect the waves. Wave **interference** occurs when two or more waves meet at the same point in the medium and momentarily combine to form a single wave. The net effect of their combined displacements will alter the positions of the particles in the medium differently from the way either wave would do alone.

For example, consider two transverse waves traveling through the medium in opposite directions. The crest of one wave has an amplitude of +2 and the other of +3. If the waves meet so that their crests merge (in phase), the energy of one joins with the energy of the other. The net effect will be to displace the particles of the medium in a manner that is the sum of the two waves. The two waves will create an amplitude of +5. When the net result is a displacement in the same direction greater than each of the individual waves, it is known as **constructive interference**. Similarly, longitudinal waves can merge compressions to produce constructive interference in sound waves.

Before interference

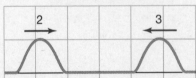

During interference

Just as two or more waves can merge constructively, they can also do so destructively. In a **destructive interference**, the joining of two out-of-phase waves cancels out all or part of the displacement of the other. This happens when the crest of one transverse waves intersects the trough of another wave. This time, the wave energies oppose one another in their effect on the particles. The result is a momentary decreased amplitude at the point of merger. If the two waves have the same amplitude, then the crest and troughs cancel each other out. In longitudinal waves, compressions and rarefactions also produce destructive interference. Interference does not end the waves. Each wave resumes propagating through the medium in its same manner after the junction.

Before interference

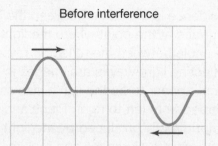

During interference

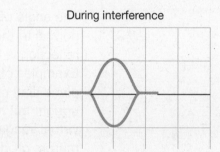

Reflection and Interference of Sound and Light Waves

As discussed in an earlier lesson in this chapter, sound waves are longitudinal waves that require a medium to propagate and are the result of a vibrating object.

There are many examples of interference in light waves caused by diffraction. When you look sideways at a shallow angle through the mesh of a window screen, bands of shadows interspersed with bands of light appear. Destructive interference of light waves, where the amplitudes of the waves are equal, eliminates the light at that point. When the amplitudes are not equal, the resulting light will be dimmer. Conversely, constructive interference results in a brighter light.

When a propagating sound or light wave encounters a new medium, three things can happen. The wave energy can pass through a transparent medium. Part or all of the wave energy can be absorbed by the medium, if it is not transparent. Finally, part or all of the wave energy can bounce off of the medium's surface and change direction as a **reflection**. For sound waves, this produces an echo. When light waves reflect, the result is glare or a mirror image. Waves will always reflect in such a way that the angle of approach (the angle of incidence) to the surface equals the angle at which they reflect off the surface. This is the basis of the law of reflection; the angle of incidence is equal to the angle of reflection. The illustration on the next page outlines the basic principals behind the law.

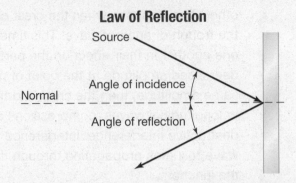

Law of Reflection

Source

Angle of incidence

Normal

Angle of reflection

The angle of incidence is the angle between the incident ray and a line normal to the surface at the point where the light strikes. The angle of reflection is the angle between the reflected ray and the normal line. Examples of reflecting light waves are images in a mirror. Images in plane (flat) mirrors appear to be the same size as the object and are upright but reversed from left to right. Plane and convex mirrors produce virtual images (not directly produced by the light waves). Concave mirrors produce both virtual images and real images.

One of the ways that we see the color of objects is due to the absorption and reflection of light waves. A banana is yellow because its surface reflects only the yellow wavelengths of light and absorbs the wavelengths of all the other colors.

Light waves, and waves in general, bend around a barrier or the edges of an opening. This bending of light waves is known as **diffraction**. The amount of bending depends on the size of the light wavelength in comparison to the size of the opening. If the opening is larger than the light's wavelength, the bending will be almost unnoticeable. If the two are closer in size or equal, the amount of bending is considerable, and easily seen with the unaided eye.

The diffraction of light waves often produces light wave interference. When a single light source is diffracted through two openings, the resultant light interference can be readily observed as areas of greater or lower light intensity. Another effect of light diffraction is to produce color. When certain wavelengths in sunlight interfere destructively, we will see the colors of the remaining wavelengths that are not affected. This can be readily observed when looking at light reflecting off thin films of bubble surfaces or oil on water.

When waves pass from one medium to another at any angle other than 90°, their direction of travel is usually bent because their speed in the new medium changes. This effect is called **refraction**. The frequency of the waves does not change. However, the wavelength does change in proportion to the change in speed. So if the speed of the waves decreases in the new medium, the wavelengths there will shorten. There will be no refraction of the waves if they enter the new medium

Test Tips . . .

Check your answers. When you have finished the test, go back and check your work.

perpendicularly. There will also be no bending of the waves if their speed does not change in the new medium.

The example of sunlight entering a glass prism to form a spectrum is a common illustration of light refraction. Suppose sunlight enters the prism at an angle other than perpendicular. The speed of light in glass is slower than in air or a vacuum. As a result, the wavelengths of light shorten and are refracted downward in the prism. Upon exiting the glass, the waves reenter the air, and the light speeds up and is refracted once again. The effect of this is to separate the different frequencies found in sunlight into the familiar colors of a spectrum. Droplets of water acting as prisms can refract light and produce the same effect in the form of a rainbow.

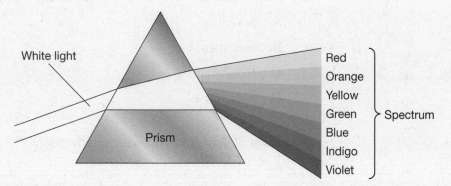

Light passing through different lens shapes will refract at various angles depending on the shape of the lens. Convex, or converging lenses, refract the light inward, concentrating it, while concave, or diverging lenses, will refract the light outwards.

DISCUSSION QUESTION

Discuss the role of refraction as it pertains to the observation of visible colors.

LESSON REVIEW

1. Which statement below MOST accurately describes wave interference in sound waves?

    A. Constructive interference makes sounds quieter.

    B. Destructive interference makes sounds louder.

    C. Destructive interference of sound waves stops the propagation of the wave.

    D. Standing waves which reinforce sound through constructive interference will make the sound louder.

Use the following illustration of the wave to answer questions 2 and 3.

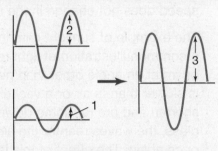

Waves are in phase

2. Which answer below accurately describes the type of interference?

   A. Standing

   B. Destructive

   C. Constructive

   D. Transverse

3. What is the net effect of the interference?

   A. +1

   B. +2

   C. +3

   D. −1

4. The diffraction of light waves can be used to create destructive or constructive interference patterns. Which statement below MOST accurately describes a characteristic of light interference?

   A. Dark areas of light interference represent constructive interference.

   B. When a color interferes destructively we will see the colors that are not interfered with destructively.

   C. Brighter areas of light interference represent destructive interference.

   D. Light cannot interfere constructively.

33 Speed of Sound and the Doppler Effect

 SPS9.e-f

Getting the Idea

Key Words

sound
echo
loudness
pitch
Doppler effect
sound quality
music
noise

You are surrounded by sounds of people talking, dogs barking, horns blowing, music playing, and machines clanking. **Sound** is a form of energy produced by vibrations of matter. Sound travels in the form of mechanical waves. They can travel from particle to particle only in a medium made of matter, either solid, liquid, or gas. The speed of sound varies as it travels through different media. Sound waves cannot exist in a vacuum because a vacuum contains no particles of matter. In this lesson, you will review some important concepts about sound.

How Sound Travels

Sound waves are longitudinal and consist of compressions and rarefactions. The speed of sound varies as it travels through different media. The condition of the medium, its temperature, pressure, density, and elastic rigidity affects the speed of sound. Sound travels faster in solids and liquids than in gases, as the table shows.

Speed of Sound

Material	Meters per Second
Carbon dioxide	259
Oxygen	316
Air	331
Water	1,482
Lead	1,960
Glass	5,640
Steel	5,960

Soft porous materials absorb sound waves. Hard rigid materials reflect some of the waves creating an echo, while transmitting the remainder of the waves. Bats use the echoes of high-pitched sounds as a sonar-like echolocation system to catch insects and avoid obstacles while flying at night. Porpoises use a similar technique in the sea.

The **loudness** of a sound depends upon the intensity or energy of the wave. This is shown by the wave's amplitude. Big amplitudes indicate loud sounds; soft sounds have small amplitudes. Loudness is measured in units called decibels. Long exposure to sounds whose loudness is over 85 decibels can cause hearing loss. Jet planes and rock concerts reach 120 decibels.

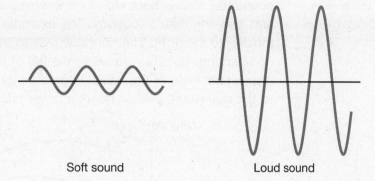

Soft sound   Loud sound

The frequency of the sound waves controls its **pitch**, how high (shrill) or low (deep) is the sound. In music, the pitch is often referred to as a note. Among singers' voices, sopranos and tenors can produce a higher frequency note such as a high C. This contrasts to the lower frequency notes of contraltos, baritones, and basses. The human ear can hear sound waves with frequencies as low as 20 hertz and as high as 20,000 hertz. Some animals can hear higher frequencies. A dog whistle can summon a pet with a sound inaudible to the pet owner.

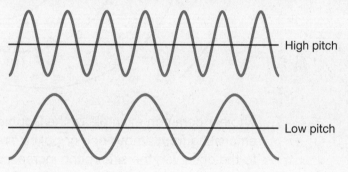

High pitch

Low pitch

The Doppler Effect

When a train approaches a grade crossing, the engineer gives a long warning blast of the horn. To the engineer, the sound has a constant pitch. However, a person waiting at the crossing hears the horn change pitch as the train comes nearer. The sound rises in pitch until the engine passes the crossing. If the horn continues to blast, the sound of the horn then drops in pitch as the engine moves farther away. This is known as **the Doppler effect**.

The Doppler effect is due to the motion of the source relative to the listener. When a stationary source produces sound waves at a constant frequency, the waves are received by a listener at that same frequency. However, when the wave source moves toward the listener, the frequency of the waves increases. This is because an approaching wave source catches up to its earlier waves. With each additional wave produced by the source, the distance between the new wave and the older wave is reduced. This creates a shorter wavelength and a higher frequency.

The opposite effect occurs when the source moves away from the listener. The listener hears a lower pitch. The new waves from the source fall farther behind the older waves increasing their wavelength and lowering their frequency. The example below shows an automobile moving to the right. The sound waves to the right of the automobile are compacting while the waves to the left of the source are expanding. The observer is front of the vehicle hears a higher pitch, while the observer to the rear of the vehicle hears a lower pitch.

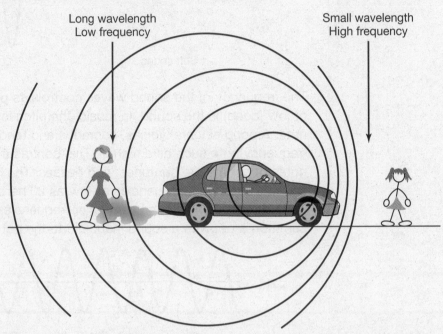

Long wavelength
Low frequency

Small wavelength
High frequency

Another common example of the Doppler effect is that of sound waves emanating from ambulance or police sirens. As the sirens speed closer to the observer, the siren pitch increases. As the siren passes and moves away from the observer, the pitch of the siren decreases. The Doppler effect also works with light waves. Astronomers observe a decrease in the frequency of light waves coming from distant stars moving away from Earth. This produces the red shift in their light since red is the lowest frequency color in the visible light spectrum. Almost all the distant stars have a red shift in their light. This is evidence that the universe is expanding.

The Sounds of Music
Music consists of a variety of sounds that are mainly pleasing to hear. Musical instruments produce sounds by creating vibrations that travel through the air. Wind instruments, such as a flute, vibrate a column of air within their body. Some woodwinds, such as a clarinet or oboe, use a reed to enhance the vibrations. Drums or xylophones are struck with a stick or other object. Stringed instruments are stroked with a bow or plucked like a guitar, as shown here.

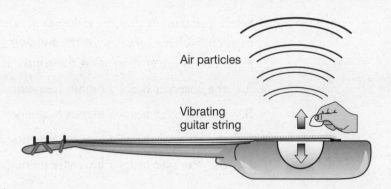

Air particles

Vibrating
guitar string

The quality of a musical sound, or timbre, is the result of overtones, a mix of vibrations producing a blend of tones that gives richness to the sound. By contrast, a pure tone often sounds boring to the listener.

Noise is the opposite of music because it consists of discordant sounds that are unpleasant to hear. The banging and clanking of heavy machinery is an example of noise. The problem of noise leads people to seek soundproofing, the stopping of sound waves from moving through a medium. Soft materials like drapes or porous tiles absorb and deaden sound. Another technique is to neutralize the sound waves by creating waves that are out of phase with the noise waves. When the rarefactions of out-of-phase waves meet the compression components of the noise, the two merge and cancel each other out leaving only the sound of silence.

Sound waves have many useful applications besides music and communication. Sonar devices are an essential tool for boats and ships to locate the sea bottom and detect underwater hazards. Seismic studies use sound waves to probe Earth's crust to determine the deep layers of rock below. This yields information about faults and earthquakes, as well as locating potential deposits of petroleum. In medicine, ultrasonic imaging allows physicians to diagnose many medical conditions using a safe noninvasive procedure.

DISCUSSION QUESTION

Discuss the situation where even the movement of the observer or the source would not create a Doppler effect.

LESSON REVIEW

1. Select a statement that MOST accurately describes the following situation: an observer hears a higher pitch than the source is producing: therefore,

   A. the source is moving toward the observer.

   B. the source is stationary.

   C. the source is moving away from the observer.

   D. the source is rotating.

2. Select a statement that most accurately describes wavelength and frequency characteristics for the following situation: an observer hears a pitch that is lower than what the source is producing, and then

   A. the observer hears a higher frequency and a longer wavelength.

   B. the observer hears a higher frequency and a shorter wavelength.

   C. the observer hears a lower frequency and a longer wavelength.

   D. the observer hears a lower frequency and a shorter wavelength.

3. Select a statement that MOST accurately describes a consequence of the following situation: when the amplitude of a sound wave increases, then

   A. its frequency decreases.

   B. its loudness increases.

   C. its pitch increases

   D. it's out of phase.

4. In which medium would a sound wave travel the fastest?

   A. air

   B. vacuum

   C. water

   D. steel

Static Electricity

 SPS10.a

Getting the Idea

Electricity is energy that can be or is transferred by electric charges, electrons, from one place to another. The build up of electric charges in an object is called **static electricity**. As you will find out in this lesson, the buildup of static electricity can cause the movement of electrons with very dramatic effects.

Key Words

static electricity
negative charge
positive charge
friction
electric force field
induction
conduction
electric discharge

Static electricity

Static electricity is usually produced by an accumulation of electrons in a given object. Electrons are particles that possess a **negative charge**. Here are two experiments that demonstrate the movement of electrons and the negative charge each electron carries.

Take a plastic rod and rub it with fur. The friction of the rod will pull electrons from the fur and move them to the rod. The rod then accumulates electrons and becomes negatively charged It possesses static electricity. This process is called charging by **friction**. The negatively charged rod can be used to pick up pieces of paper, which have a neutral charge. This ability will be explained below when induced charges are introduced.

Charging by friction can also be demonstrated by rubbing a glass rod with a piece of silk. The silk pulls some electrons from the rod, leaving the rod positively charged because it now has more positively charged protons on its surface than negatively charged electrons. Remember, protons are particles that have a **positive charge**. The protons in the rod are the source of the positive charge.

Objects with opposite or like charges act in predictable ways. If two negatively charged plastic rods are brought close together, they repel one another. The same thing happens using two positively charged glass rods. The repulsion of like charges is one of the fundamental characteristics of electrical charge.

Another fundamental characteristic can be observed by holding a negatively charged plastic rod near a positively charged glass rod. The two rods will pull each other closer. In contrast to like charges repelling each other, opposite charges attract. Static electric charges produce **electric fields** of force in the space around them similar to the force fields around magnets. An **electric force field** is the space where attractive and repulsive forces of charged particles are felt.

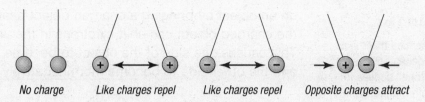

No charge *Like charges repel* *Like charges repel* *Opposite charges attract*

Like charges repel, and opposite charges attract.

One more important rule for charges is that charges are conserved just as energy is conserved. For example, when the plastic rod was rubbed with fur, it became negatively charged. This effect occurs because charge is transferred to the rod from the fur. The amount of negative charge on the rod is then equal to the amount of positive charge on the fur. This balancing effect is called the conservation of charge.

Conductors and Insulators

An electrical **conductor** is a material through which electric charges can easily flow. Metals such as copper, silver, and gold are good conductors. This is why the wires in electrical cords are usually made of copper. Silver and gold are too expensive to use as wires for common purposes.

An **insulator** is a material through which electric charges do not move easily or sometimes not at all. Plastic, rubber, and wood are good examples of insulators. That is why the wires in electrical cords are covered with rubber or plastic. The covering keeps electric charges from shocking people who handle the wires. Such shocks can cause serious injury or death. Insulation also keeps electricity from jumping from one wire to another if they should touch. Such an event is called a short circuit, which can damage appliances or cause fires.

Our bodies are conductors. That is why it is so dangerous to touch bare "live" wires carrying electrical current. The charges from the wires will move through our bodies to the ground, damaging the body along the way. Those who do not die from touching live wires are sure to experience pain.

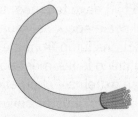

Copper wires wrapped in insulation

Induction and Conduction

Another way to transfer a charge to an object is by induction. As contrasted with charging by friction, **induction** is the buildup of an electric charge without direct contact. A static charge can be induced

Test Tips . . .

The idea that "likes repel and opposites attract" applies to both magnets and static charges. When you are studying for a test, look for ways to connect different ideas. This type of connection is known as synthesis.

on an object by bringing a charged object near to it. The electric field of the charged object can shift electrons in the uncharged object's atoms. This causes one side of the object to become more positively charged and the other side to become more negatively charged.

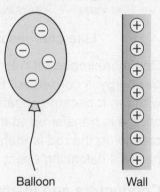

Balloon   Wall

Induction between a charged balloon and the surface of a wall

Consider a balloon. Like the plastic rod, the rubber balloon will pick up negative charges if rubbed on fur. If the charged balloon is then put against a wall, it will stick. The wood and plaster that make up walls are insulators. The balloon sticks because the charged balloon induces an opposite charge on the wall. The surface of the wall near the balloon becomes positively charged Since opposite charges attract, the balloon sticks to the wall. A similar phenomenon occurs when the negatively charged plastic rod picks up pieces of paper.

Discharge of Static Electricity

An electric charge that builds up in one object can leap to another object whose charge is opposite. You have probably experienced this phenomenon when you have touched a metal object after walking across a carpeted floor. The rubbing of your shoes on the carpet built up a static electrical charge in your body. When you touched something like a doorknob, the charge jumped between your fingers and the doorknob. You can feel this as a sharp and sudden tingle. When a charged object shifts some of its electrons to another object because the two have touched, the shift is called **conduction**. Sometimes you will see a spark as visual evidence of the **electric discharge** when electrons jump from the charged object to the uncharged object. Lightning is the most powerful discharge of static electricity. Lightning is an extremely energetic spark that streaks between two oppositely charged clouds or between a cloud and the ground, whose charges are opposite.

DISCUSSION QUESTION

Give one example of how to put a static electrical charge on an object by friction or induction.

LESSON REVIEW

1. A balloon is rubbed all over with wool. The balloon will now attract the wool because

    A. the balloon and the wool are magnets.

    B. the balloon and the wool have opposite charges.

    C. the balloon and the wool have like charges.

    D. the balloon and the wool are neutral.

2. If you hold a negatively charged plastic rod up to a ball hanging on a thread, and the ball moves away from the rod, the ball

    A. has no charge.

    B. has no matter.

    C. is positively charged.

    D. is negatively charged.

3. The rule for conservation of charge suggests that

    A. an isolated conducting sphere will hold a net charge indefinitely.

    B. if you touch a charged sphere to two neutral ones, the neutral ones will each end up with half the original charge.

    C. a piece of silk will be more positively charged after being rubbed with a glass rod.

    D. a negative charge can be produced only if an equal positive charge is also produced.

4. If a negative charge that is free to move is placed exactly between two positive charges, it will

    A. move to the left.

    B. move to the right.

    C. move up or down.

    D. not move.

35 Electric Current

SPS10.b

Getting the Idea

All electronic devices use circuits. Simple circuits are closed loops made up of elements that provide a path for electric current to flow. Conductors allow charge to flow readily, whereas insulators prevent or inhibit the flow of such charges.

Key Words

semiconductor
voltage
current
resistivity
Ohm's law
resistance
series circuit
parallel circuit

Conductivity

Materials have a broad range of conductivity. Below is a table showing some materials in order of decreasing conductivity. Electronic devices operate by combining materials of different conductivity into circuits.

Materials from Highest Conductivity to Lowest

Silver
Copper
Aluminum
Iron
Silicon
Water
Glass
Styrofoam

You can see from this table why copper is used for electrical wiring. Silver would also work well for wiring, but would be too expensive. Any material found under copper in the list would not conduct as well as copper. Silicon is a semiconductor. A **semiconductor** is a material with conductivity between a conductor and an insulator. This property makes semiconductors important for building circuits, especially those used in computer chips.

Since water is such a bad conductor of electricity, you might wonder why there are warnings not to swim during a lightning storm. The reason is that the water in pools, rivers, and oceans is not pure. It contains charged particles that conduct electricity quite well. The type of water referred to in the chart above is pure water, without any added salts or other chemicals.

Ohm's Law

In circuits, **voltage** is a measure of the force that moves charges through conducting elements. The movement of these charges is called **current**. The movement of charges, or current, is measured in amperes, and the force that moves them, voltage, is measured in volts. Current can be slower or faster depending on the conductivity of the material it is moving through.

The opposite of conductivity is called resistivity. **Resistivity** is the resistance of a material to current. This resistivity is measured in Ohms, and the symbol for Ohms is the Greek letter omega, or Ω. **Ohm's law** states that in ideal conductors, voltage is proportional to current, and that this relationship can be expressed by a constant called **resistance**. We show this relationship in mathematical form by

$$V = IR$$

where V is the voltage, I is the current, and R is the resistance.

So if voltage increases, and resistance is constant, then current must also increase. In the same way, if voltage decreases and resistance is constant, current must decrease.

Ohm's law is used to make many calculations for electrical devices, as will be shown.

Resistors

All electronic devices have one or more resistors. Take, for example, a toaster. Its resistor is its heating element, which glows orange as it heats up to toast bread In a toaster, the heating element is a piece of wire made of a material with greater resistance than copper. Recalling Ohm's law, it can be seen that if the resistance is increased while the voltage remains the same, then the current will be reduced. So as current goes through the heating element, it slows down, which causes the element to heat up.

This process is a transformation of electrical energy into thermal energy, which in the case of a toaster is useful. If the voltage source and current are known, then Ohm's law can be used to calculate the resistance of the heating element by solving for R.

For example, if a toaster has a voltage of 60 volts and a current of 2.3 amps, what is the resistance of the heating element? Ohm's law is used as follows:

$$60 \text{ V} = 2.3 \text{ } A \times R$$

$$\text{or } R = 26 \text{ } \Omega$$

Light bulbs are also resistors. They work in a similar way to toasters. In a clear light bulb, one can see a filament suspended between two conducting wires.

Did You Know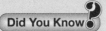

Georg Simon Ohm was born in 1787 in Germany. His parents were uneducated His father did not go to school but educated himself and his two sons. Ohm went on to earn his Ph.D., write textbooks, and teach mathematics.

A filament is suspended between two conducting wires.

This filament is made of a different material than the conducting wires, and the filament is also narrower than the wires. For these reasons, the current is slowed down just like it is in the heating element of a toaster. The filament in a light bulb gets very hot—so hot, that it gives off white light. If one were to heat up the toaster's heating element to very high temperatures, it would glow white also.

If we have a light bulb filament with a resistance of 2.1 ohms, and a current of 36 amps is passed through the filament, what is the voltage applied to the bulb? We again use Ohm's Law. This time we solve for the voltage.

$$V = 36 \, A \times 2.1 \, \Omega$$

$$\text{or } V = 76 \, V$$

Ohm's law is used by electrical engineers in designing circuits.

Series and Parallel Circuits

The two basic electrical circuit types are series and parallel. Simple series circuits are closed conducting loops that have at least one voltage source and one resistor. The components of a series circuit are wired in one path that the charges must follow. This creates a problem. If any component in a series circuit fails, all the other components shut down because the current is cut off from them. In a parallel circuit, the resistors are wired in different paths that the charges can follow. If one component fails, the other components still work because the alternate paths bring them power. Buildings are always wired in parallel circuits.

Circuits run on electrical energy from a voltage source. The usual sources are batteries or an electric socket connected to a power plant. Resistors use up energy provided by a voltage source. Electrical devices are turned on and off to stop or start the flow of current by a switch.

The best way to analyze simple circuits is to diagram them. The simplest circuit diagram includes a power source and a resistor. Adding a switch makes a circuit easier to use. Here is how a simple circuit with a switch is diagramed:

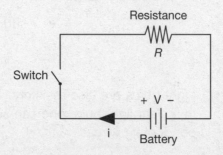

A **series circuit** is one in which more than one circuit element is included in the circuit loop. A circuit diagram for three resistors in series would look like this:

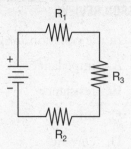

Any number of resistors can be added to a circuit loop, but the total resistance will increase for each resistor added. The total voltage will have to increase as total resistance increases. To calculate the resistance, voltage, or current of a series circuit, follow the steps outlined below. The total resistance (R_{total}) for a series circuit is the sum of the resistances in ohms. This is equal to $R_1 + R_2$ where R_1 is the first resistor and R_2 is the second resistor. The equation looks like this:

$$R_{total} = R_1 + R_2$$

The total voltage difference in the series circuit must equal the sum of the individual voltages needed to push the charges through each resistor. However, the current (I) is the same throughout a series circuit. This can be described using Ohm's law in the following equations. To calculate voltage (V_1) across the first resistor, (R_1) use this equation: $V_1 = I \times R_1$. To calculate voltage across the second resistor, use a similar equation: $V_2 = I \times R_2$. To calculate the total voltage across the circuit using the total resistance,

$$V_{total} = I \times R_{total}$$

A **parallel circuit** is one in which a simple circuit is split into more than one loop with circuit elements on each path. A parallel circuit diagram with three resistors in parallel would look like this:

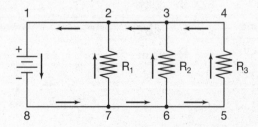

Resistors in parallel do not add plainly, as in a series. This property is due to the fact that the current is split into two different paths. The formula used to calculate the total resistance across a parallel circuit is as follows:

$$1/R_{total} = 1/R_1 + 1/R_2$$

DISCUSSION QUESTION

What resistors might be found in circuits around the house?

LESSON REVIEW

1. In the equation for Ohm's law, I is

    A. impedance.

    B. resistance.

    C. impulse.

    D. current.

2. If a simple circuit has one resistor of 3 ohms and a current of 3 amps, how many volts is the power source?

    A. 3 volts

    B. 6 volts

    C. 9 volts

    D. 19 volts

3. Of the following materials, which would be the BEST choice for insulating copper wire?

    A. aluminum foil

    B. iron

    C. glass

    D. silicon

4. If you have an electrical circuit made of copper, which material below would make a good heating element?

    A. pure water

    B. glass

    C. silver

    D. iron

36 # AC versus DC Current

 SPS10.b

Getting the Idea

Two of the most common voltage sources are batteries and generators. Batteries transform chemical energy into electrical energy. Generators transform mechanical energy into electrical energy. The electrical currents created by these two sources are different and used for different purposes. Direct current (DC) electricity produced from batteries flows continuously through a circuit in one direction only. Alternating current (AC) electricity produced from generators constantly alternates its direction of movement back and forth in a circuit.

Direct Current

The voltage output of a battery is constant over time. Because of this, a battery creates a constant current of electrons that flow in only one direction along a circuit. This type of current is called **direct current**. All of the circuits discussed in previous lessons have used direct current. This kind of current is abbreviated DC.

Here is the circuit diagram for a simple circuit with direct current. The arrows show the direction of current.

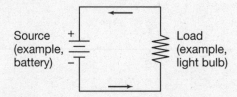

Source (example, battery) Load (example, light bulb)

How a Battery Works

Batteries are common sources of direct current. Batteries are of two types: dry cells and wet cells. Each is a container for electrochemical reactions. The reactions transfer some electrons from atoms that are more stable without them to other atoms that are more stable with them. The battery is designed so that the first group of atoms is near the negative terminal and the second group is near the positive terminal. A wall in the battery separates the groups and blocks any direct transfer of electrons inside the battery. This keeps the battery fresh. Wet cells used in automobiles contain acids that react with metal plates to produce ion flow in two directions. Positive ions flow to the negative electrode, negative ions flow to the positive electrode. Dry cells contain similar materials in paste form. Electrons carried by the negative ions flow into the electrode and out the wire.

Key Words
direct current
alternating current

When a wire is connected to both terminals, the electrons from the first group of atoms can flow out of the battery to reach the other group that needs them. The movement of charged particles is called current. As long as there are atoms with some electrons to lose left inside the battery, current will flow through the connecting wire.

If there is only a wire without resistors connecting the terminals, the battery is being short circuited The current will flow quickly, heating up the wire and draining the battery wastefully. Normally there is some resistor in the form of a light bulb or a motor connected to the battery.

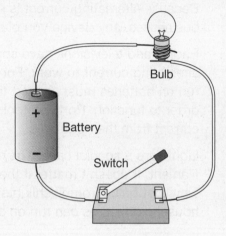

These devices are called resistors. They use the energy from the current to operate. In this way, the energy in the battery is used more slowly, and the battery is drained over a longer period of time.

Alternating Current

The current produced by a generator is called **alternating current** because its voltage difference and its current constantly change directions over regular intervals of time. You can think of the electrons in the circuit as sloshing back and forth in the conductor. Their motion is like a rapid vibration instead of a flow. However, this vibration transfers energy and power very well. Alternating current is often abbreviated as AC.

The circuit diagram for a simple circuit with alternating current is shown below.

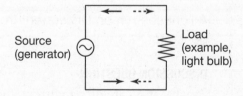

The current amperage increases and decreases. It starts at zero and quickly reaches its maximum value. Then it quickly drops back to zero again. It then repeats this process in the opposite direction of the current loop. A graph of this process over time is a sine wave.

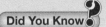

A complete cycle is finished when it has gone up to the maximum and dropped back down again in both directions. The number of complete cycles the current makes in a second is called frequency.

The current that the power company sends to your home, school, and businesses in your community is alternating current. It has a frequency of 60 hertz. This means it goes through 60 complete cycles per second.

Hertz is the unit of measurement for frequency. It is named after Heinrich Hertz, the scientist who discovered radio waves.

Because alternating current is supplied to homes, schools, and businesses, any device you plug into the wall uses alternating current.

Radios and televisions have special circuit elements that require alternating current to work. For this reason, any radio or television that is run on batteries must convert the direct current to alternating current in order to function. Portable tools have DC motors that run on the direct current from their batteries.

Lights are a special case. They only need current to flow through the filament. It doesn't matter if the current is direct or alternating. That is why light bulbs from flashlights can run on batteries, and light bulbs in household fixtures can run on alternating current.

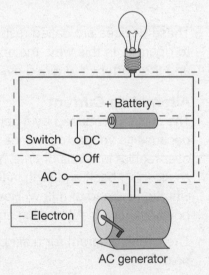

A light can run on DC current from a battery or AC current from a generator.

DISCUSSION QUESTION

In what ways are direct current and alternating current different?

LESSON REVIEW

1. How does the voltage provided by a battery vary over time?

    A. It increases gradually over time.

    B. It decreases gradually over time.

    C. It increases and decreases periodically over time.

    D. It does not vary over time.

2. A circuit has alternating current where the current goes in direction A along the circuit for 0.01 seconds before it reverses and goes in direction B along the circuit. If the current begins in direction A when it is switched on, which direction will it be going in 0.035 seconds?

    A. A

    B. B

    C. neither A nor B

    D. both A and B

3. For the example above, which direction will the current be going after exactly 0.04 seconds?

    A. A

    B. B

    C. neither A nor B

    D. both A and B

4. Which of the following devices MOST likely uses direct current?

    A. cordless electric drill

    B. dishwasher

    C. blender

    D. 60-inch television set

37 Magnetism, Motors, and Generators

 SPS10.c

Getting the Idea

Magnetism is a force that can be used to produce electricity. In turn, electricity can be used to produce magnetism. The discoveries of these relationships in the early 19th Century by English physicist Michael Faraday and Danish physicist Hans Christian Oersted led to the development of two machines that changed the lives of Earth's peoples. Those machines are the electric generator, which produces electricity in power plants, and the electric motor, which drives a multitude of appliances and other devices that make human lives easier.

Electromagnetism

The relationship between electricity and magnetism is called **electromagnetism**. The relationship is based on the following facts: an electric current is surrounded by a magnetic field, and a **magnetic field** is an area of space in which magnetic forces of attraction and repulsion are observed. **Magnetism** is the general term for the magnetic forces of attraction and repulsion. These are produced by electrons as they spin on their axes like toy tops. Lodestones, composed of a magnetic form of iron oxide, are natural permanent magnets known in ancient times. When an electric current is run through a wire loop, an **electromagnet** is produced that can be turned on or off. Electromagnets can move charged particles that are near them, which is why motors and generators work.

Magnetic Domains

An iron bar can be made into a magnet because small groups of its atoms form into **magnetic domains**. Within a magnetic domain, the atoms have their magnetic poles aligned in the same direction so the domain becomes a miniature magnet. However, the many domains are aligned in different directions. This neutralizes the magnetic forces. Rubbing the iron with a magnet or passing it through an electromagnetic field makes most of the unaligned domains line up. When this happens, the iron bar becomes a magnet. If the magnetism remains in the bar, it becomes a permanent magnet. Some metal alloys make very strong **permanent magnets**. Alnico, an alloy of aluminum, nickel, and cobalt, is an example.

Magnets are used in many different ways. You might have them on your refrigerator holding up notes and oven mitts, but they are mostly used in stereo speakers, electronic equipment, electric motors, and generators.

Electromagnets

An electromagnet is made by winding a coil of wire around an iron rod. When an electric current is passed through the coil, the iron rod becomes magnetized and produces a magnetic field. This turns the rod into a powerful, if temporary, electromagnet. The strength of the magnet is directly proportional to the number of turns of wire in the coil and the strength of the current. The two ends of the electromagnet are different. One end is called the north pole, and the other end is called the south pole. Every magnet has a north pole and a south pole.

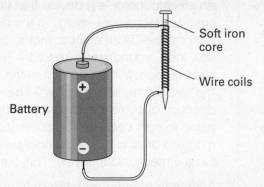

Magnetic poles behave like electric charges. Like poles repel each other; opposite poles attract each other. So if you place two north poles together, they push each other away. If you move the south pole of one magnet near the north pole of another magnet, they attract each other and stick together.

Magnets attract iron that isn't magnetic by inducing the domains in the iron to align themselves temporarily. This produces a second magnet with its temporary poles opposite to those of the permanent magnet. This is how magnets stick to the refrigerator.

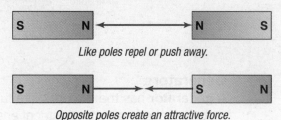

Like poles repel or push away.

Opposite poles create an attractive force.

How a Compass Works

First of all, our planet, Earth, is surrounded by a magnetic field probably caused by the rotation of its molten iron-nickel core. Earth acts as if a giant bar magnet ran between its magnetic north and south poles. Earth's magnetic poles are close to its geographic poles, the points around which Earth rotates.

To better understand how a compass works, picture a bar magnet suspended from a wire. It will twist so that the north-seeking pole of the magnet points in the direction of the Earth's magnetic north pole. The north-seeking pole of the magnet is called the magnet's north pole. However, the rule that only opposite poles attract tells us that one of these two north poles must be a south pole. The north pole of the magnet is really the opposite of Earth's magnetic north pole.

A compass contains a narrow needle-shaped magnet suspended on a pivot that is free to rotate. The north-seeking pole of the magnet is painted red It points to Earth's magnetic north pole. In this way, we can use a compass to tell us which way is north.

Motors

An electric motor is a device that converts electrical energy into mechanical energy. Mechanical energy is the energy of motion. The parts of an electric motor move. In an electric motor, an electric current flows through a wire loop around a soft iron core. The current turns the iron core into an electromagnet. If the current in the wire coil is an alternating current, then the electromagnet's poles will change back and forth with the alternating direction of current. If magnets surround the wire coil, the wire coil will begin to spin because it is alternately being repelled and attracted by the magnets around it. The spinning wire coil is connected to an armature that turns a mechanical device. This combination of parts is called a **motor**.

A kitchen blender, electric drill, or electric train are an examples of how an electrical motor can be used. The mechanical armature of the motor turns the blades that chop, mix, or puree the food, turn the drill bit, or turn the wheels of the train.

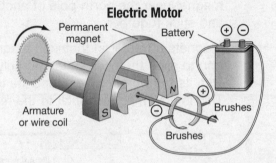

Electric Motor

Generators

A **generator** has the the opposite function of a motor. It transforms mechanical energy into electrical energy. Instead of running a current through the wire coil to move the armature, mechanical energy is used to turn the armature. This energy might come from falling water in a dam, pressurized steam from a boiler, or the spinning blades of a windmill.

Turning the armature spins the wire coil so that it cuts through the lines of force of the magnetic field coming from surrounding magnets. The magnetic field induces the electrons in the wire to move, which produces an electric current in the coil. This is known as **electromagnetic induction**. The electrons will move in one direction and then reverse and go in the other direction. This creates an alternating electrical current.

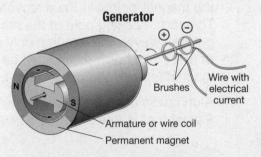

Generator

The alternating electrical current can then be sent through power lines from power plants to communities, homes, schools, businesses, and factories to run electrical devices such as blenders, radios, televisions, computers, street lights, and factory machines.

DISCUSSION QUESTION

What are some sources of mechanical energy that might be used to run a generator?

LESSON REVIEW

1. An electric motor

   A. is used to make your television screen work.

   B. does not require a voltage source.

   C. is needed to turn the blades of an electric fan.

   D. takes mechanical energy and transforms it into electrical energy.

2. Which of the following does not normally have magnetic properties?

   A. piece of iron   C. iron atom

   B. wire loop with current D. plastic loop

3. Magnetism comes from

   A. static charged particles.   C. generators.

   B. neutrons.   D. electron motion.

4. If you bring the north pole of a magnet near the south pole of another magnet, what will happen?

   A. They will attract each other.

   B. They will repel each other.

   C. They will do nothing.

   D. They will release a spark between them.

5. Which of the following devices does not commonly use a magnet?

   A. stereo speaker

   B. kitchen blender

   C. light fixture

   D. computer

EOCT Review

1. Which of the following involves the conversion of chemical energy directly into light energy?

   A. incandescent bulb
   B. burning candle
   C. fluorescent bulb
   D. halogen bulb

2. Thelma is preparing a large metal pot of vegetable soup for supper. The pot has two metal handles. Thelma is about to lift the pot with both of her hands when she remembers to use pot holders to protect her hands. What is she protecting herself from?

   A. heat transfer by radiation
   B. heat transfer by convection
   C. heat transfer by conduction
   D. heat transfer by evaporation

Answer question 3 by using the graph pictured below. The graph was prepared from data collected by the students in Ms. Lincoln's physical science class. Different groups of students carefully heated an unknown substance X and recorded its temperature as it went through several changes. They averaged their results to reduce the degree of error and then plotted them on the graph.

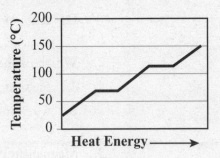

3. What is the phase of substance X when its temperature is 100 °C?

   A. gas
   B. liquid
   C. solid
   D. it is changing from a gas to a liquid

4. What is the specific heat of a substance if it takes 200 kilojoules of heat energy to raise the temperature of 20 kilograms of it from 23°C to 25°C?

   A. 5 kJ/kg·°C
   B. 20 kJ/kg·°C
   C. 100 kJ/kg·°C
   D. 200 kJ/kg·°C

5. **Which one of the following is NOT an example of an electromagnetic wave?**

   A. sound waves
   B. radio waves
   C. ultraviolet waves
   D. gamma rays

Use the diagram of the wave shown below to answer question 6 and 7.

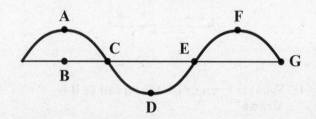

6. **Which letter indicates the trough of the wave?**

   A. A
   B. B
   C. C
   D. D

7. **Which sequence of letters in the diagram of the wave indicates the amplitude of the wave?**

   A. AB
   B. BC
   C. CE
   D. AC

8. **How does polarized light differ from ordinary light waves?**

   A. Polarized light cannot travel through a vacuum.
   B. Polarized light only vibrates in one direction minimizing glare.
   C. Polarized light travels in the form of longitudinal waves.
   D. Polarized light travels in the form of mechanical waves.

9. **A bass drum is struck and sends out 100 vibrations in 5 seconds. What is the frequency of its sound waves in hertz?**

   A. 20 hertz
   B. 100 hertz
   C. 105 hertz
   D. 500 hertz

10. **What interaction will occur when two out of phase sound waves or two out of phase light waves meet and merge into a single sound or light wave?**

    A. refraction
    B. reflection
    C. constructive interference
    D. destructive interference

Interpret the data in the following table as they relate to the speed of sound in different media. Rely only on the data in the table. Do not use any other data that you have learned.

Speed of Sound in Different Media

Medium	Speed of Sound (meters/second)
Air (20°C)	343
Water (20°C)	1,482
Glass	5,640

11. **Based on the Table, sound waves travel fastest in media that are**

    A. liquid
    B. solid.
    C. gas.
    D. warm.

12. Tonya would hear a change in pitch of the sound of an ambulance siren if she were

A. riding in the ambulance.
B. listening to the ambulance before it started to move.
C. listening to the ambulance approaching.
D. riding in another car driving side by side with the ambulance.

13. The friction involved in rubbing a glass or plastic rod with silk, wool, or fur produces a static electric charge by transferring

A. electrons.
B. protons.
C. atoms.
D. molecules.

14. Ohm's law is represented by which one of the following equations?

A. $I = VR$
B. $R = IV$
C. $R = IV^2$
D. $V = IR$

Use the circuit diagram pictured below to answer question 15.

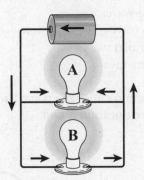

15. What is wrong with the circuit as it is drawn?

A. Direct current electrons cannot flow in opposite directions.
B. The circuit is open, so it is impossible for any current to flow.
C. Bulb B should not be lit.
D. The circuit is using alternating current from the battery.

16. What is the current supplied by a 1.5 volt battery to a flashlight bulb which has a resistance of 3 ohms in a simple series circuit?

A. 4.5 amperes
B. 2 amperes
C. 1.5 amperes
D. 0.5 amperes

17. An electromagnet becomes stronger when

A. its iron core is made thicker.
B. the number of coils of wire around its iron core are increased.
C. a higher resistance wire material is used.
D. a heavier iron core is used.

Georgia GPS Edition Coach, Standards-Based Instruction, Physical Science

POSTTEST

Name: _____

Directions:

This test is similar to the Georgia End-of-Course Test, Physical Science. Read each question carefully and then choose the best answer.

Be sure that the question number on the answer sheet matches the number on the test. Then mark your answer by filling in the circle on your answer sheet. If you do not know the answer to a question, skip it and go on. You may return to it later if time permits.

If you need to change an answer on your answer sheet, erase your first mark completely. Do not make any stray marks on the answer sheet.

If you finish the section of the test early, you may review your answers in that section only. You may not go on to the next section or return to a previous section.

PHYSICAL SCIENCE

POSTTEST

SECTION 1

1. Robert is doing an experiment that calls for the addition of 1 liter of water to a larger vessel. Robert has four different containers to choose from. Which one of the following four containers would be the most accurate and also the most practical way of doing this?

   A. a 2-liter container with a 2-liter mark on it
   B. an empty 1-liter soda bottle without volume marks on it
   C. a 500-ml container with a 500 ml mark
   D. a 5-ml graduated cylinder with 1 ml marks on it

2. Dr. Yuri Eker is studying a severe form of cancer. He injects a laboratory animal that has the cancer with a new drug. Seven days later, the animal is free of the cancer. Which of the following steps should Dr. Eker follow next?

   A. repeat the experiment many times over a few months
   B. call a press conference reporting the amazing results
   C. write a report for a prestigious science journal
   D. prepare an acceptance speech for the expected award of the Nobel prize

3. Tina tests the slope of a 1-meter long hill on the speed of a toy car. She measures the elapsed times at angles of 5° and 10°. Which one is the dependent variable?

   A. 1-meter long hill
   B. 5° slope
   C. 10° slope
   D. elapsed times

4. In the above experiment, the toy car's times were 4 sec and 2.5 sec. Which of the following choices is NOT supported by evidence?

   A. rolling friction is less than sliding friction
   B. steeper slopes increased potential energy
   C. steeper slopes increase average speed
   D. the slope length is constant

5. Which one of the following is an SI unit of weight?

   A. kilogram
   B. joule
   C. newton
   D. milliliter

Go On

PHYSICAL SCIENCE

6. Which one of the following is equal to 125 milliliters?

   A. 1.25 centiliters
   B. 0.125 liters
   C. 12.5 liters
   D. 0.013 liters

   Answer question 7 by using the diagram below.

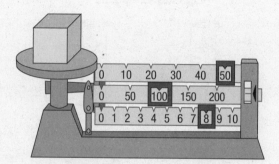

7. Which one of the following choices BEST describes the data being determined in the diagram above?

   A. the box weighs 158 kg
   B. the box's mass is 158 N
   C. the box's mass is 158 g
   D. the box weighs 158 g

8. A beaker of water's volume is 87.6 ml. Four students made three measurements each. Which set of data is precise but NOT accurate?

   A. 85.2 ml, 89.8 ml, 86.1 ml
   B. 87.7 ml. 87.6 ml, 87.5 ml
   C. 87.0 ml, 88.1 ml, 88.1 ml
   D. 85.5 ml, 85.6 ml, 85.5 ml

9. Which one of the following methods of presenting information is the clearest for showing how parts relate to the whole?

   A. line graph
   B. bar graph
   C. circle graph
   D. scatter plot

10. Which one of the following choices is a poor scientific question?

   A. Does cheesecake taste better than seven layer cake?
   B. Does saltwater stunt the growth of alfalfa?
   C. What has been the average December daytime temperature of Atlanta since 1990?
   D. How many calories are there in a 200 g barbecue sandwich?

Go On

PHYSICAL SCIENCE

11. A radio talk show host says that global warming is definitely not due to human activity because global warming has occurred many times in the past before humans existed on Earth. How would you research this claim?

   A. consult a dictionary
   B. read newspapers and magazines
   C. look up global warming in the encyclopedia
   D. look up science sites on the Internet for expert opinions

12. When heating a test tube of water over a burner, what piece of safety equipment would be the MOST important?

   A. goggles
   B. apron
   C. safety shoes
   D. latex gloves

The piece of metal on the balance was also placed in the graduated cylinder. The cylinder is shown in a before and after view. Answer questions 13 and 14 by referring to the diagram below.

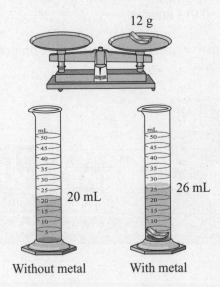

Without metal   With metal

13. What is the volume of the piece of metal in the graduated cylinder?

   A. 26 ml
   B. 20 ml
   C. 12 ml
   D. 6 ml

14. What is the density of the piece of metal?

   A. 2 g/ml
   B. 6 g/ml
   C. 12 g/ml
   D. 14 g/ml

Go On

15. An unknown gas is colorless, odorless, and tasteless. The gas turns moist iron filings reddish-brown. It condenses to a liquid at −183°C. Which fact is a chemical property of the gas?

   A. It condenses at −183°C
   B It turns iron reddish-brown.
   C. It is odorless.
   D. It is colorless.

16. Which state of matter does NOT have a definite shape or a definite volume?

   A. solid
   B. liquid
   C. gas
   D. ice cubes

17. Which one of the following choices is an example of a physical change?

   A. Solid ice cubes change into liquid water when they melt at 0°C.
   B. An egg in the hot pan on the gas burner changes from liquid to solid after it cooks.
   C. A piece of paper burns when it is thrown into a fire.
   D. A green plant transforms carbon dioxide and water into glucose during photosynthesis.

18. Marshall stirs 4 grams of salt and 10 grams of sand together in a paper cup. He then stirs 5 grams of salt and 4 grams of sand in another cup. He asks Maxine what she observes in the cups. She reports seeing grains of salt and grains of sand. What has Marshall made?

   A. two homogeneous mixtures
   B. two heterogeneous mixtures
   C. two different substances
   D. two different compounds

19. Margaret adds 25 grams of salt to a one-liter glass beaker filled up to its volume mark with pure water. She stirs the water until the salt crystals disappear. She shows the beaker to Marcus and tells him what she did. Then she challenges him to make a correct statement about the beaker's contents. Which one of the four choices below is NOT correct?

   A. It is a homogeneous mixture.
   B. It is a solution.
   C. Water is the solvent and salt is the solute.
   D. Its molecular formula is $NaClH_2O$.

20. The smallest particles of an element that has all the properties of the element is a(n)

   A. atom
   B. compound
   C. molecule
   D. gram

Go On

PHYSICAL SCIENCE

21. A liter of water has a mass of 1,000 grams. How much does a liter of water weigh?

    A. 1 kg
    B. 9.8 N
    C. 1,000 g
    D. 9800 N

22. The chemical formula for the sucrose molecule is $C_{12}H_{22}O_{11}$. How many atoms of hydrogen are in the sucrose molecule?

    A. 1
    B. 12
    C. 22
    D. 11

23. The densities of three immiscible liquid substances are as follows:

    substance X: 1.00 g/ml

    substance Y: 0.78 g/ml

    substance Z: 1.45 g/ml

    The three liquids are poured slowly into a tall graduated cylinder and allowed to separate into three distinct layers. Which one of the following arrangements starting from the top layer on down shows the correct order of the substances?

    A. XYZ
    B. ZYX
    C. XZY
    D. YXZ

24. Infer the property of water that is shown by the diagram below.

    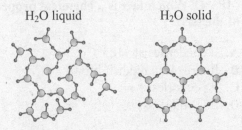
    H₂O liquid   H₂O solid

    A. Ice is less dense than liquid water.
    B. Ice and liquid water are composed of different molecules.
    C. Ice is denser than liquid water.
    D. Liquid water contracts when it freezes.

25. Which one of the following is NOT a chemical change?

    A. boiling
    B. combustion
    C. electrolysis
    D. metabolism

Go On

26. A radioactive substance has a half-life of 40 years. What fraction of the sample will remain at the end of 160 years?

   A. 1/2
   B. 1/4
   C. 1/8
   D. 1/16

27. Which subatomic particle is correctly paired with its properties?

   A. electron: negatively charged, mass about equal to a neutron
   B. proton: positively charged, mass about equal to that of an electron
   C. neutron: mass about equal to that of a proton, no electric charge
   D. positron: negatively charged, mass about equal to that of a proton

28. Where on the periodic table are the MOST reactive nonmetals found?

   A. the upper left
   B. the lower left
   C. the upper right
   D. the lower right

29. Water is a polar molecule while carbon dioxide is nonpolar. How do the molecular arrangements in the diagram below show this difference?

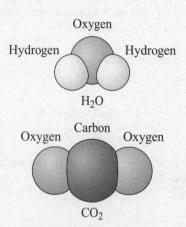

   A. The water molecule contains only three atoms in its structure.
   B. Water molecules are unsymetrically arranged making the H_2 end more positive and the O end more negative.
   C. Carbon dioxide has only one carbon atom in its molecule.
   D. Water has only one oxygen atom in its molecule.

Go On

PHYSICAL SCIENCE

Refer to the periodic table of elements to answer questions 30 through 34.

30. In the periodic table, which group or family of elements has only one valence electron in its outer shell?

   A. the alkali metals
   B. the noble gases
   C. the halogens
   D. the alkaline earth elements

31. How many neutrons are in the sodium nucleus?

   A. 12
   B. 11
   C. 23
   D. none

32. The dream of the ancient alchemists was to transform lead into gold. Today, it is theoretically possible to make the dream come true. Which one of the following choices would allow lead to be transformed in to gold?

   A. chemical reaction
   B. physical change
   C. combustion
   D. nuclear fission

33. Below are some nuclei containing different numbers of protons and neutrons. Which one is an isotope of potassium?

   A. 20 protons 20 neutrons
   B. 17 protons 22 neutrons
   C. 18 protons 21 neutrons
   D. 19 protons 19 neutrons

34. Which one of the following ions would be negatively charged with a charge of 2-?

   A. 18 electrons, 16 neutrons
   B. 10 electrons, 8 protons
   C. 0 electrons, 2 protons
   D. 6 electrons, 8 protons

Go On

35. Radioactive isotopes find practical use in all of the following applications except

A. biomedical tracers.
B. smoke detectors.
C. household cleaning agents.
D. cancer treatment.

36. Which two elements have similar chemical properties according to the periodic table?

A. helium and argon
B. oxygen and nitrogen
C. lithium and calcium
D. boron and aluminum

37. Based on the diagram below, what is the atomic mass of this atom?

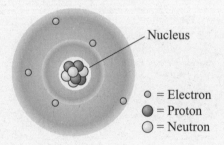

Nucleus

○ = Electron
● = Proton
○ = Neutron

A. 4
B. 8
C. 5
D. 13

38. How would an atom of chlorine MOST likely obtain a full outer shell of electrons?

A. lose 7 electrons
B. gain 7 electrons
C. lose 1 electron
D. gain 1 electron

39. Balance the chemical equation shown below by determining the missing coefficients where indicated by the blank write-on lines. Select the choice with the correct coefficients.

$$\_\ Na + F_2 \rightarrow \_\ NaF$$

A. 2, 2
B 3, 2
C. 4. 2
D. 4, 4

40. A mole is the unit used to keep track of the vast number of atoms or molecules that take part in chemical reactions. It is an essential quantity in chemistry. There are 6×10^{23} particles in a mole. If a sample of H_2SO_4 contains 12×10^{23} particles, how many moles does this represent?

A. 2
B. 4
C. 8
D. 14

Go On

PHYSICAL SCIENCE

POSTTEST

41. Plastics are materials that find wide use in everyday life. This is because their properties can be changed by rearranging their molecular structure or adding reinforcing materials. Which one of the following applications is not yet suitable for plastics?

   A. food storage containers
   B. pots and pans
   C. building siding
   D. automobile bumpers

42. What is the name of the substance whose chemical formula is NaCl?

   A. monosodium momochloride
   B. sodium chloride
   C. sodium chlorate
   D. sodium chlorine

43. Which one of the following is NOT the formula of a hydrocarbon molecule?

   A. C_8H_{18}
   B. C_3H_8
   C. CH_4
   D. C_2H_5OH

44. The relationship between the volume of a gas and the temperature in degrees Kelvin at constant pressure and mass is known as

   A. Avagadro's law.
   B. Boyle's law.
   C. Charles' law.
   D. Einstein's law.

45. Which reaction is an example of synthesis?

   A. $2H_2O \rightarrow 2H_2 + O_2$
   B. $Na_2CO_3 \rightarrow Na_2O + CO_2$
   C. $2Fe_2O_3 + 3C \rightarrow 4Fe + 3CO_2$
   D. $2H_2 + O_2 \rightarrow 2H_2O$

SECTION 2

Use the two reaction energy graphs below to answer questions 46 and 47.

Reaction 1

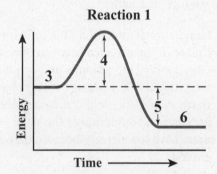

Reaction 2

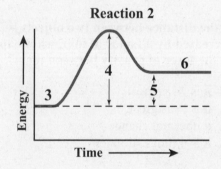

46. What number on the graphs represents the activation energy of the reaction?

A. 2
B. 3
C. 4
D. 5

47. Which number indicates the net energy absorbed or produced by the completed reactions?

A. 6
B. 5
C. 4
D. 3

48. At constant temperature, the volume of a gas is inversely proportional to

A. the pressure on it.
B. its atomic number.
C. its molecular weight.
D. its mass.

49. The diagram below shows a carbon atom combining with an oxygen molecule. Which one of the choices below is an INCORRECT statement about the reaction?

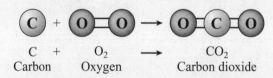

A. Carbon and oxygen are nonmetals.
B. Oxygen atoms form an oxygen molecule by covalent bonding.
C. Old bonds may need to be broken so that new bonds can form.
D. Carbon atoms transfer electrons to oxygen atoms in order to bond.

50. Which one of the following correctly shows the bonding that holds the atoms together?

A. CaO: metallic bond
B. SO_2 : ionic bond
C. KCl: ionic bond
D. $MgCl_2$: covalent bond

Go On

PHYSICAL SCIENCE

51. Which atom is correctly linked with its valence number?

A   Na, –7
B. Cl, +7
C. Ar, –8
D. Ca, +2

52. Use the diagram to answer the question. Isaac Newton proposed three laws of motion. Which one of the following statements MOST correctly describes the diagram.

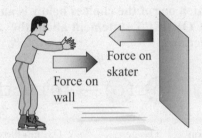

Force on skater

Force on wall

A. Acceleration is proportional to the net force on an object.
B. For every action, there is an equal and opposite reaction.
C. Acceleration is inversely proportional to the mass of an object.
D. Momentum is proportional to the mass of an object.

53. Newton's law of universal gravitation describes the force of attraction that every object in the universe exerts on every other object. There are billions of stars in the Milky Way galaxy. Which statement explains why the combined forces of gravity of the stars is unable to pull you off the surface of Earth?

A. Gravitational attraction falls off with the square of the distance between objects.
B. Gravitational attraction is proportional to the product of the masses of two objects.
C. Earth's magnetic field counteracts the gravitational attraction of the stars.
D. Stars have low density because they are gaseous.

54. If the distance between two objects is increased by a factor of four, what happens to the force of gravity between them?

A. it is $\frac{1}{16}$ as great
B. it is $\frac{1}{4}$ as great
C. it does not change
D. it is 4 times stronger

55. If the combined masses of two objects double, what happens to the force of the gravity between them?

A. it is 2 times as strong
B. it is 4 times as strong
C. it is 16 times as strong
D. it does not change

Go On

56. **In what way are electric charges and magnetic materials similar?**

   A. Distance does not affect them.
   B. Both are insulators.
   C. Opposite charges and opposite magnetic poles attract, and like charges and like magnetic poles repel.
   D. Opposite charges and opposite magnetic poles repel, and like charges and like magnetic poles attract.

57. **Which is NOT an example of processes related to electric charges in every day life?**

   A. static cling
   B. lighting a match
   C. plugging a radio into the wall socket
   D. a lightning bolt

58. **Use the diagram to answer the question. What is it in the atom's nucleus that makes a very strong binding force essential?**

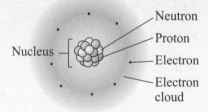

   A. All neutrons have a positive charge and should fly apart.
   B. All neutrons have a negative charge and should fly apart.
   C. All protons have a positive charge and should fly apart.
   D. All protons have a negative charge and should fly apart.

59. **Use the diagram to answer the question. Select the choice which best explains the difference in the skid lengths of the two cars.**

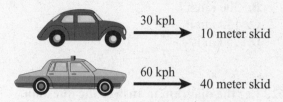

30 kph → 10 meter skid

60 kph → 40 meter skid

   A. Momentum is proportional to speed and mass.
   B. Rolling friction is less than sliding friction.
   C. Weight is due to the force of gravity.
   D. A longer car skids farther.

60. **A box weighing 40 N rests on a floor which pushes back with an equal force. What is the net force on the box?**

   A. 0 N
   B. 1 N
   C. 40 N
   D. 80 N

Go On

PHYSICAL SCIENCE

61. An unbalanced force propels a car 300 km in 4 hours. What is the average speed of the car?

    A. 1200 km/h
    B. 300 km/h
    C. 150 km/h
    D. 75 km/h

62. Use the diagram to answer the question. Opposing forces are affecting the motion of the box. What is the net force on the box?

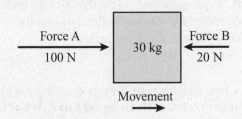

    Force A   Force B
    100 N   30 kg   20 N

              Movement →

    A. 100 N to the right
    B. 80 N to the right
    C. 20 N to the left
    D. 0 N

63. Two sailors tried to pull a heavy boat onto the beach, but it got stuck. They used a spring scale to measure the force of their pull that got the boat to move. The spring scale then showed a measurement of 240 N. What force did the 240 N represent?

    A. the weight of the boat
    B. the force of gravity on the boat
    C. the static frictional force
    D. the sliding frictional force

64. A wagon changes velocity from 2 km/hr to 6 km/hr over a period of 2 hours. What is the acceleration of the wagon?

    A. 2 km/hr2
    B. 4 km/hr2
    C. 6 km/hr2
    D. 8 km/hr2

65. An automobile has an energy use efficiency estimated at between 10 and 20%. Using the midpoint of 15% as the energy efficiency of the car, what is the actual work output if the total work input is 7500 kilojoules?

    A. 500 kilojoules
    B. 750 kilojoules
    C. 1125 kilojoules
    D. 7500 kilojoules

Go On

66. A group of workers use a single stationary pulley to raise a scaffold that weighs 800 N to a height of 20 meters. A worker measures the length of rope that came through the pulley. What was its length?

   A. 20 m
   B. 40 m
   C. 160 m
   D. 800 m

67. Use the diagram to answer the question. Which one of the choices below is the BEST description of a pair of scissors?

   A. wedge and lever
   B. a pulley system
   C. wheel and axle
   D. wheel and axle and wedge

68. Use the diagram to answer the question. In which position does the spring have the greatest potential energy?

Position 1

Position 2

Position 3

Position 4

Position 5

   A. position 1
   B. position 2
   C. position 3
   D. position 5

69. Which one of the following energy sources is renewable and has minimal environmental impact?

   A. solar energy
   B. coal
   C. uranium
   D. oil

70. An element is heated to a temperature high enough to raise the kinetic energy of its molecules to a level where they can completely break free of the binding forces holding them together. What term is used to describe that temperature?

   A. decomposition point
   B. melting point
   C. freezing point
   D. boiling point

Go On

PHYSICAL SCIENCE

71. As a sled slides down a hill, potential energy is converted to kinetic energy. However, after the ride is over, the amount of kinetic energy does not equal the amount of potential energy. This fact appears to contradict the law of conservation of energy. Why is this NOT true?

    A. The measurements are incorrect.
    B. The "missing" energy was converted to heat energy because of sliding friction.
    C. The law of conservation of energy has exceptions.
    D. Some of the potential energy was converted to mass as the sled slid down the hill.

72. Without anyone helping her, Irma lifted her suitcase weighing 98 N a distance of 1.5 meters onto the luggage rack of the train car. How much work did she do?

    A. 65.3 joules
    B. 65.3 newton-meters
    C. 147 newton-meters
    D. 147 newtons

73. Enrico stacked 200 cans, each weighing 5N, on shelves 1 meter high in only 100 seconds. How much power did he use for the task?

    A. 1000 watts
    B. 10 watts
    C. 2 watts
    D. 0.01 watts

74. How is heat energy transferred through a liquid?

    A. by convection
    B. by conduction
    C. by electromagnetic waves
    D. by radiation

75. Use the diagram to answer the question. Lucy is using the pulley system to lift a load that is too heavy for her to do without help. What is the mechanical advantage of the pulley system Lucy is using?

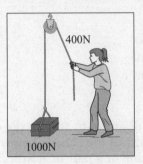

    A. 4000   C. 400
    B. 1000   D. 2.5

76. A simple machine has an efficiency of only 80%. Its work on the loading dock is to lift crates weighing 1000 N onto a platform 2 meters high. What is its work input on each crate?

    A. 2500 joules   C. 1000 joules
    B. 2000 joules   D. 800 joules

77. Use the diagram to answer the question. What is the approximate temperature when substance X melts or freezes?

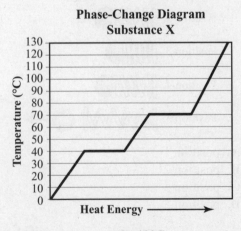

    A. 0°C   C. 40°C
    B. 32°C   D. 70°C

Go On

78. Leona was planning her project on series circuits. She wanted to find a combination of resistances and voltage sources that would produce the greatest current. Which one of these combinations will have the largest current?

    A. 120 V and 24 Ω
    B. 120 V and 12 Ω
    C. 110 V and 22 Ω
    D. 110 V and 110 Ω

79. What does the electric current in a metal wire consist of according to modern electrical theories?

    A. a flow of electrons
    B. a flow of neutrons
    C. a flow of protons
    D. a flow of ions

80. Use the diagram to answer the question. What would a person standing in the intersection hear as the three cars speed off with their horns blaring?

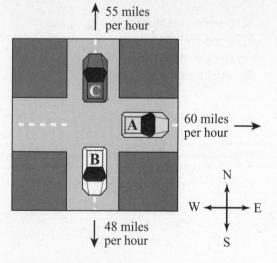

    A. a lowering of the pitch
    B. a rise in volume
    C. no change in the pitch
    D. a rise in the pitch

81. The volume of a sound is due to which one of the following components of the sound wave?

    A. its speed   B. its amplitude
    C. its frequency   D. its wavelength

82. The speed of sound waves in different media varies. In which media do sound waves generally travel fastest?

    A. empty space   C. liquids
    B. gases   D. solids

83. The use of echoes of sound waves to locate objects not otherwise visible is applied by all of the following except

    A. sonar
    B. ultrasonic imaging devices
    C. radar
    D. bats

84. Use the diagram to answer the question. Which two waves would have the highest and lowest frequencies, respectively?

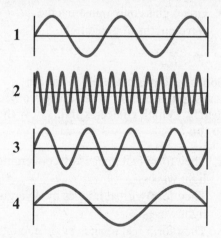

    A. 3 and 4   C. 2 and 4
    B. 1 and 2   D. 3 and 1

Go On

PHYSICAL SCIENCE

85. The electromagnetic spectrum includes all of the different wavelengths of light from the longest to the shortest. As the wavelengths get shorter, the energy of the wave

   A. drops to zero.
   B. increases.
   C. remains the same.
   D. decreases, but not to zero.

86. Use the diagram to answer the question. White light is a mixture of wavelengths that form the visible light spectrum. Which one of the choices below is the best explanation of what is happening in the diagram?

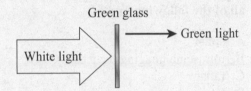

   A. Green glass absorbs only the wavelengths of green light.
   B. Green glass reflects only the wavelengths of green light.
   C. Green glass diffracts only the wavelengths of green light.
   D. Green glass only transmits the wavelengths of green light.

87. Concave lenses are used to enable nearsighted people to see distant objects clearly. Which choice explains how they do this?

   A. They form real images by converging light waves.
   B. They form virtual images by diverging light waves.
   C. They form real images by diffracting light waves.
   D. They form both real and virtual images by constructive interference of light waves.

88. The two resistances in a series circuit are each 10 ohms. The current in the circuit is 6 amperes. What is the voltage in the circuit?

   A. 10 volts
   B. 16 volts
   C. 60 volts
   D. 120 volts

89. An electromagnet can be turned on and off with a switch. This occurs because when the electric current flows, it

   A. transforms electrical energy into heat energy
   B. changes electric energy into chemical energy
   C. produces a magnetic field intensified by a soft iron core
   D. changes the iron core's electron spins to point in all directions.

90. An electric current consisting of positive and negative ions flowing in different directions can be found in

   A. a wet cell battery
   B. a copper wire
   C. an electromagnetic wave
   D. an aluminum wire

Glossary

acceleration the rate of change in velocity measured in m/sec^2 (Lesson 22)

acceleration of gravity (ag) the force of Earth's gravity on an object equivalent to 9.8 m/s^2 (Lesson 24)

accuracy a quality that compares how close a measurement is to the real or accepted value (Lesson 5)

acid any substance that releases hydrogen ions (H$^+$) in solution (Lesson 21)

affiliation where someone work or who they work for (Lesson 11)

alpha particle a particle that consists of two protons and two neutrons, which is the equivalent of a helium nucleus (Lesson 17)

alternating current generated electric currents that alternate direction in the conductor (Lesson 36)

amplitude the maximum displacement of an energy wave from its rest or equilibrium position (Lesson 30)

astronomy the study of the universe beyond Earth's atmosphere (Lesson 10)

atmospheres (atm) a unit of pressure equal to the pressure of air at sea level (Lesson 20)

atom the basic building block of all matter that is the smallest unit of an element that still has the chemical properties of that element (Lesson 12)

atomic mass a weighted averages of the masses of the naturally occurring isotopes for an element (Lesson 12)

atomic mass unit (amu) a unit of mass that compare the relative amounts of matter in atoms (Lesson 12)

atomic number the number of protons in an element (Lesson 12)

atomic number the number of protons in an element's nucleus and it is different for each element (Lesson 18)

average speed the distance traveled divided by the elapsed time (Lesson 22)

average velocity the distance traveled in some diretion divided by the elapsed time (Lesson 22)

balanced describes an equation in which each side of the equation has the same number of atoms of each element and mass is conserved (Lesson 16)

bar graph a graph that represents numbers using thick bars to compare data points (Lesson 3)

base any substance that releases hydroxide ions (OH$^-$) in solution (Lesson 21)

beta particle an electron (Lesson 17)

bias a personal prejudice or preconceived idea that may favor a particular point of view; the opposite of objectivity (Lesson 9)

binary compounds compounds that consist of only two elements (Lesson 15)

biology the study of living things (Lesson 10)

Boyle's law the gas law that states that for a fixed amount of gas at constant temperature, the volume of the gas increases as the pressure decreases (Lesson 20)

chain reaction self-sustaining series of nuclear fission reactions (Lesson 17)

Charles's law the gas law that states that for a fixed amount of gas at constant pressure, the volume of the gas increases as the temperature increases (Lesson 20)

chemical bonding a joining together of atoms by forces of attraction (Lesson 13)

chemical change any change that results in the formation of new substances (Lesson 14)

chemical formula a shorthand notation for identifying a compound, consisting of the symbols of the elements that make up the compound and subscripts (Lesson 15)

chemical property a description of the potential that a substance has to undergo a change that alters the composition of the substance (Lesson 14)

chemical reaction a process that results in the rearrangement of atoms and bonds in chemical substances (Lesson 16)

chemistry the science of what substances are made of and how they interact with energy and each other (Lesson 10)

circle graph allows you to compare parts, or percentages, of a whole (Lesson 3)

compound a pure substance composed of more than one type of element chemically combined in a fixed proportion (Lesson 15)

compound machines a machine combining two or more simple machines (Lesson 26)

compressible easily pushed into a smaller space (Lesson 20)

compression the area of a longitudinal wave where the particles are more densely clustered (Lesson 30)

compressional wave a mechanical longitudinal wave (Lesson 30)

concentration a measure of the amount of solute dissolved in certain volume of solvent (Lesson 21)

conclusion a final analysis of results that applies what was observed during the experiment to answer the original question and evaluates any preliminary explanation the scientist had before conducting the experiment (Lesson 1)

conduction the vibratory movement of particles of matter transferring heat energy in solids (Lesson 28)

conduction the flow of electrons transferring electric charge that forms electric currents (Lesson 34)

conductivity a measure of a material's ability to conduct electrical current, or allow the movement of electrical changes through it (Lesson 14, Lesson 21)

conductors the materials that allow electrons or other charged particles to flow through them (Lesson 28)

constructive interference the increase in energy when in-phase waves merge (Lesson 32)

control group group in a controlled experiment to which all other groups are compared (Lesson 8)

covalent bond the force of the attraction between two positive nuclei and the shared electrons between them (Lesson 13)

convection the transfer of heat energy in fluids by thermal currents of heated particles (Lesson 28)

crest the point of maximum displacement above the rest position in transverse waves (Lesson 30)

critical mass in fission, the mass of U-235 required for the chain reaction to occur (Lesson 17)

current a directional flow of particles in fluids or of electrons in conductors (Lesson 35)

data information collected through scientific research and inquiry (Lesson 4)

decomposition reaction a chemical reaction in which a single compound is broken down into two or more simpler substances, usually written in the form: $AB \rightarrow A + B$ (Lesson 16)

density the mass of a substance per unit volume (Lesson 14)

dependent variable the variable in a controlled experiment that responds to changes in the independent variable (Lesson 8)

destructive interference the reduction in energy when out-of-phase waves merge (Lesson 32)

diffraction the spreading out of light or sound waves after passing through an opening (Lesson 32)

dimensional analysis a system of calculation used to change one unit of measurement into another (Lesson 3)

direct current the flow of electrons in a conductor in one direction only (Lesson 36)

displacement the amount of movement in the particles of the medium a waves energy produces (Lesson 31)

distance the measured change in position traveled by a moving object (Lesson 22)

Doppler effect the apparent change in frequency of waves emitted by an object moving toward or away from an observer (Lesson 33)

double replacement reaction a chemical reaction in which the ions in two compounds exchange bonding partners, usually written in the form: $AB + CD \rightarrow AC + BD$ (Lesson 16)

echo the reflection of sound waves by a new medium's surface (Lesson 33)

editorial an article that expresses an opinion (Lesson 11)

efficiency the amount of work output divided by the work input expressed as a percentage (Lesson 26)

effort distance the distance an input force moves in a simple machine (Lesson 26)

effort the input force in a simple machine (Lesson 26)

electric discharge the sudden flow of built-up static electric charges to another site (Lesson 34)

electric force field the space where attractive and repulsive forces of charged particles are felt (Lesson 34)

electric motor a device that converts electrical energy into mechanical energy (Lesson 37)

electromagnet a device that concentrates the magnetic field produced by an electric current in a coil of wire containing an iron core (Lesson 37)

electromagnetic induction the effect of a moving magnetic field to produce an electric current in a conductor (Lesson 37)

electromagnetic spectrum the full range of electromagnetic energy wavelengths and frequencies from radio waves to gamma rays (Lesson 31)

electromagnetic wave a traveling disturbance in the electric and magnetic fields that permeate space (Lesson 30)

electromagnetism the relationship between electricity and magnetism (Lesson 37)

electron cloud a region surrounding the nucleus of an atom and consisting of the electrons (Lesson 12)

electron configuration the organization of electrons in energy levels (Lesson 13)

electrons negatively charged subatomic particles that surround the nucleus of an atom (Lesson 12)

element any substance made up of only one type of atom; there are 117 known elements (Lesson 12)

energy the ability to do work (Lesson 10, Lesson 27)

energy levels specific locations that electrons can be found within an atom of an element (Lesson 18)

equation a shorthand description, using symbols and formulas, depicting the reactants and products involved in a reaction (Lesson 16)

experiment a test that uses controlled conditions to demonstrate the validity of an explanation for an observation (Lesson 1)

experimental design the plan for a research study (Lesson 8)

experimental group group in a controlled experiment that has an independent variable that changes (Lesson 8)

family a vertical column of elements on the periodic table (Lesson 18)

force a push or pull on an object (Lesson 24)

formula a mathematical statement or equation, usually expressed in algebraic symbols (Lesson 3)

fraud the falsification of research findings through lying, omitting data, or hiding logical weaknesses (Lesson 6)

frequency the number of wavelengths per second passing a point measured in hertz (Lesson 30)

friction the drag forces produced by contact between two objects (Lesson 23, Lesson 34)

gamma ray high-energy light emission from a nuclear reaction (Lesson 17)

gas the phase of matter that has both indefinite shape and indefinite volume (Lesson 19)

Gay-Lussac's law the gas law that states that for a fixed amount of gas at constant volume, the pressure of the gas increases as the temperature increases (Lesson 20)

geology the study of the structure of Earth and the processes that shape it (Lesson 10)

generator a device that converts mechanical energy into electrical energy (Lesson 37)

graduated cylinders tall glass containers used to measure the volume of liquids (Lesson 2)

graph a chart that plots numerical data on two axes (Lesson 3)

gravity the force of attraction between any two objects (Lesson 24)

group a vertical column of elements on the periodic table (Lesson 18)

half-life the amount of time it takes for half of the nuclei in a sample of radioactive atoms to undergo nuclear decay (Lesson 17)

heat capacity the amount of heat energy required to change the temperature of a mass of any substance 1°C (Lesson 29)

heat energy the work done by the kinetic energy of particles of matter (Lesson 29)

heat transfer the transfer of kinetic energy from warmer to cooler objects (Lesson 28)

helium structure the electron configuration of a helium atom that has two electrons in the outside energy level (Lesson 13)

hertz (hz) the unit of frequency in complete wave cycles per second (Lesson 30)

hypothesis a possible explanation or tentative answer to the question being investigated (Lessons 1, Lesson 4, Lesson 7)

independent variable the variable in a controlled experiment that the scientist changes or manipulates (Lesson 8)

inference an idea that follows logically from observations (Lesson 1)

induction the effect of a charged object on a neutral object to cause it to become oppositely charged (Lesson 34)

inertia the resistance of a body to a change in its state of rest or motion (Lesson 23)

instantaneous speed the speed of an object at any moment of time (Lesson 22)

instantaneous velocity the velocity of an object at any moment of time (Lesson 22)

insulators materials which resist the flow of electrons or the transfer of heat through them (Lesson 28)

interference the combining of two or more waves into a single wave with changed properties (Lesson 32)

International System of Units (SI) the standard unit of measurement, based on multiples of 10, used by scientists around the world (Lesson 5)

ion an atom or group of atoms carrying an overall positive or negative charge (Lesson 13)

ionic bonds the force of the attraction between two ions of opposite charge (Lesson 13)

ionic crystal the rigid structure formed by positively and negatively charged ions that make up an ionic compound, bonded tightly together in a three-dimensional crystal lattice (Lesson 13)

isotopes atoms with the same number of protons but different numbers of neutrons (Lesson 12)

kinetic energy the energy of motion of particles of matter (Lesson 27)

lab report a form of scientific communication that shows how an investigator followed the steps of the scientific method (Lesson 6)

law of action and reaction for every action there is an equal and opposite reaction (Lesson 23)

law of conservation of mass law that states that atoms that existed before a reaction takes place must exist after the reaction takes place; the mass of reactants equals the mass of products in a chemical reaction (Lesson 16)

law of universal gravitation every body in the universe attracts every other body with a force equal to the products of their masses divided by the square of the distance between them (Lesson 24)

length the distance between two points (Lesson 5)

line graph a graph that connects data points with lines that allow you to see trends among that data (Lesson 3)

liquid the phase of matter that has an indefinite shape but a definite volume (Lesson 19)

longitudinal wave mechanical waves vibrating in the same direction as the wave motion (Lesson 30)

loudness the intensity of sound measured in decibels (Lesson 33)

magnetic domains areas where the magnetic poles of unpaired electrons are aligned (Lesson 37)

magnetic field the space where the attraction and repulsion of a magnet's poles are felt (Lesson 37)

magnetism the forces of attraction and repulsion arising from electron motion (Lesson 37)

mass the amount of matter in an object (Lesson 5, Lesson 14)

mass number the total number of protons and neutrons in an atom (Lesson 12)

mathematics the science of the properties and manipulation of numbers (Lesson 3)

matter anything that takes up space and has mass (Lesson 10; Lesson 14)

measurement errors mistakes made in using or reading measuring tools (Lesson 5)

mechanical advantage the output force of a machine divided by the input force (Lesson 26)

mechanical wave a disturbance of particles in a material medium (Lesson 30)

mechanism a description of the process that explains how something happens (Lesson 1)

medium the material (or electromagnetic fields in space) through which a wave travels (Lesson 30)

meniscus curved surface of the top of a liquid in a container (Lesson 5)

metalloids elements that have characteristics of metals and nonmetals and are known for being good semiconductors (Lesson 18)

metals those elements grouped on the left side of the periodic table that have one, two, or three more than the number of electrons that they need in order to have a stable arrangement (Lesson 13, Lesson 18)

meteorology is the study of weather in Earth's atmosphere (Lesson 10)

model a physical or mathematical representation of an object or process (Lesson 3)

motion a change in position over time (Lesson 22)

music sounds which are pleasant to hear (Lesson 33)

negative acceleration a reduction in the rate of speed (Lesson 22)

negative charge the electric charge of an electron (Lesson 34)

negative ion an atom that has gained electrons producing an overall negative charge (Lesson 13)

net force the unbalanced force remaining from the combined forces acting on an object (Lesson 23)

neutron neutral subatomic particles that are located in the nucleus of an atom (Lesson 12)

newton (N) the standard unit of force equals one kilogram-meter per second^2 (Lesson 23)

noble gas electron configuration the electron configuration of a noble gas atom that has eight electrons in the outside energy level (Lesson 13)

noise unpleasant sounds (Lesson 33)

nonmetals those elements grouped on the right side of the periodic table that have less than the number of electrons that they need in order to have a stable arrangement (Lesson 13)

nuclear decay process in which one or more particles in the nuclei of unstable atoms change and emit energy or particles to produce a more stable nucleus (Lesson 17)

nuclear fission the splitting of a heavy nucleus into two lighter nuclei, releasing a tremendous amount of energy (Lesson 17)

nuclear fusion nuclear reaction that occurs when small nuclei fuse, or combine, to form a larger, single nucleus (Lesson 17)

nuclear reactions reactions that take place in the nucleus of atoms and involve changes in the number of protons and neutrons; the products of nuclear reactions contain different elements than the reactants (Lesson 17)

objective based on facts and free of bias (Lesson 9)

observation a record or note made by studying something using the senses or equipment (Lesson 1, Lesson 4)

oceanography the study of Earth's oceans (Lesson 10)

Ohm's law the relationship between voltage (*V*), current (*I*), and resistance (*R*): $V = IR$ (Lesson 35)

outlier a plotted point that falls outside the typical location of all of the other data points (Lesson 3)

parallel circuit a circuit in which a simple circuit is split into more than one loop with circuit elements on each path (Lesson 35)

peer review a process in which an article is sent to knowledgeable scientists who review the procedures and conclusions of the investigation (Lesson 6, Lesson 9)

period a horizontal row of elements on the periodic table (Lesson 18); the time it takes to complete one full wave cycle (Lesson 31)

permanent magnet A magnet that retains its magnetism for a longtime (Lesson 37)

personal protective equipment (PPE) safety gear that is worn in the science laboratory (Lesson 2)

pH scale a way to measure the concentration of hydrogen ions in solution; the pH range is from 0 to 14 (Lesson 21)

phase whether matter is a solid, liquid, gas, or plasma (Lesson 29)

phase change changing from solid to liquid to gas in any direction or combination (Lesson 19, 29)

phase diagram a graph of phase changes relating temperature and heat energy (Lesson 29)

physical change any change in a substance in which the composition of the substance does not change (Lesson 14)

physical property a characteristic of a substance that can be observed directly or measured with a tool without changing the composition of the substance (Lesson 14)

physical science the study of nonliving systems; physical scientists study matter and how it interacts with energy (Lesson 10)

physics the study of energy and how it affects matter (Lesson 10)

plasma the phase of matter that consists of positively and negatively charged particles (Lesson 19)

pitch the frequency of a sound wave (Lesson 33)

polarized light waves that vibrate in only one direction perpendicular to the wave direction (Lesson 30)

positive acceleration an increase in the rate of speed (Lesson 22)

positive charge the electric charge on a proton (Lesson 34)

positive ion an atom that has lost electrons producing an overall positive charge (Lesson 13)

potential energy the stored energy in a system due to position or chemical bonds (Lesson 27)

power the rate at which work is done (Lesson 26)

precision a quality that compares how close the measurements are to each other (Lesson 5)

prediction a guess about the future based on facts or data (Lesson 1)

pressure an amount of force exerted over a certain area (Lesson 20)

procedural errors errors that involve mistakes made in conducting an experiment (Lesson 5)

protons positively charged subatomic particles that are located in the nucleus of an atom (Lesson 12)

qualitative data information obtained by using the senses (Lesson 5)

quantitative data measurement information obtained by using scientific instruments (Lesson 5)

radiation energy or particles that are emitted from the decaying nucleus (Lesson 17); the transfer of energy by electromagnetic waves (Lesson 28)

rarefaction the region of lowest particle density in a longitudinal wave (Lesson 30)

reflection the bouncing back of energy waves from the surface of a newly contacted medium (Lesson 32)

refraction the bending of light waves when they pass from one medium to another (Lesson 32)

resistance the opposition to the flow of electrical current through material measured in ohms (Lesson 35)

resistance distance the distance the output force moves the resistance (Lesson 26)

resistance force the force applied by a machine to move the resistance (Lesson 26)

resistivity a measure of a material's electrical resistance in units of ohm-meters (Lesson 35)

rest position/equilibrium the median line between a wave's maximum displacements (Lesson 30)

science the study of anything related to the natural world (Lesson 4)

scientific journals weekly or monthly publications that print scientific papers and reports of experiments (Lesson 11)

scientific method the process of inquiry and investigation that researchers use to gain knowledge and to understand the natural world around them better (Lesson 1, Lesson 4, and Lesson 7)

scientific questions questions that can be studied through further observation, testing, and analysis (Lesson 4)

series circuit a circuit in which more than one circuit element is included in the circuit loop (Lesson 35)

significant figures numbers that represent the amount of precision recorded in a measurement (Lesson 5)

single replacement reaction a chemical reaction in which an element replaces an ion in a compound, usually written in the form: A + BC → AB + C **(Lesson 16)**

semiconductor a material whose limited conductivity is useful in solid state electronics **(Lesson 35)**

simple machines ones that work with one movement **(Lesson 26)**

solid the phase of matter that has a definite shape and a definite volume **(Lesson 19)**

solubility the maximum amount of solute that will dissolve in a given solvent at a particular temperature and pressure **(Lesson 14; Lesson 21)**

solute the substance that dissolves in a solution **(Lesson 21)**

solution an evenly distributed mixture of two or more substances **(Lesson 21)**

solvent the dissolving substance in a solution **(Lesson 21)**

sound the audible form of energy propagated by mechanical longitudinal waves **(Lesson 33)**

sound quality the fullness of a sound due to complex overtones in the waves **(Lesson 33)**

specific heat the amount of heat energy required to change the temperature of a unit mass of substance 1°C **(Lesson 29)**

speed the rate of motion as measured by distance traveled divided by elapsed time **(Lesson 22)**

stability describes atoms that do not readily bond because they have filled outside energy levels **(Lesson 13)**

stable describes an element whose nucleus has enough neutrons to block the repulsive forces between protons **(Lesson 12)**

static electricity the build up of electric charges in an object **(Lesson 34)**

statistics a set of mathematical methods and procedures that help scientists compare data sets **(Lesson 3)**

subatomic particles particles that make up atoms, including protons, neutrons, and electrons **(Lesson 12)**

sublimation the physical change that occurs when a solid changes directly into a gas without going through the liquid state **(Lesson 19)**

subscripts small numbers that tell how many atoms (or ions) of that element are in each molecule (or unit) of the compound **(Lesson 15)**

surface wave a combination of transverse and longitudinal waves such as ocean waves **(Lesson 30)**

synthesis reaction a chemical reaction in which a combination of two or more substances that form a new compound, usually written in the form: A + B → AB **(Lesson 16)**

table a chart that organizes information into boxed columns **(Lesson 3)**

temperature a measure of the average kinetic energy of the particles in a substance **(Lesson 19, 20, and 29)**

theory a hypothesis that has been tested several times and in several different ways; a broad explanation that ties together a range of observations and ideas about how processes are thought to occur **(Lesson 4 and Lesson 7)**

trials repetitions of an experiment with the same conditions **(Lesson 8)**

triple beam balances a laboratory instrument the consists of balanced beams and a pan used to measure mass **(Lesson 2)**

transverse wave a wave whose vibrations in the medium are at right angles to the wave motion **(Lesson 30)**

trough the lowest point of maximum displacement in a transverse wave **(Lesson 30)**

unstable describes an isotope whose nucleus does not contain enough neutrons to block the repulsive forces between protons **(Lesson 12)**

valence electrons electrons that are found in the outer-most energy level of atoms; the bonding electrons **(Lesson 18)**

variable the factor in a controlled experiment that might affect the outcome of the test **(Lesson 8)**

velocity the speed and direction of anything moving: $v = d/t$ east **(Lesson 22)**

viscosity a physical property of fluids that is a measure of a fluid's resistance to flow **(Lesson 14)**

volume the amount of space an object occupies **(Lesson 5; Lesson 14)**

voltage the potential energy difference between two points in a circuit **(Lesson 35)**

wave a vibrational disturbance in a medium that transfers energy but not mass **(Lesson 30)**

wavelength the length of a complete wave cycle: one mid-crest to the next mid-crest **(Lesson 30)**

weight the force of gravity on an objects mass measured in newtons **(Lesson 25)**

work the energy used in moving a mass in the same direction as the motive force **(Lesson 26, Lesson 27)**

work input the product of the input force and its displacement measured in joules **(Lesson 26)**

work output the product of the output force and its displacement measured in joules **(Lesson 26)**

Physical Science Reference Sheet

Formulas

Force, Mass and Motion

Velocity = $\dfrac{\text{displacement}}{\text{time}}$ $\left(v = \dfrac{d}{t}\right)$

Acceleration = $\dfrac{\text{final velocity} - \text{initial velocity}}{\text{time}}$ $\left(a = \dfrac{v_f - v_i}{t}\right)$

Weight = mass × acceleration of gravity $(w = mg)$

Force = mass × acceleration $(F = ma)$

Work = force × distance $(W = Fd)$

Mechanical advantage = $\dfrac{\text{effort distance}}{\text{resistance distance}} = \dfrac{\text{resistance force}}{\text{effort force}}$ $\left(MA = \dfrac{d_e}{d_r} = \dfrac{f_r}{f_e}\right)$

Chemical Reactions and Properties of Matter

Density = $\dfrac{\text{mass}}{\text{volume}}$ $\left(D = \dfrac{m}{V}\right)$

Volume of a rectangular solid = length × width × height $(V = lwh)$

Heat lost or gained = mass × specific heat capacity × change in temperature $(Q = mc\Delta T)$

Waves, Electricity and Magnetism

Voltage = current × resistance $(V = IR)$

Constants and Relationships

Kelvin = °Celsius + 273 $(K = °C + 273)$

Acceleration due to gravity: g ≈ 10 $\dfrac{m}{\text{sec}^2}$

newton: 1 N = 1 kg $\bullet$ $\dfrac{m}{s^2}$

joule: 1 J = 1 N $\bullet$ m

Turn over for the Periodic Table of the Elements.

Georgia Physical Science End-of-Course Test

Periodic Table

Key

- Atomic number — 29
- Element symbol — **Cu**
- Element name — Copper
- Average atomic mass — 63.55

1	2	3	4	5	6	7	8	9	10	11	12	13	14	15	16	17	18
1 **H** Hydrogen 1.01																	2 **He** Helium 4.00
3 **Li** Lithium 6.94	4 **Be** Beryllium 9.01											5 **B** Boron 10.81	6 **C** Carbon 12.01	7 **N** Nitrogen 14.01	8 **O** Oxygen 16.00	9 **F** Fluorine 19.00	10 **Ne** Neon 20.18
11 **Na** Sodium 22.99	12 **Mg** Magnesium 24.31											13 **Al** Aluminum 26.98	14 **Si** Silicon 28.09	15 **P** Phosphorus 30.97	16 **S** Sulfur 32.07	17 **Cl** Chlorine 35.45	18 **Ar** Argon 39.95
19 **K** Potassium 39.10	20 **Ca** Calcium 40.08	21 **Sc** Scandium 44.96	22 **Ti** Titanium 47.87	23 **V** Vanadium 50.94	24 **Cr** Chromium 52.00	25 **Mn** Manganese 54.94	26 **Fe** Iron 55.85	27 **Co** Cobalt 58.93	28 **Ni** Nickel 58.69	29 **Cu** Copper 63.55	30 **Zn** Zinc 65.39	31 **Ga** Gallium 69.72	32 **Ge** Germanium 72.61	33 **As** Arsenic 74.92	34 **Se** Selenium 78.96	35 **Br** Bromine 79.90	36 **Kr** Krypton 83.80
37 **Rb** Rubidium 85.47	38 **Sr** Strontium 87.62	39 **Y** Yttrium 88.91	40 **Zr** Zirconium 91.22	41 **Nb** Niobium 92.91	42 **Mo** Molybdenum 95.94	43 **Tc** Technetium (98)	44 **Ru** Ruthenium 101.07	45 **Rh** Rhodium 102.91	46 **Pd** Palladium 106.42	47 **Ag** Silver 107.87	48 **Cd** Cadmium 112.41	49 **In** Indium 114.82	50 **Sn** Tin 118.71	51 **Sb** Antimony 121.76	52 **Te** Tellurium 127.60	53 **I** Iodine 126.90	54 **Xe** Xenon 131.29
55 **Cs** Cesium 132.91	56 **Ba** Barium 137.33	57-71 ☆	72 **Hf** Hafnium 178.49	73 **Ta** Tantalum 180.95	74 **W** Tungsten 183.84	75 **Re** Rhenium 186.21	76 **Os** Osmium 190.23	77 **Ir** Iridium 192.22	78 **Pt** Platinum 195.08	79 **Au** Gold 196.97	80 **Hg** Mercury 200.59	81 **Tl** Thallium 204.38	82 **Pb** Lead 207.2	83 **Bi** Bismuth 208.98	84 **Po** Polonium (209)	85 **At** Astatine (210)	86 **Rn** Radon (222)
87 **Fr** Francium (223)	88 **Ra** Radium (226)	89-103 ☆☆	104 **Rf** Rutherfordium (261)	105 **Db** Dubnium (262)	106 **Sg** Seaborgium (266)	107 **Bh** Bohrium (264)	108 **Hs** Hassium (269)	109 **Mt** Meitnerium (268)	110 **Ds** Darmstadtium (281)	111 **Rg** Roentgenium (272)	112 **Uub** Ununbium (285)	113 **Uut** Ununtrium (284)	114 **Uuq** Ununquadium (289)	115 **Uup** Ununpentium (288)			

☆ Lanthanide series

57 **La** Lanthanum 138.91	58 **Ce** Cerium 140.12	59 **Pr** Praseodymium 140.91	60 **Nd** Neodymium 144.24	61 **Pm** Promethium (145)	62 **Sm** Samarium 150.36	63 **Eu** Europium 151.96	64 **Gd** Gadolinium 157.25	65 **Tb** Terbium 158.93	66 **Dy** Dysprosium 162.50	67 **Ho** Holmium 164.93	68 **Er** Erbium 167.26	69 **Tm** Thulium 168.93	70 **Yb** Ytterbium 173.04	71 **Lu** Lutetium 174.97

☆☆ Actinide series

89 **Ac** Actinium (227)	90 **Th** Thorium 232.04	91 **Pa** Protactinium 231.04	92 **U** Uranium 238.03	93 **Np** Neptunium (237)	94 **Pu** Plutonium (244)	95 **Am** Americium (243)	96 **Cm** Curium (247)	97 **Bk** Berkelium (247)	98 **Cf** Californium (251)	99 **Es** Einsteinium (252)	100 **Fm** Fermium (257)	101 **Md** Mendelevium (258)	102 **No** Nobelium (259)	103 **Lr** Lawrencium (262)